# Unleashing the Lion

Eric Petrie was born and educated in Walthamstow, London. After various jobs including that of milkman, apprentice electronics engineer, part-time roadie/poet/folksinger, door-to-door salesman and residential child care officer, he took a degree in theology and then trained as a teacher. He worked as an RE teacher in South London for five years before moving into special education in Herefordshire. At present he is priest in charge of Salwarpe and Hindlip with Martin Hussingtree and coordinating chaplain to West Mercia Police. He is married with two children and is a regular on blues-harp at the annual blues jam at the Greenbelt Festival. His previous publications have been two books of poetry and a play, as well as *Keep Music Legal* (with Simon Law) a guide to copyright law for musicians.

With grateful thanks to Heather, Alice & Aidan, Chris & Chris, Mel & Simon, Simon, Sarah & Lydia, Mark, Jane, Jemma & Ben, Dave, Jackie, Matt, Tom & Jonners, Ian & Becca, Revd Dr Brian Easter, Revd Dr David Bryan, Revd Peter Ashby and the staff and residents of Winslow Court.

AMDG

and

In memory of Revd Canon K. H. Druitt (1900–1990)

# Unleashing the Lion

## THE POWER OF GOD IN
## HEALTH AND HEALING

I. R. Eric Petrie

First published in Great Britain 2000
Society for Promoting Christian Knowledge
Holy Trinity Church
Marylebone Road
London NW1 4DU

British Library Cataloguing in Publication Data

A catalogue record for this book is available
from the British Library

ISBN 0-281-05324-3

Typeset by David Gregson Associates, Beccles, Suffolk
Printed in Great Britain by
Redwood Books, Trowbridge, Wiltshire

# *Contents*

"Aslan a man!" said Mr Beaver sternly. "Certainly not. I tell you he is the King of the wood and the son of the great Emperor-beyond-the-sea. Don't you know who is the King of Beasts? Aslan is a lion – *the* Lion, the great Lion."

"Ooh!" said Susan, "I'd thought he was a man. Is he – quite safe? I'd feel rather nervous about meeting a lion."

"That you will, dearie, and no mistake," said Mrs Beaver, "if there's anyone who can appear before Aslan without their knees knocking, they're either braver than most or else just silly."

"Then he isn't safe?" said Lucy.

"Safe?" said Mr Beaver, "don't you hear what Mrs Beaver tells you? Who said anything about safe? 'Course he isn't safe ..."

(C. S. Lewis, *The Lion, the Witch & the Wardrobe*)

He pounced on me like a lion. He chased me off the road, tore me to pieces, and left me.

(Lamentations 3.10–11)

Almighty God,
who enlightened your holy Church through the inspired
witness of your evangelist Saint Mark:
grant that we, being firmly grounded in the truth of the gospel,
may be faithful to its teaching both in word and deed;
through Jesus Christ your Son our Lord. Amen.

(from *Calendar, Lectionary and Collects*, 25 April
The symbol of St Mark is a wingéd lion.)

# Introduction

# *David, a true story*

A true story. Only the names, as they say, have been changed. I was teaching in a special school for young people with severe learning difficulties, those who would once upon a time have been described as being mentally handicapped. In addition to this the young people had emotional and behavioural difficulties.

Their behaviour was so difficult that most of the young people lived at the school for fifty-two weeks of the year. Their challenging behaviour, as it is called, was so extreme that, unfortunately, many of the young people are unlikely ever to fit into the wider community. Many of the youngsters were occasionally violent, in sudden outbursts of intense frustration. This is understandable but, even if one understands it, it is unacceptable behaviour. And it still hurts!

David was about seventeen, with very fair hair that flopped over his face and very pale skin. Apart from a slightly withdrawn look there was nothing to mark him out from any other lad of his age. I had chosen him as the subject of a special study that I was doing, part of a training course. He had one particular piece of behaviour that precisely fitted my needs. For fully twenty per cent of his waking time, for a total of twelve minutes in every hour, one minute in every five, he would drum with his fingers. He would drum on the table, the chair, his legs, his chest, his head. He would drum on my legs, my chest and my head. He would, defying obvious danger signals, drum on Allen's desk, chair, and even, very dangerously, on Allen himself.

David's fingers were swollen and, in places, raw and chafed. The drumming was so hard and prolonged that it was causing physical harm. One of the reasons for his being placed in residential care was simply that his parents (and neighbours) couldn't stand it any longer. I began to look for causes of the behaviour and soon

1

realized that one of the causes was stress. David's face was a mask of distress and fear the whole time. He had no spoken language, would use very few signs and did not appear to want to learn others. Instead he would drum us out.

He would demand endless cups of tea, particularly from female members of staff, bullying them into making drinks for him. We could find little else except hot drinks to interest him. One day when our attention was elsewhere he drank eight cups of hot chocolate in one go. He had to be coerced into eating anything other than meat. And for fully twenty per cent of the day he would drum out his frustrations.

I did three different methods of statistical analysis to see how much of David's day was spent drumming. And whichever method I used, I came up with around twenty per cent. I thought that if I could find something else for him to do, to occupy his hands, he wouldn't be able to drum at the same time. In the professional language of the course it was a 'mutually exclusive activity'. I thought, perhaps, simple frame weaving would do the trick and keep his hands too busy.

I presented my analysis to the psychologist who was my tutor and explained my future plans. I would slowly build up the mutually exclusive activity until I had reduced the drumming to fifteen per cent of David's waking day. This may not sound much but it meant an extra three minutes in every hour, nearly an hour in a whole day – nearly seven hours a week!

The following week, I planned to work intensively on David and, at one stage, sent my two assistants off for a walk with the other three pupils. This would naturally reduce the noise and any tensions being built up in the group, among staff as well as young people. I had been using aromatherapy and massage for a few months, coupled with stress-reduction and relaxation therapy, so, taking advantage of the quiet, I began to work.

Personally, I am dubious about any intrinsic value in the essential oils that create the aromas, but we had a qualified aromatherapist on the staff who made up individual massage oils. I think that the value is in the touching and aromatherapy massage is a positive and appropriate way to touch another person. However, the very smells of the scented oils do seem to give one bit of a lift.

I put on some quiet classical music, probably Vaughan Williams' 'Lark Ascending', as that was usually in the classroom, and in a gentle reassuring voice talked to David. I massaged his hands, which of course stopped the drumming for a while, at least from one hand at a time. And let me say here that my motive for cutting the drumming down was not entirely altruistic – it was getting on my nerves, and Becci, one of my assistants, got really worked up by it. Although I had proved that the drumming was taking up twenty per cent of David's time, it came as a surprise to us. Like any irritating habit that someone else has, it was fast becoming intolerable. Although it only actually took up twenty per cent of the time, we were anticipating it for eighty per cent. It took up part of our minds the whole time!

I was suddenly struck by an urge to pray for David, for healing, while I was massaging his shoulders. This was not something that I really expected, and luckily it was not some sort of Joan of Arc voice – that would have really worried me! It was just an impulse, a feeling, that I ought to do it.

And as I prayed I saw what appeared to be a ring of blue light about fifteen centimetres across, centred on the spine below the shoulder blades. I felt I ought to massage around the edge of the circle, and, using my thumbs, I did. There was nothing extraordinary about it. No angels singing. No big fanfare of trumpets. No sickly sweet Hollywood production number. No Mormon Tabernacle Choir. It was totally matter of fact. An impulse, a circle of blue light, a feeling that I ought to massage it and so I did.

Immediately, and I still feel sceptical about it – it took a militant atheist friend to convince me that I might be being *too* sceptical! – David became relaxed. The drumming stopped. I felt worn out and the frightened look went out of David's face. Still no fanfare, angel voices, orchestra. If anything it was quite dull and boring!

Over the next week I analysed David's drumming again. It was now taking up less than one per cent of his waking day. I was unable to explain it. Except to tell the story as I have told it above. What it did do was ruin my special study.

Instead of a slow step-by-step reduction, the drumming had disappeared almost completely. Instead of mutually exclusive activities progressively taking up more and more of David's time – instead of weaving, sewing, jigsaws, gardening and so on being introduced to stop the drumming – they had to be introduced to fill the newly available time. If anything David was, perhaps, a little more receptive to new skills! It was totally on its head. And I had to go cap-in-hand to the psychologist and explain why my figures didn't tally.

This set me thinking about healing. I began to wonder what healing is, and what health is. If David was healed, then why has he still got learning disabilities? Why does he still need coercion to eat his vegetables? I began to wonder about whether this God that, week after week, as a preacher in the local parish church, I would describe as causing wonderful things to happen, could still do his stuff.

Stories abound, those fantastic tales of miraculous healings, the incredible, the fabulous, the bizarre even. I knew someone who had recovered from a seemingly fatal illness after his church had prayed for him. But still I remain sceptical. The stories in the Bible are full of Jesus healing everybody in sight willy-nilly. But that was then, this is now. And there is a deep gulf between the two.

# 1

# *Field trip!*

The Spirit of the Lord is upon me, because he has anointed me to preach good news to the poor. He has sent me to proclaim release to the captives and recovering of sight to the blind, to set at liberty those who are oppressed, and proclaim the acceptable year of the Lord.

(Luke 4.18–19)
[J. B. Phillips altered]

This is how Luke's Gospel describes what Jesus said that his mission in life was going to be. It is a quotation from the Jewish prophet Isaiah. Luke's Jesus uses the Scriptures because that was what was expected of a prophet or a rabbi, in first-century Palestine. It would have been pointless to have spoken in terms of our modern, scientific, post-Enlightenment age to the age in which he lived, even if he had been able to. His contemporaries would not have understood it. Like us, Jesus was a product of the age in which he lived, or in technical language he was *contextualized*.

To understand the context in which Jesus spoke is in many ways a task that is almost impossible. Layer upon layer of different people's interpretation is involved. Our knowledge of Jesus in the Bible is at the best second-hand, probably at a further remove than that.

Our world-view is entirely different from that of the ancient world. We live in a post-industrial society; theirs was largely agrarian. We have a rigid view of the universe; theirs was negotiable. Our culture is defined by immediacy; theirs was defined by distance. We have miracle drugs; they sought healing miracles. And so on.

5

However, taking these things into account can help us to attempt to make a connection across the differences between now and then. So to begin with it might be useful to look at the reasons that the Gospel writers put pen to paper in the first place. What are their concerns? Are they the same as ours? We do not have any direct, unbiased, first-hand accounts of anything that Jesus said or did. Everything is coloured by the writers of the Gospels looking back from after Easter. In the light of their understanding of the resurrection the writers of the New Testament selected particular events in the life of Jesus. They had a motive and it was not that of a modern biographer. The Gospel writers were concerned with the meaning of Jesus' life, not the facts. Their overriding concern was helping their readers to interpret the life, death, and resurrection of Jesus. If it helped the reader (or probably the hearer – the Gospels were certainly read aloud) to a proper understanding then facts became secondary. The Gospel writers wrote works of faith presenting Jesus in the best possible light, as propaganda, in order that the reader 'may believe' (John 20.31).

This is not a problem except in the way we read the Gospels. It is not a fault in the writers' technique. They were not trying to be biographers or historians. They were, in a very positive sense, propagandists, publishing underground radical pamphlets.

The Gospel writers may have elaborated and written what should have been said in a particular situation. Luke may possibly have put a speech into the mouth of Paul in Athens. It was appropriate in that setting to record what was right rather than bare facts. This was in much the same way that ancient generals would have had heroic pre-battle speeches put into their mouths by their biographers. For they are not meant to be read as objectively as a modern history – questionable as that is. The importance is in the truth that underlies the bare facts, the gospel. They are meant to bring one face to face with Jesus Christ. Gospels are not histories, or biographies, they are Good News. They provoke the response of faith.

The world-view of the first century was very different to ours. According to Stephen Hawking most of us have a very simplified scientific world-view, on a par with that of Galileo.[1] To all intents and purposes, we believe that the world around us has laws that are scientific. If we drop something it follows the law of gravity and falls to the ground. The idea of something happening to break those rules is either impossible, or is a miracle (and we tend to see

6

miracles as superstition or simply bad observation), or is the result of an as yet undiscovered *new* rule.

We believe the sun to be the centre of the solar system circled by the planets. The solar system is on the edge of a galaxy, shaped something like a lens. In turn the galaxy is part of the universe, and so on, beyond comprehension. Everything is natural. Up there is just space and down there is the ground.

The ancient world, at least in the traditional biblical view, was peopled with a God, or gods, humans, and spirits. It was flat. Above the earth was a dome, both being supported by the pillars of the earth (1 Samuel 2.8). This was the sky and heaven. On the inside of the dome were the sun, moon and stars that went across the sky every day or night, racing back to the beginning as soon as they were out of sight (Genesis 1.14f., Psalm 139.9). The sun could also stop moving (Joshua 10.13). The dome, called the firmament, was something like a colander turned upside down. It was full of holes which allowed the rain to come in through the 'floodgates of heaven' (Genesis 7.11). Above the dome were the waters above the firmament and below the earth was more water (Genesis 1.7). The firmament was the area where the gods lived. The earth was where human beings existed. Between the two lived spirits, who were forces for good. Under the earth was the realm of death and evil powers (Job 11.8).

While we see our universe in terms of non-personal, natural, scientific rules, the people of the ancient world saw the world as a personal place. We believe that the earth orbits the sun, a natural phenomenon. Many first-century people saw the sun as a being in its own right, *Sol Invicta*; consequently, the halo around Jesus' head in art represents the disc of the sun. We see all the rules as fixed and permanent; they saw the world as a place that was negotiable. We see natural disasters as being horrific, yet impersonal. The ancients saw a natural disaster as the visitation of some non-human being. According to the book of Genesis, the disaster that overtook Sodom and Gomorrah was the occasion of Abraham plea-bargaining with God. Unsuccessful, yet still worth a try!

There were people in the ancient world, of course, who believed in natural laws. Hippocrates (whose oath until recently bound doctors) taught that epilepsy was natural and natural cures were available. Conversely, many people in our world seem to believe that germs are a kind of personalized affliction, much as demons were in the ancient world. But, generally, where we rely on miracle drugs such as antibiotics they relied on miracle-workers.

The scale of our world is radically different from that of the ancients, so vastly different that the two worlds are incomparable. The ancient world was not only flat but the Americas, Australasia, much of northern Europe, southern Africa and eastern Asia were unknown to the people of the ancient Mediterranean. To go beyond the Pillars of Hercules, out of the Mediterranean, was to venture into the realms of the unknown. *Ultima Thule*, the very last land on the earth before you fell off the edge, was only six days' sailing beyond Britain. And a day's sailing in the first century was meant literally. Mariners would rarely sail after dark because they couldn't see where they were going. Even during the day they rarely ventured far from land. Jesus, as an adult, probably went no farther than a hundred miles from home. Nazareth to Jerusalem, for instance, is about sixty miles, much less than many moderns commute to and from work. The whole of St Paul's missionary journeys were less than ten thousand miles while the modern average annual car mileage is about thirteen thousand miles.

The population in the time of Jesus was largely involved in agrarian pursuits. Even many whose income was not directly from farming indirectly lived from agriculture. Jesus, as a carpenter and jobbing builder, would have built stables and other farm buildings, made cart-wheels and handles for tools, and so on. Jesus time and again refers to sheep, corn, vines or other agricultural themes. To the majority of urban-dwellers in Britain sheep are white blobs, corn that green blur (or pale golden blur in summer) that whips past the car on the way to Tesco's to buy wine! Faith the size of a mustard seed doesn't grow out of a bottle of Sainsbury's Dijon. 'I am the gate for the sheep' is completely meaningless when buying a leg of Safeway's lamb. Gates in Britain are not human beings, no-one sleeps across gateways to keep wolves out! There is probably only a tenuous connection between a frozen leg of lamb and a live sheep in our minds anyway.

The population of the world in biblical times was considerably smaller and, obviously, that of the known world smaller still. Much of Europe was covered with a forest that was nearly impenetrable and very sparsely populated. The majority of first-century cities were little larger than modern villages. Palestine was a comparatively crowded country but did not have a population anywhere near that of today. Joachim Jeremias puts the normal population of Jerusalem at about 25–30,000.[2] At major festivals, however, this figure would have been much inflated.

The age of the population is steadily increasing; there are now close to two million people over the age of eighty in Britain. Assuming that the population as a whole remains at about 56 million, this means about four in every hundred people will be over the age of eighty. And nearly a quarter of the population will be over sixty-five. This has implications for society on a scale never known before. J. D. Crossan, quoting Thomas Carney, suggests that in a pre-industrial society less than three per cent of people reached sixty.[3] More than half of those born alive died before reaching sixteen.

In our modern world we think globally. News broadcasting is nearly instantaneous. A famine in Somalia? Everyone knows. We might not do anything but we know. The world is both larger and smaller. Until relatively recently the far side of the world was at least six weeks away by fast ship; now it is next door. When Jesus was asked, 'Who is my neighbour?' he told the story of the good Samaritan. The Samaritan came into close contact with the victim. Even the Priest and the Levite came within yards of him. Coming so close caused the Samaritan to feel something, to do something. The Samaritan, the Priest and the Levite made decisions based on something touching their world.

We are faced, in our own homes, with images of war, of famine, of disease. The scale of the horrors that we witness daily is beyond even that of the Roman amphitheatre, beyond even that of the Nazi concentration camps. Forty million people in Africa alone are suffering from the effects of famine. The immense scale of natural horror is beyond comprehension. We feel helpless in the face of it all. Hope becomes a futile gesture in the face of such horror. The future looks increasingly bleak.

The concerns of a hugely wider world become our concerns. Not only do we wake in the middle of the night to worry whether there is enough money to pay the mortgage or whether the gas bill has been paid. We wake to mourn for a dead child on the other side of the country, on the other side of a continent, on the other side of the planet. We are touched by an ever increasing need for compassion. And as our compassion is increased it thins. As it flows ever wider into such genuine areas of need it is wasted by being less and less effective. Hope seems futile. We are helpless. Unlike the Samaritan our compassion cannot be translated into action. We become the Priest and the Levite, pouring out our compassion but uselessly.

Until the end of the Middle Ages all books were not only written by hand but every single copy of every single book was a handmade, hand-written copy. Surrounding me on the walls of my study are more books than in many medieval libraries. Supermarkets sell books. So do newsagents and even churches. In the Middle Ages most churches only had one copy of each of the five or six service books that they needed, each one hand-written. By Tudor times printing began to make an impact on society. In 1549, when Thomas Cranmer published his first English Prayer Book, a law was passed to force every church to buy a copy. The price of this printed book was three shillings and eight pence, the monthly wage of an agricultural labourer!

At the time of Jesus there was a professional class of letter-writers. Much as we would use a word-processor and a laser printer to prepare a CV in order to impress a future employer, in the first century people would use a scribe to prepare an impressive-looking letter. Scribes and copyists wrote letters, made copies of documents, and copied books and papers, all with remarkable accuracy.

We live in an age when the news reports in the media are rarely more than a day or so old in national newspapers. Live coverage is seen on the television. Reporters are on the spot, reporting as it happens. It really is new. Until this century much news was weeks old by the time it appeared in the press. The news of Jesus' life was not reported in the next day's *Sun*, it was carried by word of mouth along the major trading routes of the Roman Empire. Instead of hours or days, in rural areas, it was still news years after the events! Instant reporting has had a major impact on the society in which we live. We no longer need to go out gossiping with neighbours, in fact local gossip is largely irrelevant. The news that we gather is much wider. News and gossip are regional, national and international. This has the effect of enclosing us in the cocoon of our homes and, at the same time, exposing us to the world in a way never seen before.

Palestine at the time of Jesus was an occupied country. The *Pax Romana*, for all its benefits, and there were many, was nonetheless an imposed peace. Early Christians were less impressed: the book of

# Field trip!

Revelation paints a different picture of Rome and her supposedly benevolent rule. As Richard Bauckham points out:

> Rome is a harlot because her associations with the peoples of her empire are for her own economic benefit. [...] she offers the supposed benefits of the *Pax Romana*, [...] unity, security, stability, the conditions of prosperity. But in John's view these benefits are not what they seem: they are the favours of a prostitute, purchased at a high price. The *Pax Romana* is really a system of economic exploitation of the empire. Rome's subjects give far more to her than she gives to them.[4]

The pages of the New Testament are full of Romans: soldiers, officials, and Roman puppets. The foreign Herods were appointed kings over the Jewish people – they were from Idumea, the hated Edom of the Old Testament.

Even worse was tax collection. A Roman official was given charge of an area with a quota to collect. Anything he managed to collect on top of the quota was profit. He, in turn, appointed gatherers to collect. They were unpaid and again had to skim from the top. The whole system was utterly corrupt! The Pharisee who thanked God that he was not a sinner like the tax-collector had a real point.

At least one of Jesus' disciples was part of an anti-Roman resistance movement – Simon, a terrorist, a Zealot. Perhaps Judas Iscariot too: he may have been named after his favourite method of assassination – a *sikarios*, a thin-bladed stiletto. Jesus' family was almost certainly part of an anti-occupation sub-culture, though not necessarily actively involved. Jesus' and his brothers' names reflect a nationalistic fervour. Jesus is a form of Joshua, meaning 'Yahweh is Salvation', and is the name of a hero who liberated the promised land. Jesus' brothers' names similarly echo a desire for liberation: Simon and Judas were named after heroes of the Maccabaean revolt; James (or Jacob) and Joseph were named after two of the Patriarchs, founders of the nation. They lived in Galilee which, John Marsh suggests, was more militantly nationalistic than Judea.[5]

J. Massyngbaerde Ford points to the centrality of a class-struggle in the gospels.[6] She suggests that, in Jesus' era, nationalism was a way in which the lower classes could find an identity apart from the Roman Empire. Nationalists projected God as king. This took three forms. First, God was the universal sovereign. God was ruler over Romans too and, therefore, all people were equally subject to the Law. Secondly, God was King of Israel and would overthrow the present regime. Finally, God was the eschatological King; his Kingdom is not of this world. Each of these ideas can be found in the New Testament, applied to Jesus. There is, for example, the King of kings and Lord of lords (Revelation 19.16), a universal ruler. There is the inscription over Jesus' head, 'This is the King of the Jews' (Matthew 27.37, etc.), and the statement of Jesus, 'My kingdom is not of this world' (John 18.36). The idea of a politically subversive element within the group of disciples is quite likely. What is surprising is that in the Synoptic Gospels, Jesus does not appear to show any unwillingness to pay taxes or even handle the hated foreign coins with their pagan symbols and idolatrous images. Jesus, in the Gospels, is no classic class-warrior, but neither does he accept the status quo uncritically.

St Paul, on the other hand, was one of the elite of the Roman Empire. Society was divided into three broad social classes: slaves, the masses, and Roman citizens. Most citizens were, of course, Italians, but as the empire expanded leading provincial citizens were allowed to buy citizenship. And if you survived the twenty-five-year enlistment in the legions citizenship was part of your pension! Paul, by inheritance as a citizen of 'no mean city', was allowed to appeal to the emperor for justice. This was denied to Jesus, a commoner. Jesus was crucified – a punishment for slaves and non-citizens – and Paul beheaded, a privilege, if it can be called that, of citizenship!

Women have been denied equality in Britain by legal and structural means – only relatively recently have they not been the legal property of men. The attitude of Jesus to women in a more repressive society than our own, especially as it was reported exclusively by the men who wrote the Gospels, is all the more remarkable. Incidentally, the Pauline statement that in Christ there is neither male nor female (Galatians 3.28) cannot be seen as empowering women so much as restricting men. In the ancient world a man committing adultery was not seen as being serious compared to adultery in a woman. The reason is largely to do with inheritance: if a child was born to a woman who committed adultery, its paternity is uncertain and so the inheritance may pass to someone not entitled to it. The children fathered by an adulterous man were simply not his problem! Paul doesn't allow women to have the same freedom as men – men should be continent too.

The Jewish people in biblical times were not very tolerant of non-Jews, and this has continued to the present day. So the attitude of Jesus to the outsider, the non-Jew, even allowing for the deliberate slanting of the Gospel writers to make Jesus accessible to Gentiles, is remarkably enlightened. That this enlightenment has not been a historical feature of the Church is unpardonable.

Finally, our world is a place that is interconnected economically in a way that the world never has been before. A fall in coffee prices in Europe means economic ruin in Brazil or Kenya. An end to a civil war in Africa means three thousand more on the dole in Liverpool, say, where the weapon guidance systems are made. The very scale of the potential harm that can be done to the eco-structure of the planet is beyond anything that has ever happened before.

In the first century, the Roman Empire was, similarily, an economically interdependent structure. A poor grain harvest in Egypt could mean a famine in Rome. With a population of between 800,000 and one million in the first century, making it the largest city in the Western world until eighteenth-century London, the Roman preoccupation with bread (and circuses) is understandable. 'The very life of the Roman people is daily at the hazard of wind and wave,' said the Emperor Tiberius. The fact that Rome was so dependent upon imported grain became the subject of an imperial edict telling landowners to stop planting vineyards and grow wheat and barley instead. Nonetheless, the level of interdependence was nothing like as extensive as it is today.

The Roman army could lay waste a whole region, salting the fields, destroying crops, causing long-term deprivation to the population. A war would be followed by starvation and disease. Compared to those available to us, these weapons were negligible. Both deliberately and accidentally the scale of any potential ecological damage is limited by resources and abilities. Those of our world are infinitely more deadly in their scope.

The whole view of economics was different in the ancient world. In modern society, particularly in the post-industrial West, the economic base is the commercial transaction. Money is borrowed, at interest, and then invested in trade or industry to create more wealth. The capitalist ideal is that there is a trickle-down effect that increases the wealth of all people. This would not only have seemed ludicrous to the Roman world, it would also have been immoral. Their ideal was to be a farmer – a rich farmer with lots of land and slaves to do the actual work, but nonetheless a farmer. Cato points out that someone who lent money to others as a profession, a usurer or money-lender, was the lowest of the low. 'Our ancestors held', he wrote, that the thief be fined 'double and the usurer four-fold [. . .] one may judge from this [. . .] how much less desirable a citizen they considered the usurer than the thief.'[7] This model for citizenship has contained within it a moral hierarchy as well as a social one. At the summit is the gentleman-farmer, then the merchant (preferably the gentleman making a one-off venture), then the thief, and, at the very bottom, the money-lender.

The Christian Church did not really begin to challenge slavery until the fourth century. As a system it was complex and paradoxical. Although the work and life of an agricultural slave was harsh and frequently brutal, household slaves were treated quite differently. Agriculture was extremely labour-intensive and farm-slaves were treated as 'articulate' animals. They were frequently branded with an owner's mark and supplied with a bare minimum of food and clothing; slave-revolts were the only option. On the other hand, slavery was not a barrier to social advancement in the towns: a number of bishops had been slaves, notably Callistus, a fourth-century Pope.

Roman aristocrats had body-slaves who were literally trusted with their master's life. Trusted servants would hold a blade to their owner's throat while shaving them. The body-slave was frequently viewed more as a friend and confidant, doubling as a personal secretary or trusted emissary, than as property. Marcus Tullius Cicero, the philosopher, had a slave called Tiro who was very close. When Tiro became ill Cicero sent him a series of letters that are certainly not what one would expect. 'You must now be well in mind so as to be so in body, I beg of you to ensure this as much for my sake as for your own,' he wrote on 10 April 53 BCE.[8] 'You could not believe how anxious I am about your health,' he wrote two days later.[9] Tiro recovered, was freed and took the name Marcus Tullius Tiro in order to show his gratitude and his continuing client status. Paul obviously had a very close relationship with the runaway, Onesimus. The relative status of Roman citizen and slave is largely irrelevant: 'I am sending him back to you now, and

14

with him goes my heart [. . .] How much he means to me!' (Philemon 12, 16)

Small-scale factories existed, for instance in the manufacture of roof-tiles or pottery, but these were not factories in the modern sense. Whole households worked at the craft trades, passing the skills on from generation to generation. Among the poorer people were the day labourers who were available to work on farms or to do labouring work for building projects. The parable of the workers in the vineyard in Matthew 20 sets their daily wage at one denarius, though work was uncertain and probably seasonal. There was no job-security in labouring. The labourers would have been, in the main, poor, unskilled workers without enough land to support their families.

Roman policy was not to generate more wealth through increased production or trade; instead it sought to redistribute existing wealth. Through taxation or plunder the empire redistributed wealth from the conquered nations to the centre. Practically, this meant that the empire had to expand, increase the tax burden or suffer economic collapse. Inside the empire there was only a finite amount of wealth, and with no philosophy of wealth creation, the only way to increase this wealth was to increase the size of the empire itself.

To maintain itself a slave-owning culture needs a continual influx of fresh slaves to replace the dead. When the Jewish revolt of 68–70 CE was suppressed 70,000 new slaves were suddenly made available, from all classes and degrees of learning and culture. It is a particular feature of slavery, illness and pregnancy being economically unproductive, that the ante- and post-natal mortality rate is extraordinarily high. Cato wrote: 'Sell [. . .] an old slave, a sickly slave, and whatever else is super-fluous.'[10] This meant that in many ways the society had to sustain a policy of military expansionism.

The Roman world may be viewed as having a socio-economic structure shaped something like a series of distorted pyramids. At the top was the patron who had clients: servants, slaves or free, who depended upon him or her directly. These clients would all be part of the household of rich patrons, perhaps eating at their table and being housed, clothed and fed at their expense. These clients in turn would be in the position of exercising a form of patronage over others, perhaps by a less direct method. Jesus' parables of the unforgiving servant in Matthew 18.23ff. and the unrighteous steward in Luke 16 both show examples of this form of hierarchy. The servant and the steward are themselves clients but call in the favours owed to them by their own subordinates. Society was founded more upon obligation than on simple finance. Although cash was used it could not wholly cancel a debt. One was still obligated to one's patron for the kindness of loaning the money or whatever in the first instance.

Social mobility was by way of becoming part of the household of a rich and powerful patron. By increasing the patron's wealth, perhaps, by the slightly *infra dig* method of trade, one was allowed by the patron to rise too. And while one remained a client the idea was to gain the goodwill of one's patron who would then shower one with responsibility and power. The parable of the pounds in Luke 19.12ff. gives a picture of the patron increasing the authority of the good servants. For their performance they receive the authority over ten or five cities. The negative side is that the one who doesn't do well receives the anger of the aristocrat. The same parable when recounted in Matthew has the 'useless servant' thrown out of the household to become an outcast. He is now someone outside of the economic system, with no-one to feed him, clothe him or give him shelter. It is no wonder that 'he will cry and grind his teeth' (Matthew 25.30).

The view of the world that we hold – our science, our geography, our communications and mass media, our social, political and economic view, is different from that of the people in the Bible. Our world is not their world and we can have no real connection with theirs unless we attempt to build a bridge of our imagination, taking into account both their world and ours.

Then Jesus went to Nazareth, where he had been brought up, and on the Sabbath he went as usual to the synagogue. He stood up to read the Scriptures and was handed the book of the prophet Isaiah. He unrolled the scroll and found the place where it is written: 'The Spirit of the Lord is upon me, because he has chosen me to bring good news to the poor. He has sent me to proclaim liberty to the captives and recovery of sight to the blind; to set free the oppressed and announce that the time has come when the Lord will save his people.'

Jesus rolled up the scroll, gave it back to the attendant, and sat down. All the people in the synagogue had their eyes fixed on him, as he said to them, 'This passage of scripture has come true today, as you heard it being read.'

They were all well impressed with him and marvelled at the eloquent words that he spoke. They said, 'Isn't he the son of Joseph?'

He said to them, 'I am sure that you will quote this proverb to me, "Doctor, heal yourself." You will also tell me to do here in my home town the same things you heard were done in Capernaum. I tell you this,' Jesus added, 'prophets are never welcomed in their home town.

'Listen to me: it is true that there were many widows in Israel during the time of Elijah, when there was no rain for three and a half years and a severe famine spread throughout the whole land. Yet Elijah was not sent to any one living in Israel, but only to a widow living in Zarephath in the territory of Sidon. And there were many people suffering from the dread skin disease who lived in Israel during the time of the prophet Elisha; yet not one of them was healed, but only Naaman the Syrian.'

When the people in the synagogue heard this, they were filled with anger. They rose up, dragged Jesus out of the town, and took him up to the top of the hill on which their town was built. They meant to throw him over the cliff, but he walked through the middle of the crowd and went his way.

(Luke 4.16–30)

Luke sets Jesus' declaration in Nazareth, the place where he grew up. It was the Sabbath so Jesus went to the synagogue. Archaeological evidence suggests that in first-century Palestine women were excluded from day-to-day synagogue worship. They were allowed to view worship through a removable screen on special occasions but, to all intents and purposes, the synagogue was a male preserve. The description of the ritual in the synagogue in Nazareth is similar to that still found in many Orthodox synagogues. Chaim Raphael says that synagogues are 'meeting places for hearing the *Torah* read, usually with commentary and sermonic interpretation'.[11]

The official in charge of the synagogue was known in Hebrew as a *Chazzan*, and was a mixture of caretaker and schoolteacher. His job was to take care of the synagogue, to keep it clean, to teach the children and to take care of the scrolls that the scriptures were written on. He would give the hand-written scroll to the reader and put it away after the reading. The scroll was so valuable that the surface was not to be touched and a pointer was (and is) used to follow the words.

When Jesus finished reading the passage from Isaiah he sat down. In our culture it is usual for people to stand to speak. In first-century Palestine the Rabbi would sit to teach; in modern universities the Professor has a chair reflecting this ancient tradition. So when Jesus sat down, Luke has everyone look, 'their eyes fixed on him'. They would have been filled with anticipation, expecting an interpretation of the passage. Like a modern church congregation, or a football crowd, or those watching a soap opera, they knew what would happen next. They carried baggage with them: their past, their aspirations, history, social and political context, and so on. When Jesus did not match their expectations he created conflict. After all, Jesus was supposed to be one of them. He had grown up here. Everybody knew him – he went to the synagogue as usual. People looked at each other confused – 'Isn't this the son of Joseph?' They were not expecting some local nobody to suddenly say that a five-hundred-year-old prophecy had been fulfilled. Not right there in front of them!

Claus Westermann, with some exaggeration, describes the passage as being 'the last occasion in the history of Israel on which a prophet expressed his certainty of having been sent by God with a message to his nation with such freedom and conviction'.[12] And suddenly, in the middle of ordinary Sabbath worship, this person everyone had known from childhood says it is fulfilled. Here and now. Shocking, to say the least.

It is morning, barely. The unborn sun is just beginning to lighten the night sky. The stars are fading in the firmament. As the sky becomes purple, then pink, men are hurrying past, moving silently in the dawn. You join them. Ahead is a low, single-storey building. The tiny windows high up in the walls are alight with welcome.

As you enter the porch you pull your fringed scarf, your *tallith*, up over your head. Perhaps you think of Samson, who had such pride in the length of his hair that he walked about with his head uncovered. Or Absalom, think what his pride led to! Better to be humble and cover your head. You wind the leather straps of the *tephilim* around your left arm, the one nearest the heart, and on to your forehead. And as the tiny leather boxes touch remember that you worship God with all your heart and all your mind!

As you enter the doorway you reach up and touch the small box containing words of Scripture with your right hand. You kiss the fingertips and pass on. Inside the building is smoky and the lamps are spitting and flickering. About forty or fifty men are crammed into the room, there are benches to sit on along the walls but everyone is standing. You recognize most of the people, it's a small town and strangers are rare. You work your way through the crowd to stand with some friends.

The *Chazzan* begins the service as the sun lights up the horizon, sending beams of glorious light through the tiny windows. Everyone – you, Ephraim the baker, Jacob the rich Pharisee who has as many as *ten* servants, Joshua the weaver (you know, the one who can get the occasional lamb, no questions asked), and all of the others – joins in the familiar words. After all, you have recited them three times a day for the whole of your adult life – ever since your thirteenth birthday. They were the first words you ever heard, whispered into your ear just after you were born. And, hopefully – pray God you'll die of old age in your bed – they'll be the last words you'll ever say before seeing God face to face.

*Shema Yisrael Adonai Eloheynu Adonai Echad.*

(Hear, O Israel: The Lord our God, The Lord is one.)

The prayers follow the *Shema*; perhaps everyone takes three steps backwards and then forwards again. After all, Moses had to pass through three halting-places on his way up the mountain to receive the law, the *Torah*: through the darkness; through the cloud; and through the thick darkness. The prayers are called the *Amidah* or standing because you say the eighteen prayers blessing God standing up.

Then comes the portion of Scripture appointed to be read from the Law. Perhaps you are one of those that the elders have asked to read part of the Law. The *Chazzan* goes to the ark or cupboard in the wall and takes out a scroll. He carefully unwraps the coverings and places the scroll on the desk ready for you. He hands you the special pointer so that you can follow the reading without touching the precious vellum.

All week, in your everyday life, you have spoken in Aramaic. Your notes about the grain that you buy and sell have been in Aramaic. Your children speak Aramaic. Your wife speaks Aramaic.

And now, here in front of you, is this portion of Scripture – and it is written in Hebrew. Not that you can't read Hebrew or anything, but it is not as familiar to you as it was when you were learning to read it daily at school. You struggle through it, with the *Chazzan* giving an Aramaic translation as you go along. Finally it is over and as you return to your place a few friends gently pat you on the shoulder. Well done, they mouth silently. You redden a little and feel a little bit smug, just a bit self-satisfied. Yes! I can still do it! Now, let's see if old Habbakuk can do it anywhere near as well.

Then it is the turn of this young man, his beard is untouched by grey as yet. I know who he is, Joseph's son, the builder, did cousin Miriam's new place out Capernaum way. Neat bit of joinery. Nicely done, mmm. This is the free choice of a piece from one of the Prophets. Isaiah, jolly good. Oh, that bit. Yes. Life is hard but if we put up with it for a while longer those that oppress us now will get their come-uppance. We might be slaving away for no return – that's the fault of these Romans and their tax-collectors. The day of God's favour is coming. Yes, we'll drive the bloody Romans into the sea and we'll be free. Liberty for the captives, yes. We'll get our liberty when we get rid of these foreigners who oppress us. Oops, he's sat down. I'd better sit on the floor. Still, he can't have anything new to say. Let's fight the Romans and we'll be ready for the year of Jubilee. Get all our old debts sorted out then, eh?

Who does he think he is? 'This passage of scripture has come true today, as you heard it being read.' How can he know what it means? It's about fighting the Romans, boy, not building houses! How can it have come true? What does he know? He's just Joseph's son. A common builder. I watched him grow up; he was nothing special then! And he's bloody rude! Don't you come quoting stories about Elijah and Elisha and them foreigners to me, sonny. If you really were any good you could heal the sick here, but no. It's all right healing the sick in Capernaum, what about here, eh? Not enough publicity, is it?

And now you've got the damn cheek to accuse us of not being good enough to hear this good news. Insolent and rude. Fancy, saying that foreigners are better than we are, the people that you grew up with. Stoning's too good for him, I say. Let's throw him off the top of the hill.

And everyone joins in and bundles him off. It's blasphemy, or as good as, to say that we, God's chosen people, are going to take second place to foreigners. But he looks straight at you, eye to eye. And our arms drop. We can't do it. And one by one we go home. Ashamed of ourselves.

Luke's is not the only Gospel to describe Jesus' conflict with the people of his home town; they all do – even John mentions it in passing. Luke, however, makes conflict the fulfilment of Isaiah's prophecy. Luke begins his 'orderly account' of Jesus' ministry with this keynote speech.

It has been suggested that Jesus was a preacher, announcing God's Kingdom. This relegates the healing ministry to second place; healing becomes a testimony to the words. However, Luke's Jesus lists the priorities, giving each equal weight. Bringing sight to the blind is as important as bringing good news to the poor, which is as important as proclaiming release to the captives. They are part and parcel of each other.

Isaiah's prophecy would have been heard by first-century Galileans as God's declaration of war on the Romans. The very next phrase in Isaiah (not quoted by Luke) is that God will save his people 'and defeat their enemies'. Even if Jesus didn't quote this part, and he probably would have done, the complete prophecy would have been well known. Listeners would have supplied the unspoken agenda for themselves. The land would soon enjoy the wealth of other nations and the oppressors go. All would be turned upside down. These cursed foreigners will become slaves and do the work!

The phrase about restoring of sight for the blind is not found in the extant Hebrew versions of Isaiah; the Hebrew is confused. The Masoretic Text reads, 'to open wide the gates of darkness', usually thought to mean 'opening the eyes of those who are imprisoned by blindness'. However, the Greek version known as the Septuagint has both releasing the prisoners and restoring sight to the blind, probably because they too were unsure of the meaning.

By referring to restoring sight the essentially passive prophecy becomes a manifesto of action. One no longer needs to wait for God to put things right in the future. The future is now; it is beginning.

Jesus has been healing in Capernaum. The year of Jubilee, when all debts were written off; all land returned to its former owner, has already begun there. The people of Capernaum don't get talk; they get action. And yet Jesus is not prepared to heal here. And this is supposed to be his home, he grew up with these people. He owed them something. No wonder they were a bit miffed!

Coming from Galilee with its rebellions and resentments, did Jesus have ambitions to be a political messiah, a warrior-king? Did he think that his role was to lead the people in armed revolt against the Romans? Or perhaps, like Gandhi, lead peaceful civil disobedience? Or was he beyond politics, a spiritual leader whose other-worldly kingdom was above power-plays?

Many of the portraits of Jesus that have been painted over the past thirty or so years have reflected less of the first century than the twentieth. We have made Jesus in our own image! In the 1960s John Allegro portrayed Jesus as a hippie, hallucinating on magic mushrooms. In the seventies Jesus became a political revolutionary, a kind of early Che Guevara. In eighties Britain Jesus became a central figure in the conflict between the ruling right wing and the radical left. He was an individual who dealt with individuals, on an individual basis – Margaret Thatcher argued that there is no such thing as society. And he was the social Christ – embodied in the solidarity within movements such as the miners' unions. In the 1990s Stevan L. Davies described Jesus as a New Age shaman who uses psycho-therapy to cast out demons.[13]

So we have to be careful how we build our model of Jesus. Lame Deer, a medicine man of the native American Lakota people, wrote:

You have made a blondie out of Jesus. I don't care for those blonde, blue-eyed pictures of a sanitised, Cloroxed, Ajaxed Christ. How would you like it if I put braids on Jesus and stuck a feather in his hair? You would call me a very crazy Indian, wouldn't you? Jesus was a Jew. He wasn't a yellow-haired Anglo. [...] His religion came out of the desert in which he lived, out of his kind of mountains, his kind of animals, his kind of plants. You've tried to make him into [...] a long-haired Billy Graham in a fancy night-shirt, and that's why he doesn't work for you anymore.[14]

Lame Deer shows a Europeanized, distorted view of Jesus, not applicable to First Americans. The Jesus of the European settlers was one of them! And as Lame Deer points out, as a Jew, Jesus was hardly the type they would meet socially. And they wouldn't let their daughters marry him! Our search must be for Jesus in the authentic setting of his own time.

The Gospels portray Jesus as being perceived as a political threat to the power of Rome – once their attention was drawn to it. The chief priests and Sanhedrin saw Jesus as a blasphemer. Although we would see those as separate categories, in the first century things were not so easily separated. The emperor was also a religious figure; he was frequently also *Pontifex Maximus*, the head of the Roman state religion. The emperors were also venerated as gods, so they were often in the peculiar position of being chief priest in their own cult!

There was no distinction between religious and other areas of life, particularly among Jewish people. The law of Moses, the *Torah*, governed all life. Medicine, healthcare, diet, and economic, social and sexual relationships, were integrated in the *Torah*; and inter-spersed were religious rituals. There was no distinction between commands to lend money to the poor without interest and rules concerning the animals for sacrifice. Life was life and no distinction could be made.

Jesus would not have seen himself as a political revolutionary, as an agent of social change or as a spiritual leader. To have over-thrown the Roman overlords would have been seen as a religious act. All life was governed by the laws that God gave to Moses, in this land that was given to the Jewish people by God. Luke's tradition of Jesus' manifesto makes his task all-embracing, covering all life. And there is no reason why we should seriously doubt that Luke is echoing a tradition that goes back to Jesus.

In a later reference to the same prophecy Jesus answers a query about whether he was the great deliverer that John the Baptist expected. Jesus' actions did not match John's ideas of a deliverer and he was concerned.

Go back and tell John what you have seen and heard: the blind can see, the lame can walk, those who suffer from dreaded skin diseases are made clean, the deaf can hear, the dead are raised to life, and the Good News is preached to the poor.

(Luke 7.22)

John the Baptist was seen by the early church as a witness to Jesus. As, in this story, he is shown as doubting, if not actually hostile to Jesus, the story is probably early and reflects a real sense of conflict between the cousins. John was expecting a war-lord, a mighty warrior, a Day of the Lord judgement-figure. He expected Jesus to come armed with a metaphorical winnowing-shovel to stir things up, beginning the end times. The chaff, the Romans, would be discarded, consumed in a fire. The people of Palestine, the good grain, would be saved.

Instead Jesus backs away from any role imposed on him. He declares that he restores those left out, returning those who are completely marginalized to the centre of things – the sick, the dead, and, the poor. He maintains his integrity by choosing not to be moulded by another person's ideology. Jesus' mission had great urgency. It was no a theoretical mission proclaiming some distant pie in the sky when we die. There is no time to waste. Jesus saw his mission in terms of God's endgame. The Kingdom of God is here and now. So when he favours the people on the edge, it is because of the frightening urgency. The poor and sick must come first; they have no time to waste. Their very lives are at risk. Their needs are desperate.

This is the justice and righteousness that God requires. The blind recover their sight; the deaf hear; the lame walk; the person with the dreaded skin disease is cleansed. This leprosy-like dreaded skin disease was not only physically disfiguring, it was socially disfiguring as well, the result of moral uncleanness, needing isolation. Paralysed people were isolated *in* the community that they depended on. Illness meant isolation at all levels: physical, social, spiritual and ritual, it encompassed the whole person. Jesus addressed this immediate situation. He was not against the rich, it was merely that the poor have no time to lose. Jesus brings liberation – from the power of disease; from the power of outside forces; from internal chaos. And liberation creates conflict.

Jesus conflicted with the people of his home town. He and John the Baptist are portrayed in a very early tradition as not seeing eye to eye. Much of Jesus' ministry (all according to some scholars[15]) can be seen as conflict. There are situations of conflict with the scribes and Pharisees; conflicts with demons and spirits; a conflict which escalated into a violent assault upon the sanctuary traders in the Temple; conflict within himself in the Garden of Gethsemane; conflicts with the chief priests and the Romans; and, finally, a successful conflict with death itself. The idea of a gentle Jesus meek and mild flies in the face of the evidence. Jesus was a figure of controversy; conflict centred upon him.

## NOTES

1 Filkin, D., *Stephen Hawking's Universe: the cosmos explained.* BBC Books, London, 1997, p. 16.
2 Jeremias, J., *Jerusalem in the time of Jesus.* SCM, London, 1985, p. 84.
3 Crossan, J. D., *The Historical Jesus: the life and times of a Mediterranean Jewish peasant.* T. & T. Clark, Edinburgh, 1991, p. 4.
4 Bauckham, R., *The Climax of Prophecy: studies in the Book of Revelation.* T. & T. Clark, Edinburgh, 1993, p. 347.
5 Marsh, J., *Jesus in his Lifetime.* Sidgwick & Jackson, London, 1981, p. 89.
6 Massyngbaerde Ford, J., *My Enemy is my Guest: Jesus and violence in Luke.* Orbis, Maryknoll, NY, 1984, pp. 4f., etc.
7 Marcus Porcius Cato, *On Agriculture* 1, cited in Crossan, *The Historical Jesus*, p. 51.
8 Cicero, *Letters to his Friends* 16. 14, cited in Crossan, *The Historical Jesus*, p. 48.
9 Cicero, *Letters to his Friends* 16. 15, cited in Crossan, *The Historical Jesus*, p. 49.
10 Cato, *On Agriculture* 2. 7, cited in Crossan, *The Historical Jesus*, p. 47.
11 Raphael, C., *The Springs of Jewish Life.* Chatto & Windus, London, 1983, p. 155.
12 Westerman, C., *Isaiah 40–66, a commentary.* SCM, London, 1969, p. 367.
13 Davies, S., *Jesus the Healer.* SCM, London, 1995, pp. 116–19, etc.
14 Lame Deer and Erdoes, R., *Lame Deer: Sioux Medicine Man,* quoted in Hodgson, J. and Kothare, J., *Vision Quest: Native Spirituality and the Church in Canada.* Anglican Book Centre, Toronto, 1990, pp. 162f.
15 For example, Myers, C., *Binding the Strong Man: a political reading of Mark's story of Jesus.* Orbis, Maryknoll, NY, 1988.

# 2

# *Case conferences*

Doctors will often call a case conference for particularly complicated problems. They call together a group of experts, each
hopefully having something to contribute, to restore the patient
to full health. The most important experts that we have for Jesus'
cases are the four Gospel writers, and the oral traditions underlying
the Gospels. Their contribution will be central but there are a
number of experts in history, biblical studies and medicine who,
hopefully, may also shed light on Jesus' ministry. The Gospels
record thirty-eight incidents of healing: raising the dead, healing
the sick, and exorcising the spirits which control the possessed.
Twenty-six accounts describe individual healings and twelve refer
to groups – the latter are scanty in detail, saying only, for instance,
that 'he healed them'. Thus the individual healings must form the
basis of our case studies.

The individuals recorded as being healed suffered from a variety
of complaints and illnesses. There were eleven people with the
dreaded skin disease (which the older translations of the Bible
call leprosy – probably vitiligo or psoriasis, not Hansen's Disease
or true leprosy, which was rare in first-century Palestine); five who
were blind; two with paralysis; someone with a withered hand; a
person with deaf-mutism; a woman with a haemorrhage. There are
a further eight who have demon possession, plus Mary of Magdala
who was released from seven demons. And three people who were,
according to the Gospel accounts, raised from the dead.

The Greek Gospels use two types of word for sickness, those
which refer to specific areas, like *cholos* meaning lameness, and
general words, similar to those used in modern English. The
Greek *kakos echontes* literally means in a bad way. *Astheneia*
means without strength, weak. These are too vague to give much

idea of Jesus' activity. Therefore we must concentrate on more specific diagnoses. There are also different words used to describe healing: the basic Greek words are *therapeuo, iaomai, sozo,* or *diasozo,* and *apokathistemi.* The first two are general verbs meaning to heal. *Therapeuo* is the service of a physician, closely related to the idea of serving. *Iaomai* is from the same root as the word for physician and means to act as a physician, to cure. The writers of the first three Gospels prefer word *therapeuo* whereas John tends to use *iaomai.* Luke, however, uses the two almost interchangeably (*therapeuo* fourteen times and *iaomai* twelve). Mark, on the other hand, only uses *iaomai* once but uses *sozo* as often as *therapeuo* – six times each.

Mark was probably the earliest of the Gospels (at least in its first redaction or edition) and, interestingly, uses the word *sozo* most frequently. This verb has a wide range of meanings: to save or to keep, especially to keep alive or preserve from harm; to keep or observe the Law; to keep in mind or remember. It is often used with the additional sense of motion: 'to bring one safe to, to escape to a place' or to carry off to safety, to rescue from war or to rescue a country from the enemy.

*Sozo* and its related words are used in the Greek Septuagint as an equivalent to the Hebrew *shalom* which has a whole spectrum of meanings: strength, wholeness, peace, long life, salvation, right-eousness, soundness, well-being, prosperity, completeness. John Wilkinson comments, 'Healing is never purely physical, and the salvation of the soul is never purely spiritual, but both are fore-shadowed and illustrated in the healing miracles of Jesus in the Gospels.'[1]

## CASE I

### THE MAN WITH PARALYSIS

A few days later Jesus went back to Capernaum, and the news spread that he was at home. So many people came together that there was no room left, not even out in front of the door. Jesus was preaching the message to them when four men arrived, carrying a paralysed man to Jesus. Because of the crowd, however, they could not get the man to him. So they made a hole in the roof right above the place where Jesus was.

27

When they had made an opening, they let the man down, lying on his mat.

Seeing how much faith they had, Jesus said to the paralysed man, 'My son, your sins are forgiven.'

Some teachers of the Law who were sitting there thought to themselves, 'How does he dare to talk like this? This is blasphemy! God is the only one who can forgive sins!'

At once Jesus knew what they were thinking, so he said to them, 'Why do you think such things? Is it easier to say to this paralysed man, 'Your sins are forgiven', or to say, 'Get up, pick up your mat, and walk'? I will prove to you, then, that the Son of Man has authority on earth to forgive sins.' So he said to the paralysed man, 'I tell you, get up, pick up your mat, and go home!'

While they all watched, the man got up, picked up his mat, and hurried away. They were all completely amazed and praised God, saying, 'We have never seen anything like this!'

(Mark 2.1–12)

It was often argued that Jesus did not heal at all and these narratives were fictional additions to the story of a simple teacher. More recently, however, evidence has begun to emerge that Jesus was one healer in a culture where other healers performed similar acts. The Jewish people were renowned throughout the empire for their exorcisms. A generation after Jesus, the Jewish historian Josephus boasted of their power over demons.[2]

This man is described as having paralysis and so being carried everywhere. Apart from any pain and distress he suffered, the effects of his illness were devastating. There were only a handful of hospitals in the whole known world, there was no National Insurance or Sickness Benefit (or even private health insurance!). Unless sick people were independently wealthy, and did not have to work, they had no income. We can assume that this man was not wealthy as friends carried him not servants, and rich people sent for Jesus! He was a burden on the tiny community of family and friends. Their resources, depleted by the loss of his income, were further stretched by the cost of caring. This cannot be measured in purely financial terms – there is also a human cost.

The man couldn't walk because of his paralysis. To go anywhere his friends carried him. Unable to walk, he required constant attendance to perform bodily functions. And even were he fully continent someone had to fetch the utensils and, perhaps, help him use them. This meant twenty-four-hour care. And twenty-four-hour care means just that. There is no break from it. It goes on day after day, week after week, month after month, year after year, interminably.

The effect on family and friends of long-term illness is devastating. Initial enthusiasm wanes and becomes duty. The sick person has done nothing and seen no-one since the last visit. With no new stimuli, conversation becomes repetition – creating boredom, then tension, and irritation in everyone involved. Finally, anticipation causes irritation to begin even before a visit. This lack of enthusiasm and irritation develops, more seriously, into guilt. This is projected on to the sick person. The sickness, and therefore the sick person, cause your guilt. They are responsible, not you. It becomes easier not to visit, placing even more strain on the immediate family who, imprisoned by the illness, cannot escape.

So, hearing that Jesus is in Capernaum, you go. Perhaps after his treatment in Nazareth, Jesus set up home in friendlier Capernaum. Perhaps he already had, causing rejection in Nazareth! Mark suggests that Jesus was at his own home but this author is frequently vague about time and place. He inherited an oral tradition less interested in where and when than about faith in the living Lord. Traditionally, Mark records Peter's teaching, stringing together Peter's stories into one narrative. So Mark is full of 'immediately', 'then', or as here, 'a few days later', making the narrative flow. There is a breathless quality to it, a kind of 'and then ... and then ... and then ...' A Gospel for those on the edge, with no time to spare. It is short and fast-moving; people in crisis have no time for explanations. It is a headlong rush to the cross. At Jesus' baptism the cross is on the horizon. From the transfiguration it is inescapable. Mark's immediacy has a carefully composed structure which favours those whose needs have deadly haste.

There are crowds – with no hospitals those who suffered from long-term debilitating illnesses would have been commonplace. The person who was blind, or deaf, who had paralysis or demon-possession, received what care was available at home. People with acute illnesses or fevers would have either recovered, continued to be ill or died.

Although some families have been enriched and drawn closer by the experience of caring, the human cost of care is more than many families can bear. A high ratio of parents with a child having special needs, requiring long-term care and intensive monitoring, experience broken relationships. The historian Morton Smith recalls an example of the horrendous effect on one individual in 1940s Jerusalem. A person, suffering what Smith describes as lunacy, was turned out into the streets. The family was unable to cope any longer.

> The first thing I saw [...] was a lunatic, a filthy creature wearing an old burlap bag with neck and armholes cut through bottom and sides. He was having a fit. It seemed to involve a conversation with some imaginary being in front of him. He was pouring out a flood of gibberish while raising his hands as if in supplication. Soon he began to make gestures, as if trying to protect himself from blows, and howled as if being beaten. Frothing at the mouth, he fell to the ground on his face, lay there moaning and writhing, vomited, and had an attack of diarrhoea. Afterwards he was calmer but lay in his puddles of filth, whimpering gently.[3]

Morton Smith watched, rooted to the spot, but no-one else took the slightest notice. People stepped round avoiding the puddles. Finally, a shop assistant came out, poured sawdust into the puddles and kicked the man in the back a couple of times. 'He got up and staggered off still whimpering, rubbing his mouth with one hand and his back with the other. When I came to live in the "Old City" I found that he, and half a dozen like him, were familiar figures.'[4]

When rumours start about Jesus healing, crowds gather. The sick are there. Their families and friends collect – wanting healing and liberation from their intolerable burden. And there are sightseers wanting to see, to get involved in whatever happens.

So many people cram into Jesus' home you couldn't get through. You hoist your friend on to the roof and begin to dig through it. Literally, Mark says you 'unroofed the roof' which is so clumsy a phrase it is certainly from the earliest oral tradition. When Luke rewrote the story he used a word for roof tiles (with the same root as 'ceramics') to get rid of Mark's ugly phrasing and make it easier for a non-Palestinian reader. To dig through to Jesus is an act of trust, of hope, perhaps of desperation. Haste outweighs any act of destruction. Feelings at this point are far from simple. Motives are mixed, partly a desire for healing, partly hoping for the liberation of family and friends, but God's action is not limited by human motives.

The faith in this story is not in a faith-healer, nor is it that of the paralysed man. It is the faith of his friends, a micro-community representing all believers, looking back from beyond the Easter Event. The faith of the Church is in the risen Lord Jesus, and in the power of God to forgive sins. By saying, 'My child, your sins are forgiven', Jesus is not forgiving the sins – they are already forgiven. God forgives. Herman Hendrickx writes that Jesus' words should not be interpreted as forgiving; they encourage 'the one who seeks help: God forgives his sins and, therefore, Jesus can and will cure him'.[5] The Church trusts that Jesus can heal and trusts in the message that Jesus proclaims, God's mercy and forgiveness.

Forgiveness and healing are linked in this story; first-century Jews saw a link between sin and sickness. The paralysed man is forgiven as a prelude to healing. The Hebraic world-view had the concept of corporate and, in particular, family sin. In the Ten Commandments, God threatens to punish not only those who hate him but their descendants. 'Our ancestors sinned, but now they are gone, and we are suffering for their sins' (Lamentations 5.7).

R. A. Lambourne describes the Jewish idea of family, the *mishpaha*, as a horizontal concept, the family now, and a vertical concept, stretching back in time to the Patriarchs. 'There is [. . .] not merely an oscillation between the individual Israelite and corporate Israel but also between the Israelite of today and the Israelite of past history.'[6] So Paul writes, 'As in Adam all die, so in Christ all will be brought to life' (1 Corinthians 15.22 REB). The present participates in the past and anticipates the future with the new Israel to come, the eschatological Israel. In Christ is participation in the new family; the eschaton is fulfilled, he is the new *mishpaha*.

Sin isn't merely an individual act in early Christian thought. Individual actions are in the context of *mishpaha* and have cosmic ramifications. By participating in the Patriarchs, any action involves all descendants of the Patriarchs, the whole of humanity. In this sense, all sickness is caused by sin, not individual sin but that of the global family. The idea of original sin being transmitted

31

# Unleashing the lion

through the sex act came long after the New Testament, most clearly by St Augustine. In the New Testament original sin is participatory. Sickness is not a result of your parents' intercourse. It is not causal in that sense. By being born, one participates in all of humanity.

The Son of Man has 'authority on earth to forgive sins'. In the *mishpaha* the Son of Man is all humanity participating in Christ. This implicates every individual in all sin and its results. But it also allows everyone to be part of the Christ's new priestly family. All can declare God's forgiveness. If participation in the whole of human sin causes sickness, then participation in God's forgiveness is involved in the process of healing.

Matthew's conclusion comes from a different oral tradition: 'When the people saw it, they were afraid, and praised God for giving such authority to people' (Matthew 9.8). This looks forward to the period when the 'power of the keys' will be granted to the apostles. However, reading this with the idea of *mishpaha*, past and future become a participation in the present forgiveness. Everyone now participates in the authority of the great high priest. The new age is here, when God and humanity are not separated. No wonder the question of authority comes up repeatedly in these narratives. Naturally conservative religious leaders needed to stop such revolutionary ideas.

In this story there is controversy with some teachers of the Law, an undefined group of lawyers, copyists, schoolteachers and so on. Their knowledge of the Law elevated them socially and so they rivalled Jesus in interpreting the *Torah*. Here they take a central role. The story as we have it is carefully constructed. It has what is called a chiastic structure – the parts of the story balance:

(a) The crowds come to Jesus for teaching.
  (b) The paralysed man comes; his sins are forgiven.
    (c) The teachers of the Law question Jesus' authority to forgive sins.
  (d) The paralysed man is healed and goes away.
(e) The crowds respond to Jesus' teaching by praising God.

This structure suggests that the climax is conflict. Has Jesus the authority to forgive sins? But Jesus does not forgive the man, God does – through Jesus the representative of all people. The story in this form, raising the question of Jesus' authority,

32

probably reflects the concerns of the period soon after Easter. When Peter heals a man who cannot walk, 'in the name of Jesus Christ of Nazareth' (Acts 3.6), it provokes his and John's arrest. Their sentence forbade them to 'speak or teach in the name of Jesus'. This particular controversy reflects the time when Jesus' name was being used in the Church's healing ministry. As the story was told in this new situation the questions of the teachers of the Law were a serious problem. What was participation in the risen Lord? How could one experience forgiveness? The questions became interwoven in the story, probably long before Mark heard it. Pharisees are from a slightly later time again and became added to the Gospels in the same way.

There is no desire to mislead on the part of the Evangelists. God alone forgives sins. But Jesus, by his death and resurrection, is identified with Godhead, so can forgive sins as God. Mark's account is *Christological*; pointing to the risen Christ. So the story as it is now structured is centred on participating in the *mishpah* of the risen and glorified Lord, sharing his authority.

When the man's sins are forgiven he does not immediately walk away. He lies on his mat, paralysed. Jesus commands him to get up and go home. This declaration is made in active language. It is absolutely in Jesus' own authority. God forgives sins; Jesus, participating in humanity, simply and passively declares God's forgiveness. But the healing is, 'I tell you', a phrase redolent of Messianic declaration. There is no room for misinterpretation, God forgives sins but he has delegated healing to the, as yet, unglorified Jesus!

Jesus commands the non-functioning limbs to move. And the man is healed. But, much more, family and friends are healed too – they are liberated from the captivity of illness. Jesus doesn't simply heal individuals, he heals the community around them. The man is able to take responsibility for himself again. He is restored to citizenship. He is able to worship God properly. Were he incontinent, he is no longer – he can become ritually clean and take part in worship (after seven days). Incontinence didn't only affect the sufferer, all bodily discharges affected anyone who touched the person, their bed, or anything that they had touched, or even spat on. This meant the friendship shown by his friends was incredible. They were willing to cut themselves off from society, at least to some extent, for friendship.

The burden has been lifted from family and friends, community writ small. Health has been restored – health meaning release of captives, the lame walking, and family life restored. Mark doesn't use the word *sozo* but its effects are here: strength, wholeness, righteousness and an observance of the Law, soundness, prosperity, rescue from the clutches of an enemy.

## CASE 2

### THE MAN WITH THE WITHERED HAND

Then Jesus went back to the synagogue, where there was a man who had a paralysed hand. Some people were there who wanted to accuse Jesus of doing wrong; so they watched him closely to see whether he would heal the man on the Sabbath.

Jesus said to the man, 'Come up here to the front.' Then he asked the people, 'What does our Law allow us to do on the Sabbath? To help or to harm? To save someone's life or to destroy it?'

But they did not say a thing. Jesus was angry as he looked round at them, but at the same time he felt sorry for them, because they were so stubborn and wrong.

Then he said to the man, 'Stretch out your hand.' He stretched it out, and it became well again. So the Pharisees left the synagogue and met at once with some members of Herod's party, and they made plans to kill Jesus.

(Mark 3.1–6)

This man's hand was, in Greek, dried up, usually translated withered. We don't know whether this was a recent condition but in the Gospel according to the Hebrews (containing some parallel, possibly authentic elements of the oral tradition) the man says, 'I was a mason, earning my living with my hands, I beg you, Jesus, restore my health to me, so that I need not beg for my food in shame.'[7]

This story too is carefully constructed in a chiastic form:

(a) Jesus goes to the synagogue, the Pharisees are there.
   (b) Mention of man with the withered hand.
      (c) Pharisees watch Jesus.

34

(d) Questions about the Sabbath.
(e) Jesus looks at the Pharisees.
(f) The man's withered hand is restored.
(g) The Pharisees leave the synagogue, Jesus stays.

The central issue is what the Law permits, but underlying it, again, is the issue of authority. As we saw, teachers of the Law would usually be consulted in cases of dispute. Jesus' opponents in this case, however, are Pharisees and Herodians. The Pharisees are unlikely to be the original villains here. They seem to have been based in Jerusalem, opponents of the very early church. Indeed, Paul was one of their leading protagonists. The decade after the crucifixion, 30–40 CE, is a more likely time for conflict with Pharisees, and in Judea! Josephus, the Jewish historian, suggests that Galileans did not welcome Pharisees.

The Herodians were friends and supporters of Herod Antipas and not a defined party. Antipas, a son of Herod the Great, was, confusingly, called Herod whenever mentioned in the New Testament. He had a deservedly unsavoury reputation and was unpopular. He had John the Baptist executed; he was a Roman puppet ruler from a foreign family, provoking Jewish xenophobia. He built a city called Tiberias, named after the emperor, on an ancient cemetery, ritually unclean in the Jewish eyes (Numbers 19.14). So Herod imported Gentiles to live there. After John's execution his family, including Jesus, would have been watched carefully. The Herodians are probably Jesus' original antagonists, perhaps with the teachers of the Law.

The Pharisees were the persecutors of the early church, and therefore of the risen Lord – 'Saul, Saul! Why do you persecute me?' (Acts 9.4) Their appearance here is another Christological device, showing the continuation between the earthly Jesus and the risen Christ. This story is part of the inexorable march to the cross and the glory of Easter. Jesus' miracles create conflict but Mark arranged his material to show Jesus as more than a miracle-worker. Some see them and worship God, others plot. Jesus' destiny was the cross and there his nature is revealed.

The man's hand is unusable and makes him incapable of earning a living. There were no jobs for disabled people so he has to beg. He uses one hand for everything – in many cultures one hand is used for clean functions and the other for unclean ones. In parts of

Africa one refers to 'the side of the hand I eat with'. If left-handed-ness was seen by the Jews as being a disability (Ehud is literally 'restricted as to his right hand', Judges 3.15), one-handedness is worse. Unlike the paralysed man whose friends brought him, this man has to bring himself. And he has to brave conflict, becoming the target of a hostile crowd.

So Jesus says, 'Come here', and, 'Stretch out your hand.' When Jesus spoke to the man with paralysis, he said, 'I tell you, get up [...] and go home.' To the man with the withered hand he says, 'Stretch the muscles, stretch the hand, stretch out your fingers, stretch the sinews, stretch out your hand.' Jesus uses a word of power. 'Stretch out your hand' is no simple instruction to hold out the hand. Jesus is no magician. Healing happens with the response to Jesus' command. Without the response, without the paralysed man getting up, without this man stretching out his hand, there is no healing. The patient's willingness is involved. It is not enough simply to come before Jesus and expect restoration. Deliberate acts of will and body make the restoration possible. Participating in Christ is healing.

He has been healed, he enjoys freedom from slavery. When the Hebrews were enslaved in Egypt they suffered seven days a week. Slaves are not allowed a day off but part of their covenant with God insists on a day of rest. Sabbath is a symbol of freedom and now, paradoxically on the Sabbath, Jesus gives Sabbath to this man by restoring his hand. There is no day off from the slavery of sickness; one is in utter thrall to disease. So to heal the person who is sick is the same thing as setting the captive free! And it also brings good news to the poor. Now he can return to work, support his family, and help to stimulate the local economy. He returns from begging on the margins to the centre of life.

In the ancient world, the implacable laws of science which rule our universe were unknown. Illness was caused by the invisible population of the skies or the earth or the realm below the earth. In the tradition that Mark received, Jesus was angry. The anger, in Mark, is directed at the enemies plotting against him. In the oral narrative it probably went, 'Jesus was angry and said to the man ...', directing his anger against whatever being enslaved the man and caused the ailment. There is a marginal reading of Mark 1.41 in which Jesus heals a leper after being moved with anger. Paul tells us to put on God's armour against the devil. For 'we are not fighting against human beings but against the wicked spiritual forces in the heavenly world, the rulers, authorities, and cosmic powers of this dark age' (Ephesians 6.12). When Jesus heals, he challenges the will of these cosmic powers. He replaces their spiritual chains with the person's own restored will and self-determination. The captives are liberated.

# CASE 3

## THE MAN POSSESSED BY A MOB

Jesus and his disciples arrived on the other side of Lake Galilee, in the territory of Gerasa. As soon as Jesus got out of the boat, he was met by a man who came out of the burial caves there. This man had an evil spirit in him and lived among the tombs. Nobody could keep him chained up any more; many times his feet and hands had been chained, but every time he broke the chains and smashed the irons on his feet. He was too strong for anyone to control him. Day and night he wandered among the tombs and through the hills, screaming and cutting himself with stones.

He was some distance away when he saw Jesus; so he ran, fell on his knees before him, and screamed in a loud voice, 'Jesus, Son of the Most High God! What do you want with me? For God's sake, I beg you, don't punish me!' (He said this because Jesus was saying, 'Evil spirit, come out of this man!')

So Jesus asked him, 'What is your name?' The man answered, 'My name is "Mob" [Gk. *Legion*] – there are so many of us!' And he kept begging Jesus not to send the evil spirits out of that region.

There was a large herd of pigs near by, feeding on a hillside. So the spirits begged Jesus, 'Send us to the pigs, and let us go into them.' He let them go, and the evil spirits went out of the man and entered the pigs. The whole herd – about 2,000 pigs in all – rushed down the side of the cliff into the lake and was drowned. The men who had been taking care of the pigs ran away and spread the news in the town and among the farms. People went out to see what had happened, and when they came to Jesus, they saw the man who used to have the mob of

37

demons in him. He was sitting there, clothed and in his right mind; and they were all afraid. Those who had seen it told the people what had happened to the man with the demons, and about the pigs.

So they asked Jesus to leave their territory.

As Jesus was getting into the boat, the man who had had the demons begged him, 'Let me go with you!' But Jesus would not let him. Instead, he told him, 'Go back home to your family and tell them how much the Lord has done for you and how kind he has been to you.' So the man left and went all through the Ten Towns, telling what Jesus had done for him. And all who heard it were amazed.

(Mark 5.1–20)

John Wilkinson writes that 'in psychiatric terms we may diagnose the Gadarene demoniac [...] as suffering from a manic depressive psychosis'.[8] He was in a state of acute mania. He was too strong to restrain, breaking chains and smashing leg-irons. We think of these restraints as barbaric but they were probably to prevent him from harming himself. The diagnosis, manic depressive psychosis, Wilkinson suggests, merely describes the symptoms. The first-century diagnosis – sounding far-fetched and, perhaps, with the exciting chill of horror films – is demon possession.

Demonic possession seems particularly far-fetched – these symptoms are of a recognized psychiatric disorder. Personal demons are replaced by personal psyche. But, Wilkinson continues, 'the matter is not as simple as this view would suggest, for the introduction of psychiatry by no means excludes the possibility of demon possession'.[9] Psychiatric diagnoses are generally descriptive. Manic depressive psychosis describes the symptoms, not their cause. Excepting brain injury, psychiatry rarely identifies cause and, in practice, concentrates on symptoms. Psycho-analysis, however, attempts to identify the causes of disorders but cannot deal with the organic dysfunction of the brain. Analysis can help with emotional disorders (though the opposite is also true and some research suggests that those patients who recover after treatment would have done so anyway).

Morton Smith suggests that Jesus' healings were the result of magical methods 'which may have worked for psychological reasons'.[10] In his experience recounted above, he describes the

38

'lunatic' arguing with an 'imaginary being'. Smith's description denies the eidetic reality of the experience and casts doubt on the disorder. The being was imaginary in Smith's objective observation but not to the man himself – it apparently beat him up!

It is conservatively estimated that about two hundred and fifty million people world-wide suffer from *severe* mental illness. About a million people in Britain annually receive psychiatric care. In 1989, according to Stephen Pattison, sixty per cent of all National Health Service beds were devoted to the care of patients suffering from mental illness. 'In the UK no less than 11% of all men and 17% of all women are ill enough to be hospitalized in a psychiatric facility during the course of their lives.'[11] And illness affects society no less because it is rooted in the brain not the body.

Physical illness can be a secondary effect. Paralysis may be psychologically induced but long-term, without physiotherapy, it may become physical. Muscles waste and joints ossify. Even if the psychological disorder is successfully treated the paralysis remains. Physical impairments can be caused by treatment given for mental conditions. Someone with learning difficulties mutilated her own face. She tore at her skin causing quite horrifying injuries. After surgery, advice was sought from a variety of medical disciplines. The only conceivable solution was to fit restraints on her arms to prevent further injury. Over several years of wearing the restraints the joints in her arms became calcified. She can now barely bend her arms at all. Restraint is still needed as the behaviour remains unchanged.

The ancient world, we saw, was populated with beings. Possession by spirits good and bad was taken for granted. Jesus declared himself possessed by the Spirit of the Lord, proclaiming the prophecy fulfilled in Nazareth. Jesus came into contact with many who were possessed by demons. These bad spirits were thought to cause of all manner of ills. One called Leroel, apparently, brought on chills, shivering and a sore throat, and was probably a personification of a viral infection.

In the two hundred years before Jesus, when there was a tendency to correct parts of the Hebrew text which had become difficult, several unusual or corrupted words were personalized. In Genesis 3.24, God sets guards to prevent Adam and Eve returning to Eden. These are cherubim and a flaming sword. The word translated 'flaming sword' is only used once in the whole Bible. As people thought and argued about it, they personalized it. The sword, by association with angelic beings, joined them as an angel called *Lahtiel*. Saul M. Olyan describes several cases where angels have been derived from difficulties in the text: *Abaddon* – a place of perishing, a parallel to *Sheol*, the grave – is used as the name of an angel in Revelation 9.11. *Mammon*, according to Olyan, became an angel (and/or demon) in later Christian texts.[12]

There was some influence, at a popular level, on first-century Judaism from Iranian religion. Some inter-Testamental literature portrays a dualism: God versus Satan, good angels versus bad angels. In the Book of Jubilees, demons are angels that rebelled against God and were cast out of heaven. They descended to earth to continue their mischief (Jubilees 10.1). Their present task is seducing humanity from righteousness. They deliberately and maliciously inflict pain and suffering. In the first century, little distinction is made between those possessed by demons and sufferers from physical ailments (though some Gospel passages do differentiate, such as Mark 1.32).

Demons in the ancient world were expelled by power. The usual invocation was, 'I adjure you in the name of [. . .]'. The name, if that of some superior being, either God or an angel, overcame the demon.

> The twenty-ninth [demon] said 'I am called Rhyx Anoster. I unleash hysteria and cause pains in the bladder. If anyone mashes up the seeds of laurel into pure oil and massages the body with it saying, "I adjure you by Marmaraoth [an angel]," I retreat immediately.'
>
> (The Testament of Solomon 18.33)

'Exorcist' and 'exorcism' are Greek words but are never used of Jesus in the Gospels. They are only used of the sons of Sceva, some itinerant Jewish exorcists, pejoratively. They attempted an exorcism, 'in the name of Jesus, whom Paul preaches.' The demon replied, 'I know Jesus, and I know about Paul; but you – who are you?' (Acts 19.13–16) A name is not just what to call a person – it is integral to personality. Using a name uses the virtue, power and authority of the person, as shown on amulets with the inscription, 'I conjure you by the Name'. The name of God is too holy, too powerful, too virtuous, to be inscribed.

The geography of this story is confused. Mark, unfortunately, places it in Gerasa, some thirty-five miles from the sea of Galilee. Matthew and Luke edited Mark's story. Texts of Luke present three different locations: Gerasa, Gadara (echoing Matthew), only five miles away from the sea, and a small coastal town called Gergesa. Gergesa's cliffs fit the topography of the story.

The man with the evil spirit lives among the tombs for more than shelter. Living in a graveyard is appropriate – an evil spirit would inhabit the place of the dead. A spirit-controlled individual was cut off from the world of the living, existing in a morbid twilight world. Isaiah says that his contemporaries rebelled against God and went 'at night to caves and tombs to consult the spirits of the dead. They eat pork and drink broth made from meat offered in pagan sacrifices' (Isaiah 65.4). The Testament of Solomon, collecting magical texts from the first to third centuries, continually cites demons who dwell among tombs.

> I ordered another spirit to appear before me [...] saying, 'Who are you?' He replied, 'I am a lecherous spirit of a giant man who died in a massacre in the age of giants [...] My home is in inaccessible places. My activity is this: I seat myself near dead men in the tombs at midnight [and] assume the form of the dead; if I seize anyone [...] I cause him to be possessed by a demon and to gnaw his own flesh to pieces and the saliva of his jowls to flow down.'
>
> (Testament of Solomon 17.1ff.)

Is there a connection between a possessed person's self-mutilation and a flesh-eating demon? One translation of the possessed man cutting himself with stones was that he bit himself. This is an unlikely translation but not an uncommon behaviour. James, my godson, will bite his own hand when agitated.

Many scholars regard the herd of pigs as being added to the original story, arguing that the pigs are there to shelter the legion of demons. Isaiah describes eating pork in the same breath as necromancy, both being utterly repugnant to the Jewish mind. George Knight wrote 'that the Law of Moses forbade the eating of pork that was employed by some Canaanites in the worship of "underground" deities'.[13] The *Encyclopaedia Judaica* notes archaeological evidence, in the form of 'figurines and relics of bones', supporting a relationship. Eating pork and unclean animals is a deliberate realignment of loyalties away from Yahweh. To first-century Jews and Christians a connection between this story and the prophecy would have almost certainly been drawn (Paul quotes Isaiah 65.1f. in Romans 10.20f).

Pigs were loathed by Jewish people and used by pagans as part of the ritual surrounding death. Isaiah links pigs and summoning up the spirits of the dead. The area where the demon-possessed person lived is Gentile and pagan, an area where pigs were no doubt used for sacrifices and meals in the necropolis. Gundry says that because of their 'revulsion against pigs, a Jewish audience would find a humorous satisfaction in the drowning of the herd'.[14] The story of the demons infesting the pigs and throwing themselves over a cliff comes from the early oral tradition. Perhaps, at the same time or soon after Jesus expelled the demon, some pigs fell over the cliffs into the sea below and drowned. Whether Jesus was the cause of the pigs' suicidal activity or not is irrelevant: the humour made the link inevitable.

Demons, according to the New Testament (following the apocryphal Tobit where a demon is sent off into Upper Egypt), prefer desert regions (see Mark 1.12f.). Similarly, the Testament of Solomon has a demon called Asmodeus pleading, 'I beg you King Solomon do not condemn me to water' (Testament of Solomon 5.11). So the destruction of the pig or pigs in water would have been interpreted as the complete and total destruction of the demons, their final defeat, following their expulsion from the man.

The power, the essence, of a being is intimately connected with its name, so Jesus asked the demon's name. It declares, 'My name is Legion; for we are many' (RSV), which may be an evasion on the part of the demon, refusing to answer Jesus' question. Alternatively, the demon may be giving a straight answer. H. B. Swete commented that 'to a Palestinian of our Lord's time the name would connote not only vast numbers – the strength of a legion often reached 5,000–6,000 men – and submission to a superior will; but the miseries of a military occupation by a foreign power [. . . who] knew how to harass and plunder'.[15] If the man is possessed by a whole regiment of demons, how do they all fit into about two thousand pigs? A *telos* of soldiers is more likely, 2,048 men. However, *telos* and legion may have been loosely interchangeable.

Joachim Jeremias suggests, radically, that in the oral stage the story was current in Aramaic where the words 'legion' and 'legionary' are the same, *ligyôn'a*. He writes that originally a single demon called *Soldier* replied to Jesus, '*My name is soldier; since we* [the demons] *are a great host and resemble each other as soldiers do*.'[16] Jeremias is probably right to identify the demon as 'Soldier' but not one in a uniform demonic host. The demon's actions are soldierly. The afflicted man probably had stylized and ritualized behaviours which were interpreted as military by himself and his family. He becomes soldierly, resembling both a single legionary and the whole legion – a symptom of his illness was a military bearing. The transition from oral Aramaic to literary Greek dramatically inflated the number of demons.

A disorder with highly ritualized behaviour affecting about one and a half million people in Britain is Obsessive-Compulsive Disorder or OCD. Obsessive, from the Latin *obsidere* – to lay siege to – is how sufferers feel. They are besieged by a force or being beyond their control. According to Stella Carlton, OCD 'consists of a repeated and persistent intrusion of an obsession which occurs against a person's will and gradually comes to tyrannize his daily life'.[17] One sufferer said, 'I wish I could go back in time to where it first began because it now seems so out of control. What was once myself and my rituals is now my rituals first, and then myself.' The sufferer knew the rituals were illogical and unnecessary but could not stop and, trapped in a labyrinth with no escape, lived in perpetual anxiety. Dr Johnson, the eighteenth-century lexicographer, twirled and twisted, performing stylized gesticulations at every threshold, 'and as soon as he had finished, he would give a sudden spring and make an extensive stride over the threshold, as if he were trying for a wager how far he could stride'. He obsessively avoided stepping on cracks in the pavement and touched every post that he passed. There is some evidence linking OCD with *Tourette's Syndrome* – a 'disorder characterized by a variety of facial tics, muscular jerks and involuntary behaviour, sometimes involving compulsive imitation of others and use of offensive language' (*Chambers Dictionary*).

The man infested by 'Soldier' was suffering from an illness with alternating periods of mania and depression. He seems also to have suffered from OCD, and perhaps Tourette's Syndrome, which Dr J. Rapoport describes as two sides of the same coin.[18] This was evidenced by his mechanistic rituals, reminiscent of the parade ground. Perhaps he also 'swore like a trooper' if some such phrase was current! The Greek historian Polybius, writing in the second century BC, used the word *stratiotkos*, translated 'like a rude soldier', and the Decapolis, where this story happens, was Hellenized, so it is a possibility.

Diagnosing the illness does little more than describe the symptoms in a more clinical fashion. Jesus did more. He named the demon and, using his authority, subdued him. His will overcame 'Soldier', causing him to retreat from the battlefield utterly defeated. The man was restored to his right mind. Possession was turned into release from erratic behaviour and chaotic thoughts. The unclean spirit is, ironically, cast into the symbol of Gentile uncleanness, pigs: unclean was banished into unclean, and to drown the evil spirit – a demon's worst nightmare! It is a deliciously comic end to the tale.

The structure of the story is more complex but still chiastic:

(a) Jesus comes by boat/man comes impelled by demon
    (b$^1$) Symptoms described
    (b$^2$) Demon acknowledges Jesus' authority/demon challenged to leave
      (c) Pigs mentioned
        (d) Demon asks to go into pigs
          (e) JESUS GRANTS PERMISSION
        (f) Demon goes into pigs
      (g) Swineherds mentioned
    (h$^1$) Description of restored man (i.e. no symptoms)
    (h$^2$) People fear Jesus' authority/Jesus challenged to leave
(i) Jesus leaves by boat/man leaves, commissioned by Jesus

In the final written form of Mark's narrative even demons come under Jesus' jurisdiction. The demon has to ask permission: Jesus has authority to judge demons and pronounce sentence. Demons no longer act unchallenged or infect human beings with impunity.

Jesus restores the man's health and dignity; he can return to his family. By healing the individual Jesus restores the community's health. The family need no longer worry. Their guilt at being unable to care is lifted, they are restored to righteousness/health/cleanliness/purity/*shalom*.

The Kingdom of God is opened to the restored man. Jesus transcends boundaries of race – the man is almost certainly Gentile. Jesus overthrows religious boundaries – the demon is unclean. Contact with pigs and swineherds is repugnant to the first-century Jew, causing impurity. Going to a graveyard defiles the person. David Rhoades notes that 'Mark eliminates ritual purity-defilement as a demarcation and draws a line between moral and immoral behaviour as that which determines purity or pollution.'[19] Mark is full of opposites and reversals: of insiders and outsiders, rich and poor, the first and the last, male and female, and Jew and non-Jew. Jesus encompasses the demon-possessed Gentile in the Kingdom. He does not merely step over the boundaries, he takes the boundary with him.

The wilderness here echoes that of the temptations, the abode of demons. Jesus struggles with unearthly powers and defeats them utterly. Jesus returns from the wilderness empowered for his mission. The man, previously possessed by 'Soldier', is to return from the wilderness empowered for Jesus' mission, as the first sent by Jesus to proclaim the Kingdom, and from outside the boundaries. But the boundaries have been stretched by Jesus to include him: outsiders are part of the *koinonia* the participation in Christ.

The local people acknowledge Jesus' power and authority but want nothing to do with him. The kind of power that he demonstrated was not the sort of thing they wanted in their own backyards, they were frightened by it. Jesus is, once again, portrayed in a situation of conflict. This conflict is resolved with the cosmic forces, yet strangely unresolved with the fearful humanity. Cosmic drama causes human conflict – not everyone responds favourably towards the good news, as Mark's Christian community had no doubt discovered. Mark is looking forward to the culmination of Jesus' ministry: the future, the cross, is prefigured in the present. Mark intends us to see the road to the cross. Jesus is betrayed by humans while defeating principalities and powers. The future cosmic defeat of evil and Jesus' own death are shown as affecting the here and now.

## CASES 4 & 5

### JAIRUS' DAUGHTER AND THE WOMAN WITH A HAEMORRHAGE

Jesus went back across to the other side of the lake. There at the lakeside a large crowd gathered round him. Jairus, an official of the local synagogue, arrived, and when he saw

Jesus, he threw himself down at his feet and begged him earnestly, 'My little daughter is very ill. Please come and place your hands on her, so that she will get well and live!'

Then Jesus started off with him. So many people were going along with Jesus that they were crowding him from every side. There was a woman who had suffered terribly from severe bleeding for twelve years, even though she had been treated by many doctors. She had spent all her money, but instead of getting better she got worse all the time. She had heard about Jesus, so she came in the crowd behind him, saying to herself, 'If I just touch his clothes, I will get well.'

She touched his cloak, and her bleeding stopped at once; and she had the feeling inside herself that she was healed of her trouble. At once Jesus knew that power had gone out of him, so he turned round in the crowd and asked, 'Who touched my clothes?'

His disciples answered, 'You see how the people are crowding you; why do you ask who touched you?'

But Jesus kept looking round to see who had done it. The woman realized what had happened to her, so she came, trembling with fear, knelt at his feet, and told him the whole truth. Jesus said to her, 'My daughter, your faith has made you well. Go in peace, and be healed of your trouble.'

While Jesus was saying this, some messengers came from Jairus' house and told him, 'Your daughter has died. Why bother the Teacher any longer?'

Jesus paid no attention to what they said, but told him, 'Don't be afraid, only believe.' Then he did not let anyone else go on with him except Peter and James and his brother John. They arrived at Jairus' house, where Jesus saw the confusion and heard all the loud crying and wailing. He went in and said to them, 'Why all this confusion? Why are you crying? The child is not dead – she is only sleeping!'

They laughed at him, so he put them all out, took the child's father and mother and his three disciples, and went into the room where the child was lying. He took her by the hand and said to her, '*Talitha, koum,*' which means, 'Little girl, I tell you to get up!' She got up at once and started walking around. (She was twelve years old.) When this happened, they were

completely amazed. But Jesus gave them strict orders not to
tell anyone, and he said, 'Give her something to eat.'

(Mark 5.21–43)

These two healing stories may have already been dramatically
linked in the oral tradition. Jairus' daughter, critically ill, dying
before Jesus can get there, is a complete story in itself. So is that
of the woman with the uterine haemorrhage, a long-term debilitating condition. Neither is a trivial complaint.

Jairus' daughter cannot be diagnosed, there simply isn't enough
information. As the story progresses, people at Jairus' home think
she is dead. Jesus, alternatively, says she is sleeping. Is it a cataleptic
trance which Jesus diagnoses correctly? It is impossible to tell. The
Marcan author doesn't give any further detail.

Jesus' conflict with the people in this story is unusual, pointing to
its authenticity. Jesus is the subject of contemptuous laughter. It is
scathing, ridiculing Jesus, not furthering Mark's purpose of por-
traying Jesus as the soon-to-be crucified, risen and glorified Lord.
Conflict would support his overall plan, contempt would not. But
this very contradiction may indicate how consummate an artist the
author is. He portrays Jesus as contemptuous – prefiguring the
cross, where Jesus is to be ridiculed. For only in the context of
the cross can resurrection occur, Jesus' or the girl's. Mark evokes
in the reader sympathy for Jesus, perhaps that of an eyewitness.
Peter is an insider to this event and tradition describes Mark as his
literary executor.

In the Acts of the Apostles, echoing this story, Peter raises a dead
woman saying, '*Tabitha*, rise.' *Tabitha* and *Talitha* are probably the
same word, misspelled by Luke in Acts – he does not quote the
Aramaic in his account of Jairus' daughter. This double use of the
formula *Talitha Koum* may indicate that it was part of an early
healing liturgy.

Ernest Best believes Mark's purpose was pastoral, a call to discipleship, designed 'to build up his readers as Christians and show
them what true discipleship is'.[20] 'Many of Mark's readers may
have already failed through public or private persecution or other
causes; the failure of the historical disciples followed by their
eventual forgiveness and known success as missionaries (e.g.
Peter) would then be a source of great encouragement.'[21] Jesus
being ridiculed would greatly encourage persecuted believers.

Jesus emerges covered in glory while his abusers are proved wrong. Jesus is vindicated, so Mark's readers can be vindicated if they continue faithful. Laughter freezes on the condemning lips. The dramatic irony is that we, the audience, are amazed by the Lord's action in the secrecy of the girl's room and, unknown to those outside, our lives can never be the same again. So too for Mark's audience, outside their persecutors appear to be gaining the upper hand. Inside, in the Christian community, the reality is different. Here the work of the risen Lord can be seen.

Another story has parallels. Paul in Acts 20 preaches an interminable sermon and Eutychus dozes and falls out of the window. Luke, an eyewitness, pronounces him dead. Paul disagrees: 'Don't worry, he is still alive.' After Eutychus is revived, everyone eats a meal. Both stories significantly share conflicting diagnoses, and meals immediately after resuscitation. Luke and John show Jesus breaking or distributing bread as a post-resurrection experience. This is a sequence: healing (or resurrection), then a meal, possibly reflecting a simple healing liturgy. Peter's mother-in-law prepares, so presumably eats, food. St Paul after his blinding on the Damascus road, 'was able to see again. He stood up and was baptized; and after he had eaten, his strength came back' (Acts 9.18f.). The order, healing, baptism, eating, is repeated time after time.

Jairus asks Jesus to lay hands on his daughter but Jesus simply takes her by the hand. There is no precedent here for any formal practice. Nor, until now, does Mark mention the practice. Jesus touched Peter's mother-in-law and a man with a dread skin disease but not in a formal, liturgical sense. The imposition of hands was probably liturgical practice in Mark's church. Ironically, in neither of these two linked narratives does Jesus do it. In one he takes the girl by the hand, in the other he is touched. Jairus' request expresses the concerns of Mark's church. This is misplaced. Jesus gives no precedent here – that is given in Mark 6.5. (An interesting aside: Jesus did not touch people possessed of demons, whereas he touched those with physical ailments. Demons seem contagious.)

The woman had suffered uterine haemorrhage for twelve years. The chronic loss of blood was 'probably due to the presence of fibroid tumours or *fibromyomata* in the uterus'.[22] Fibroids are the commonest tumours of female genital organs: 18–24 per cent of all women over thirty-five have fibroids in the womb. They are usually benign and cause no health problems whatsoever. However, according to Dr John Wilkinson, in about 'a quarter of the cases in which they are present they cause chronic abnormal uterine bleeding'.[23] Losing blood causes anaemia and physical weakness.

In New Testament Palestine, the sufferer bore the affliction of the Levitical Law in addition to physical symptoms – anaemia, weakness and fatigue. According to Mosaic Law: 'If a woman has a flow of blood for several days outside her monthly period of if her flow continues beyond her regular period, she remains unclean, as long as the flow continues, just as she is during her monthly period' (Leviticus 15.25). For seven days following menses a Jewish woman is considered unclean. This woman probably had an intermittent blood flow, rather than constant bleeding, but any show of blood made her unclean for another week. Any bed she lay on, any seat she sat on, anyone who touched her became ritually unclean. Generally, an orthodox Jewish couple practise sexual abstinence for the duration of menstruation and seven days beyond, until the wife has a ritual bath and is purified. Theoretically, they come together with great joy, every month another honeymoon. This joy has been denied our woman and her husband for twelve years.

The woman, physically weakened, isolated culturally and religiously, despairs. She has tried every remedy available. Doctors are useless. Time has not healed. She comes behind Jesus and touches his cloak. This was a utilitarian garment, large and rectangular, thrown over one shoulder during the day and used as a blanket at night. The tradition is quite clear that it was this and not Jesus himself that the woman touched.

There and then, she is healed. The flow of blood stops. She senses healing. There have been no healing words, no healing touch. No-one has spoken. The woman alone has acted. She is the initiator and the executor. Jesus has been an unwitting partner. Mark writes that Jesus felt the power go out of him. The cloak is not magical. Power to heal comes from Jesus but is not controlled entirely by Jesus' will and can be hijacked! Other people touch Jesus and the apostles to receive healing – even Peter's shadow is described as giving healing. A gift of healing is not entirely under control.

This story is the most Jewish in Mark. Jesus is portrayed as the *scapegoat*, the Old Testament beast that carried iniquity off into the wilderness (Leviticus 16.20–8). He is the sacrifice for unintentional

sin (Leviticus 4), touched by the ritually unclean or their representative. Touch passed all impurity to the sacrifice. This idea is picked
up in Isaiah 53.11b: 'My devoted servant, with whom I am pleased,
will bear the punishment of many and for his sake I will forgive
them.' Mark has already quoted a similar passage from Isaiah at
Jesus' baptism and Jesus sees his own destiny similarly. 'The Son of
Man did not come to be served; he came to serve and to give his life
to redeem many people' (Mark 10.45). Mark alludes to sacrifice
through this story. The ritually unclean person touches the sacrifi-
cial victim, Jesus, and becomes ritually pure. Jesus' life, therefore, is
forfeit and the woman is cleansed of all ritual impurity. Here we see
Mark's pastoral skill empowering the sick person. The woman's
example gives other people strength and courage.

Many writers, wrongly, make the woman's healing conditional;
she was healed the moment she touched Jesus' cloak. Words are
secondary. Mark gives details as a creative and imaginative story-
teller, heightening the drama. He tells us the woman was trembling
with fear – a plausible detail. Anyone denied ordinary, everyday
social situations for twelve years would be withdrawn and inept.
Touching anyone would be stressful, especially as that touch would
make him unclean too. She would kneel at his feet in fear and in
gratitude and awe. Now she is clean and whole.

Jesus says to her, 'Daughter, your faith has saved you [from
*sozo*]. Go in peace [the Hebrew *shalom* is sometimes translated
*soteria* in the Septuagint] free from your whippings [*apo tes
mastigos*]'. She is healed, not merely of physical affliction – her
flagellation, as Jesus so graphically describes it – but of the
stigma, the uncleanness. Not in a week as the Law prescribes, nor
after a ritual bath. Not even after changing her clothing. Jesus
declares her not merely healed, the past event, but saved,
righteous, wealthy, all the things that *shalom* and *sozo* imply –
now, this minute.

In Luke's Gospel *sozo* and *diasozo* are only used five times. Two
are in Luke's version of these stories. One is the same as Mark, of
the woman being healed. The other use does not follow Mark and is
therefore Luke's deliberate editing. The messengers bring Jairus the
devastating news of his daughter's death. Jesus says, 'Only believe
and she shall be healed/saved/purified (*sozo*).' Both of these stories
have this concept of salvation and purity. Luke uses *sozo* independently in two other places. One describes the post-exorcism

condition of the man previously possessed by 'Soldier'. The other, where ten people with the dreaded skin disease are sent away healed by Jesus, is similar to the use here. A Samaritan comes back to Jesus. He too is saved by faith and dismissed – almost in the same words: 'Get up and go; your faith has made you well/saved you/made you pure' (Luke 17.19). There is no suggestion that the others will have their healing reversed.

Healing and salvation are linked but there is no simple one-to-one congruence. Physical and mental health are restored but salvation is a part of being healed. Luke's Gentile audience stand outside of the Law and need salvation – discovering it in response to healing. In Mark's more mixed community the link is more direct: '[T]he only ministry', writes Best of Mark, '[...] clearly recognized is one directed to the outside world, [...] healing and evangelization.'[24] Ritual purity and healing and salvation are part of living righteously.

The woman is purified, her period of barrenness, of enforced celibacy, over. No longer cursed by God, she can return into society, family, religion, sexual activity, perhaps become pregnant. Her whole life changes. No longer impure and isolated, she is now a complete human being.

There is a form to this passage though the structure seems extremely complex. Though taken as two distinct stories, the structure becomes clearer. At the heart of the pericope is the story of the woman. This is chiastic. Around this is the girl's story. The form of a story says nothing about its historicity. Form has to do with why the story is told and to what audience. A story told in a newspaper would have a style inappropriate for a Crown Court – form does not affect truth. These two stories have entirely different structures. However, grouping the people gives a dynamic to the passage, with the woman's story inserted in the centre.

(1) Jesus and the disciples;
(2) Jesus and Jairus (and daughter);
(3) Jesus and the crowd;
(4) Jesus and the inner core of disciples, i.e. Peter, James and John;
(5) Jesus and Jairus' daughter.

A useful way forward is to move from:

(I) The evangelistic community – Jesus and the disciples, to

51

(II) the new convert – Jairus or his daugher, to
(III) those who are outside the evangelistic community – the crowd, who are taught and dismissed, to
(IV) the new convert joining Jesus in the inner core with Peter, James and John, where
(V) healing and resurrection take place, followed by
(VI) a meal.

This may reflect a form of primitive liturgy relating to initiating converts into the church. It is reminiscent of those of the third and fourth centuries although one must be careful not to read back into Scripture later developments. However, this indicates early linkage between healing and baptism, physical and spiritual regeneration.

(1) Jesus is met in the midst of the evangelistic community.
(2) The new convert (Jairus or Jairus as sponsoring his daughter) comes to Jesus.
(3) The crowds (the unbaptized) receive teaching.

*The Teaching*

  (a) The woman and the doctors – no healing.
    (b) The woman talks to herself (secretly?) about touching Jesus.
      (c) The woman acts and touches Jesus.
        (d) She is healed.
      (e) Jesus responds to the woman's action.
    (f) The disciples talk among themselves (secretly?) about touching Jesus.
  (g) The woman and Jesus – salvation.

(4) The crowds (the unbaptized) are dismissed.
(5) The new convert is welcomed into the inner core, the community of the baptized.
(6) Healing and resurrection take place, followed by the Eucharistic meal.

In the worship of Mark's community this passage would apparently be used in baptism or the Eucharist. This would echo the Jewish experience of Passover year by year. By remembering historical experience, the past is encountered as living reality. The experience of conversion/baptism is realized not as memory but as participation in the events. There are no references to water, but all references to dying and rising with Christ reflect baptism. Jairus' daughter graphically dies and rises with Christ. In baptism we are symbolically dying to self and rising to new life in Christ and experience the reality of the baptismal community. This community experiences healing as the individual is healed; healing is not experienced in isolation.

## CASE 6

### THE BOY WITH EPILEPSY

When they joined the rest of the disciples, they saw a large crowd round them and some teachers of the Law arguing with them. When the people saw Jesus, they were greatly surprised, and ran to him and greeted him. Jesus asked his disciples, 'What are you arguing with them about?'

A man in the crowd answered, 'Teacher, I brought my son to you, because he has an evil spirit in him and cannot talk. Whenever the spirit attacks him, it throws him to the ground, and he foams at the mouth, grits his teeth, and becomes stiff all over. I asked your disciples to drive the spirit out, but they could not.'

Jesus said to them, 'How unbelieving you people are! How long must I stay with you? How long do I have to put up with you? Bring the boy to me!' They brought him to Jesus.

As soon as the spirit saw Jesus, it threw the boy into a fit, so that he fell on the ground and rolled round, foaming at the mouth. 'How long has he been like this?' Jesus asked the father.

'Ever since he was a child,' he replied. 'Many times the evil spirit has tried to kill him by throwing him in the fire and into water. Have pity on us and help us, if you possibly can!'

'Yes,' said Jesus, 'if you yourself can! Everything is possible for the person who has faith.'

The father at once cried out, 'I do have faith, but not enough. Help me to have more!'

Jesus noticed that the crowd was closing in on them, so he gave a command to the evil spirit. 'Deaf and dumb spirit,' he said, 'I order you to come out of the boy and never go into him again!'

The spirit screamed, threw the boy into a bad fit, and came out. The boy looked like a corpse, and everyone said, 'He is dead!' But Jesus took the boy by the hand and helped him to rise, and he stood up.

After Jesus had gone indoors, his disciples asked him privately, 'Why couldn't we drive the spirit out?'

'Only prayer can drive this kind out,' answered Jesus; 'nothing else can.'

(Mark 9.14–29)

This story raises the question of the relationship between Jesus' healings and faith, or perhaps the question: was Jesus a faith-healer? The story of the boy infested by a deaf and dumb spirit describes the boy's symptoms: he falls down, foams at the mouth, grinds his teeth and goes rigid. The fit described when he is brought to Jesus adds detail. He has convulsions, gives a loud cry and becomes unconscious. These are the classic symptoms of a clonic-tonic seizure, the epileptic fit once called *grand mal*. Some modern writers see epilepsy as evidence of learning disability but there is no evidence whatsoever for the suggestion.

This pericope causes dispute among scholars: some take the three descriptions of the fits in the story as evidence of two separate oral sources, others see one oral tradition which Mark's community inherited.[25] Now, after Mark's redaction, it appears seamless, the symptoms described cohesively. Jesus observes one fit and questions the father for the case history. However, the narrative is not simply structured. Descriptions of symptoms are intermingled with discussion of faith. Finally, the explanation – only prayer – does not fit the facts and appears as an afterthought.

When Jesus appears the disciples have already failed to exorcize the spirit and have become embroiled in an argument with some teachers of the Law. When Jesus asks, no-one will tell him what the argument is about though it is probably again about authority. The disciples have already been given authority to drive out spirits (Mark 3.15, 6.7), which presumably has not been retracted. Otherwise, why are they trying to expel this one?

Only ten verses after this story, an unknown person uses Jesus' name to cast out demons – the name relating intimately to power.

By using a name one adopted the authority of the named person. Using Jesus' name imposes a relationship on him. That a stranger exorcizes demons using Jesus' authority is an affront to the disciples. The twelve who have followed Jesus from the beginning are snubbed. They feel that Jesus' name was something to be used by the group, the relationship shared by the community of faith.

The disciples had almost certainly been invoking the name of Jesus. Jesus' authority makes them *sh^elochim*. The *sh^elochim* (*shaliach* is the singular) represent the person who sent them. In Hebrew, certain prophets such as Moses, Elijah, Elisha and Ezekiel are described as being *sh^elochim* when performing miracles that are the preserve of God alone. The *shaliach* is not someone who refers all decisions back. Instead, in a sense, it *is* the person represented. All the principal's authority and power are there in the person of the representative. In the *Talmud* 'the *shaliach* of a man is as the man himself'. Jesus certainly saw himself as God's *shaliach*: 'Whoever has seen me has seen the Father' (John 14.9). The *shaliach* concept is probably behind Mark 9.37: 'Whoever welcomes in my name one of these children, welcomes me, welcomes not only me but also the one who sent me.' In Jesus, God is fully represented, Jesus' authority *is* God's authority. So when the disciples invoke the name of Jesus, Jesus himself is there. And so by extension, is God.

The conflict is probably over whether Jesus' name may legitimately cast spirits out. It seems to be a continuation of the conflict which Jesus had in Mark 3.20–30. The scribes there accused Jesus of casting out spirits by Beelzebul, the chief demon. Jesus cast out spirits in his own authority. Here the disciples attempted to emulate him. The point of dispute, though, remains the same. By whose authority does Jesus cast out demons, and on whose authority does he allow others to cast out demons?

While the disciples are arguing Jesus arrives, hotfoot from the transfiguration, still physically changed and dressed in shining robes. The crowd, in Mark's account, are more than 'greatly surprised', they are awe-struck. The Greek word *exethambethesan* is only used of the highest stress, which Gundry describes as 'so extreme as to cause emotional distress, bodily tremors and psychological bewilderment'.[26] Mark only uses the word at times of intense emotional and physical distress: when he describes Jesus' state in the garden of Gethsemane, intensely depressed and fearing sudden violent death; and when he describes the emotional turmoil of the women discovering a young man sitting in the empty tomb. The Good News Bible has 'alarmed', but 'utterly horrified' might be better.

The disciples and the teachers are so busy arguing that they fail to remember the boy's health. The cause of the dispute, the boy, is no longer of interest to them. His epilepsy is ignored. The boy's needs and his father's are now secondary. The only matter of import is that of legitimate authority. The disciples have externalized their failure, transforming it into a display of aggression towards the scribes. The boy, the focus of their disappointment, is pushed to one side. The boy is only important to his father. So Mark has him break in. He answers the question, 'What are you arguing with them about?' To the father this is irrelevant compared with his son's health.

Jesus is angry and despairing and exasperated. He echoes the Old Testament prophets – 'How long, O Lord?' The question is eschatological. How long? Until Judgement Day. This story suggests judgement and God's endgame. There are echoes of Moses striding back, fresh from his encounter with YHWH on the mountain. He comes down finding he is changed while nothing else is. Moses, after forty days in God's presence, is still in another world. The overwhelming reality of God so transforms the seer that he cannot see how others fail to share his experience. Coming down to earth, literally and metaphorically, Jesus finds the world alienated from God – a shock after meeting the living God. Jesus is still all a-glow. The way to the cross is now certain. It is so certain that people are completely terrified by the very look of him. Mark wants his audience to see the cross now writ large on Jesus' features. From the transfiguration it is inevitable, the point of no return. Baptism began the journey but now there is no turning back. Now Mark concentrates on Jesus' words. Miracles are less important because all Jesus' life embodies miracle now. The risen Christ, the Holy One, is here in person. Mark, writing his Christological Gospel, looks from beyond Easter. The crucifixion/resurrection/Spirit-explosion event legitimizes Jesus' authority. The earthly Jesus is the risen Lord. The endgame is in play.

After experiencing God's reality it is no surprise that Jesus calls the crowd an 'unbelieving generation'. The disciples, the community of faith, are implicated. Even the boy's father is unfairly implicated. He had faith enough to bring his son to

Jesus, it wasn't his fault that Jesus wasn't there! The argument about Jesus' authority opposes the crowd and the teachers to Jesus. The crowd are seen as being outside the community of faith. The teachers care more about authority than justice and negate the Law's values. The disciples too lack faith.

Does the community need Jesus' physical presence? To Mark's church this is important. The church no longer has Jesus physically with them and yet they are a healing community. How can they understand their own situation? Jesus' 'How long do I have to put up with you?' may be a cap that fits Mark's community too! Perhaps they too have turned to internal squabbling instead of the missionary task of healing the sick and releasing captives. Mark explains that the disciples' exorcism was unsuccessful because of their faithlessness. Healings do not occur in an uncongenial setting. Even Jesus was powerless in Nazareth because of the people's lack of faith. No-one questions Jesus' faith, the faith community does not exist apart from Jesus. The community without Jesus at its centre is a community of unfaith. The disciples without Jesus are alone in the midst of unbelief. In the community of faith, with Jesus in its midst, everything is possible.

The central motif of the story is the father's heartfelt cry, 'I believe; help my unbelief!' (RSV), echoing the words of Jesus. The people are faithless and unbelieving, so too is the father. But he has a tiny, hope-against-hope, faith. Not in the risen Lord – Easter has not yet come, it is still a future event – but a faith enabling him to stand before Jesus and ask. Faith is partly an act of the will and partly a gift of God. The father's cry is, 'I have faith at this moment, I have willed faith, I cannot make more faith alone – I need God's gift, given in the faith community, the gracious gift of sustained faith.' The father does not have faith in Jesus but in the God whose *shaliach* Jesus is; God will act through the person of Jesus. And Jesus cannot act on his own, as a *shaliach* he can only act for his principal.

This narrative, too, is chiastic though perhaps more tenuous than before:

(a) Prologue: the dispute between the disciple and the teachers.
  (b) Public questions about unbelief 'How long ...?'
    (c) A description of the symptoms in action, the seizure.

57

(d) A dialogue about faith, 'Everything is possible ...'
'I do have faith but not enough. Help me to have more.'
(e) A description of faith in action, the exorcism.
(f) Private questions about unbelief. 'Why ...?'
(g) Epilogue: 'Only prayer can ...'

What the chiasmus emphasizes is faith. Faith is only possible when Jesus takes centre stage.

What relationship does Mark draw between Jesus and faith? In each story God acts. We know nothing about the man with paralysis – by virtue of his friends' faith God's forgiveness is declared. Mark does not consider the faith of the person healed. There is no information about whether the man with the withered hand went to see Jesus, implying faith, or whether he was at the synagogue and met Jesus by accident. All we know about his faith is his willingness to come up to the front and stretch out his hand as Jesus commands. The willingness to isolate oneself at the command of Jesus is, however, a mark of discipleship. Presumably the man infested with 'Soldier' is not in his right mind before healing, as he is afterwards. Mark seems to suggest that the spirit itself may have approached Jesus, though this is unlikely in view of the consequences, Mark does not provide enough evidence. It must be remembered that the man clearly wanted to become a disciple after the event. Jesus' faith, on behalf of the man, seems to be the operative factor. There is no-one else available. The man is socially, ritually and physically isolated. Jesus stretches the barriers of the community to include him and Jesus' faith allows the demonic oppression to be lifted.

The woman with the haemorrhage has faith: 'If I just touch his clothes, I will get well.' The healing faith causes her to touch Jesus but there is still a faltering step isolating her from the crowd. She initiates the action, imposing her healing upon Jesus, but only in her response to Jesus is the extent of her faith revealed. It goes beyond simple healing: a saving/purifying/releasing faith. Her faith marks her out as a disciple, a believer in more than just the healing powers of Jesus.

Jairus' daughter has no possibility of faith: in a coma or dead, she can have no say in the matter. But her father has faith enough to approach Jesus. Jesus supports his faith when the tragedy happens – 'Don't be afraid, only believe.' Both Jairus' daughter and the boy with epilepsy are healed, by virtue of their fathers' faith – in the same way as the paralysed man is healed by virtue of his friends' faith.

Obviously, healing does not require suggestion from Jesus or auto-suggestion from the patient. Jesus does not necessarily require faith from the individual concerned. A sponsor may be required, if only to bring the person to Jesus, and Jesus can, in exceptional circumstances, do that for himself. Jesus is not a faith-healer in any modern understanding. He has faith and, in a sense, he *is* faith. The patient does not need faith, for Jesus has faith and *is* faith enough. The sick are isolated from the whole community; all relationships are damaged. A sick person is, perhaps, unable to show even a rudimentary faith, as in the case of Jairus' daughter. Consciousness, however, requires faith that God will act. But this faith is simply faith enough to approach Jesus and ask, not a faith in the risen and glorified Christ.

When Jesus casts the spirit out it screams. This is the tonic stage of the tonic-clonic seizure. According to Wilkinson, 'one result of the sudden spasm of the muscles is a loud weird guttural cry which may be suddenly emitted by a person at this stage of a fit. This cry is due to the forced expiration of air through the narrowed opening between the vocal cords which results from the spasm of the muscles of the larynx.'[27] In Mark's drama it is no mere natural phenomenon, it is the final ironic demonstration of Jesus' authority. He even denies the deaf and dumb spirit its deafness and dumbness: it loses its identity and screams.

The boy goes into a state of flaccid unconsciousness. Like Jairus' daughter, he is mistaken for a corpse. He is no longer possessed; Jesus takes his hand and raises him to new life. By raising the boy and restoring him to his father, Jesus graphically prefigures resurrection. God's power is openly shown as superior to that of spirits. God's power, through his *shaliach*, is life-enhancing and life-restoring. This incident is sandwiched between two predictions of Jesus' death and two predictions of the resurrection. The road to the cross is openly written on Jesus' face, the road to disgrace and death. The cross is easy to see in Jesus' transfigured face and clothes, but resurrection is also predicted and God's power demonstrated openly.

The question that the disciples ask is of great importance to the Marcan church, a question addressed to the risen Lord by the church. 'Why couldn't we drive the spirit out?' Jesus' reply to the church is that this kind of spirit – and presumably this means deaf and dumb spirits, who can neither articulate their own name nor hear the adjuration – can only be driven out by prayer (and fasting, some ancient manuscripts add!). Most commentators observe that Jesus doesn't practise what he preaches, and doesn't pray. But this is to ignore where Mark placed the story – in the context of the transfiguration. The cross is now inescapable. Jesus' life is now that of the Father, whose *shaliach* he is. It is not that prayer is unnecessary, far from it, but there is a sense in which all of Jesus' life is now prayer. The disciples didn't persist. They didn't pray and pray and pray. One of Jesus' parables (Luke 18.1–8) tells of a woman who badgers a corrupt judge until he gives judgement in her favour. They should 'always pray and never become discouraged'. This parable may not have circulated orally in Mark's community as it perfectly encapsulates the message that Mark has for his church. Constant prayer was important to the early church; Paul urges his readers to 'pray constantly' and practise rejoicing always and giving thanks under all circumstances. Luke's parable and Mark's story give continual prayer in the community of the faithful Jesus' authority. The life of the Christian is to echo the life of Jesus. All life is to be prayer.

We have examined a sample of Mark's healing stories, probably the earliest written accounts of Jesus' healing activity. The stories give us a picture of the concerns facing one early church community. These narratives addressed the concerns of Mark's community or he would not have included them. The skill in the composition of Mark is extraordinary. When I first read Mark it seemed like the stories that I used to mark when teaching eleven-year-olds. It has that breathless quality, 'And then Jesus ... And suddenly he ... And then ... Immediately ...' What I had not reckoned on was the use as a highly sophisticated literary device. It keeps the listener on the edge of their seat. This Gospel is a thriller. Mark's consummate skill means not a single word is wasted!

Mark's main intention is a concern for the whole community. No healing is in isolation from the community. The people healed are part of a community. Healing has social, economic, sexual, spiritual and political implications. No area of life is untouched. Jesus and his disciples are a community, the precursor of the Church. They are the faith community, centred on the risen Lord. Jesus takes the boundaries of his own community with him. He doesn't cross boundaries. He extends them to include those marginalized by their situation. So the woman, outside the community for twelve years, is now encompassed by the boundaries of the new community. And there is no time to waste on ritual purification – Jesus *is* ritual purification.

The Marcan church was probably concerned with its own holiness. It was worried about the effects of its preaching and healing ministry. If anything, some of the people were worried that it was being too successful! The newer members were not particularly sympathetic to the Jewish religious traditions. There was probably the beginning of a struggle for the leadership of the community. Was the power-base of the church to be Jewish or Gentile? The balance of the members was changing. For the Jewish Christians the church seemed as though that it was becoming overwhelmingly Gentile!

The community of which Mark was a member was most probably in Rome. In 50 CE there were riots in the Jewish quarter of Rome. The behaviour, according to Edmundsen (quoted by John Wenham), was 'of such a threatening character as to force the government [...] to take strong action. This appears [...] to be nothing more than a fair interpretation of Suetonius' words – "the Jews who were continually rioting at the instigation of Chrestus he [that is Claudius] expelled from Rome".[28] If Chrestus is a corruption of Christus or Christ, then the evangelization of the Jewish community by Christians caused the tumult. When Claudius expelled all Jewish people from Rome, Jewish Christians went with them.

After the Jewish community members were expelled there would have been a power vacuum. New Gentile leaders would emerge and step in. When Claudius died and the edict was allowed to lapse Jewish Christians, like Aquila and Priscilla (Acts 18.1–3), would return to Rome. This meant a power struggle in the church between the returning Jewish Christians and the, by now, well-entrenched Gentile leaders. The question of where to draw boundaries was of paramount importance.

This is why Mark emphasizes reaching beyond Jewish ritual purity. The woman with the haemorrhage is ritually unclean. By reaching out to Jesus she becomes an active witness to his mission – she claims liberation as a woman for all women. The man with the 'Soldier' is not only ritually unclean because he lives in a cemetery with pigs: he is a Gentile, and, worse still, he is demon-possessed. These two characters epitomize the problem. If the Church accepts these impure people does it become tainted with their uncleanliness? What about the non-kosher foods that the new Gentile Christians eat, isn't the whole Church made unclean by associating with them? 'Not at all,' says Jesus.

'There is nothing that goes into a person from the outside which can make him ritually unclean. Rather, it is what comes out of a person that makes him unclean.' [Listen, then, if you have ears!]

When he left the crowd and went into the house, his disciples asked him to explain this saying. 'You are no more intelligent than the others,' Jesus said to them. 'Don't you understand? Nothing that goes into a person from the outside can really make him unclean, because it does not go into his heart but into his stomach and then goes on out of the body.' (In saying this, Jesus declared that all foods are fit to be eaten.)

And he went on to say, 'It is what comes out of a person that makes him unclean'.

(Mark 7.15–20)

The boundaries can be expanded by Jesus to include everyone. By partaking in the risen Lord, Mark's community becomes and remains ritually pure whoever it brings in! This does not mean licence, far from it: once one has become an insider the moral code is strict. The Christian Church of which Mark was a member believed it had at its heart a gospel of action, called by its Lord to the dual ministry of healing and proclamation.

## NOTES

1 Wilkinson, J., *Health and Healing*. Handsel, Edinburgh, 1980, p. 33.
2 See Vermes, G., *Jesus the Jew: a historian's reading of the Gospels*. William Collins Sons and Co, Glasgow, 1973, pp. 58–82.
3 Smith, M., *Jesus the Magician*. Victor Gollancz, London, 1978, p. 9.

Case conferences

4 Smith, M., *Jesus the Magician*, p. 9.
5 Hendrickx, H., *The Miracle Stories of the Synoptic Gospels*. Geoffrey Chapman, London, 1984, p. 115.
6 Lambourne, R. A., *Community, Church and Healing: a study of some of the corporate aspects of the Church's ministry to the sick*. DLT, London, 1963, p. 28.
7 James, M. R., *The Apocryphal New Testament*. Oxford University Press, London, 1924, p. 5.
8 Wilkinson, *Health and Healing*, p. 26.
9 Wilkinson, *Health and Healing*, p. 26.
10 Smith, *Jesus the Magician*, p. 152.
11 Pattison, S., *Alive and Kicking: towards a practical theology of illness and healing*. SCM, London, 1989, pp. 103f.
12 See Olyan, S., *A Thousand Thousands Served Him*. Mohr, Tübingen, 1993.
13 Knight, G., *The New Israel: a commentary on the Book of Isaiah 55–66*. Handsel, Edinburgh, 1985, p. 91.
14 Gundry, R. H., *Mark: a commentary on his apology of the cross*. Eerdmans, Grand Rapids, 1992, p. 262.
15 Swete, H. B., *The Gospel According to St Mark*. Macmillan, London, 1898, p. 91.
16 Jeremias, J., *Jesus' Promise to the Nations*. SCM, London, 1958, p. 31n.
17 Carlton, S., *The Other Side of Autism: a positive approach*. Self Publishing Association, Hanley Swan, Worcester, 1993, p. 58.
18 Rapoport, J. L., *The Boy who could not stop washing*, cited in Carlton, *The Other Side of Autism*, p. 63.
19 Rhoades, D., 'Social Criticism: crossing boundaries', in Anderson, J. C. and Moore, S. D. (eds), *Mark and Method: new approaches in biblical studies*. Fortress Press, Minneapolis, 1992, p. 158.
20 Best, E., *Following Jesus: discipleship in the gospel of Mark*. JSNT, Sheffield, 1981, p. 12.
21 Best, *Following Jesus*, p. 12.
22 Wilkinson, *Health and Healing*, p. 53.
23 Wilkinson, *Health and Healing*, p. 53.
24 Best, *Following Jesus*, p. 243.
25 Pryke, E. J., *Redactional Style in the Marcan Gospel*. Cambridge University Press, Cambridge, 1978, p. 158.
26 Gundry, *Mark*, p. 487.
27 Wilkinson, *Health and Healing*, p. 65.
28 Edmundson, G., *The Church in Rome in the First Century*, cited in Wenham, J., *Redating Matthew, Mark and Luke: a fresh assault on the synoptic problem*. Hodder & Stoughton, London, 1991, p. 149.

# 3

# *Life, the consulting room and everything!*

Dark, rain-swept roads. Wipers sweep, revealing glimpses of chaos. Blue lights flash, hurtling through the blanketing rain. Everything pulls over, letting the ambulance through. A pregnant woman in one car begins to moan. Sirens wail, frantic minutes lost. Traffic nose-to-tail, it is twenty-five past five of a winter's evening. A paramedic works with measured professional calm, juddering from side to side. On the stretcher, a bloody mess, once human. Limbs in odd and strangely eerie positions. The face indistinguishable.

Braking, reversing and doors thrown open. The trolley is wheeled through double doors into A & E. The harassed triage officer assigns a cubicle. Panic, bleep the crash team. 222. Priority! A young nurse, pretty and innocent, first shift on casualty, caring and naive, retches violently. Someone shouts, 'Not in here. Get out!' The trolley is rushed through while hands try to massage the failing heart. Electrical paddles are placed on the chest and the Casualty Officer calls, 'All clear?' The body convulses, as the shock hits the heart. Stethoscopes listen.

Drama unfolds and yet another hospital soap rattles its way into our televisions. Compelled, we watch. All human life is here! Sex is hinted at. Romance, played for all it's worth. Life and death decisions made weekly. There are goodies, nurses and doctors. And baddies, administrators, penny-pinching pencil-pushers more interested in pounds than patients' lives. If only we had a ...! We could've saved that seventeen-year-old accident victim, that three-year-old asthma attack, that mother of three.

The overworked young doctor is saved from a ghastly mistake by the young nurse we left a while ago being sick – romance in the wind? And nine times out of ten, death, the ultimate baddie, is defeated and the patient saved – looking brave and noble in a wheelchair, full recovery guaranteed! And we become involved in their story.

The doctor has mystique, authority. Wearing the priestly garb of the Aesculapian: white lab coat reveals that doctor equals SCIENTIST (in block capitals, with the mythological aura of romance); stethoscope hanging casually from a pocket – careful understatement, emphasizing power. The 'greens' of surgeons equally aweful – what could inspire more awe than someone dressed to rummage inside a broken body and bring resurrection? A long way from the blood-stained bandage stripes of the barbers' pole, their mystique another weapon in the arsenal against disease and death. Authority to cast out illness plays an important part in the healing process.

Physicians and surgeons are portrayed as high priests in the medical cult, and the nurses are acolytes. And, although the majority of entrants to medicine are now women, the image is still of the handsome young (male) doctor and the pretty young (female) nurse swooning on command! Hospitals are the cathedrals of medicine, those of the Victorian period built to the greater glory of Progress. And, like cathedrals, many now have a shabby, down-at-heel look. The confessional, the consulting room, has done somewhat better. The story of medicine is one of magic and witch-craft; herbalism and folk-remedies; accident and misunderstanding; religion and, perhaps, a little science.

Since pre-history humans have been conscious of illness and have attempted to cure disease and stop pain. The attempt to control symptoms and avoid dying have been paramount since the beginning of sentient life. Many animals learned to lick wounds clean; human beings will absent-mindedly suck a bleeding finger. A cat uses grass as an emetic to get rid of hair-balls. There is a species of bear that has learned over generations to eat certain berries after hibernation; the laxative effect kick-starts a digestive system that has been dormant all winter.

From the earliest times humanity has used both preventative and curative medicines, practising methods that accorded with the prevalent world-view. In the ancient world events were ascribed a supernatural cause. The editorial slant of the chronicler decided whether the cause was good or evil – a census in the Old Testament is ascribed to both God and Satan (God in 2 Samuel

24 and Satan in 1 Chronicles 21). Illness and accident were ascribed to friendly or malevolent beings according to whether they affected friend or enemy. Thus medicine became a function of the supernatural professional, the priesthood. In the *Torah* are rules for public health, cultic practice, personal hygiene and diet, all intermixed. This supernatural element meant that prayer had a medical function and so prayers became attached to tasks like mixing medicines.

In ancient Mesopotamia there were written guidelines for physicians. The Code of Hammurabi warns that a doctor causing a patient's death will have his fingers cut off. In Babylon laws regulated how close cattle-sheds could be to houses, stipulated the distance cemeteries had to be from settlements, and made rules about clean drinking water. Babylonians also incinerated clothes worn by people with infectious diseases. Their Chinese contemporaries catalogued herbal remedies, many of which are still used, practised acupuncture and gave massage treatments. In India surgery was highly developed. Antiseptics and anaesthetics were used for surgery and fresh surgical clothing worn. (In the modern West surgeons wore filthy, blood-spattered clothing until very recently. Lister, who published the first important works on antiseptic, merely took off his coat, rolled up his sleeves, pinned on an unsterilized towel to protect his waistcoat from blood splashes and operated!) In India, three thousand years earlier, surgical instruments were boiled. The surgeon, with over a hundred different instruments to choose from, was instructed to keep fingernails short and hands scrubbed clean. They, apparently, recognized a relationship between mosquitoes and malaria, and used inoculations against smallpox.

A Greek physician of the fifth century BCE, Hippocrates, has the reputation of founding the modern science of medicine. 'Hippocratics prided themselves on their clinical acuity, being quick to pick up telltale symptoms, as with the *facies hippocratica*, the facial look of the dying: "a protrusive nose, hollow eyes, sunken temples, cold ears that are drawn in with the lobes turned outward, the forehead's skin rough and tense like parchment, and the whole face greenish or black or blue-grey or leaden."'[1] Single-handedly Hippocrates (whose writings are not of one person but of a school of thought) changed the nature of medicine. Natural causes were identified for ailments: stagnant water was associated with dysentery and diarrhoea; strokes are more likely to occur with increasing age; those over fifty, one Hippocrates wrote, are liable to hemiplegia – they suddenly become 'sunstruck' or cold. Another author using Hippocrates' name suggested that epilepsy (the sacred disease – associated with emperors and royalty) is no more divine or sacred than any other disease but has specific characteristics and a definite cause. He noted that many people who suffer from epilepsy have a warning of a seizure and find a safe place to fall and have convulsions. This premonitory stage is absent in the boy of the Gospel, who frequently fell into danger.

Hippocrates is famous for his oath, used until fairly recently. But, as doctor and novelist Richard Gordon comments, it is an oath 'which few doctors can recite or even recall beyond a friendly discouragement to avoid sex with their patients'.[2] It includes a promise to support fellow physicians against outsiders – perhaps that is why Luke ignored Mark's comment about the physicians' uselessness for the woman with the menorrhagia? Oath-takers promise not to divulge professional secrets to outsiders and not to use the knife.

The Hippocratic school brought medicine a proper scientific method – precise observation and accurate description. The physician was trained to note symptoms and, by building a complete picture, give a prognosis, forecasting the course of the disease. Careful observation allowed the value of treatments to be assessed and either added to the pharmacopoeia or not as the case warranted. Hippocrates' advances were, however, limited by the current concept of humours. Unfortunately this remained the dominant model for the next two thousand years. Humours were adopted unquestioningly and with the authority of sacred writ. They were unquestioned because, Hippocrates taught, it was impertinent to question your physician's treatment – doctor knows best! This paternalism allowed medics to reject anything that challenged them, especially if made by a non-doctor!

Galen (circa 129–99 CE) was the most influential doctor whoever lived – his ideas remained dominant for nearly fifteen hundred years. He was appointed, soon after qualifying as a physician, to be surgeon to a gladiatorial school. This gave him the opportunity to observe anatomical dissections without having to wield the blade personally. While the sword is not so delicate a tool for anatomical work as the scalpel, any dissection work done to human subjects was frowned upon as being socially unacceptable. (Sword-fighting, on the other hand, was perfectly OK!) However, Galen did both dissection and vivisection on animals and he described the function of the kidneys in both living and dead, in great detail. Galen's major difficulty lay in the rhetorical model of logic used to test his theories. He would set out alternatives, showing each to be logically false, and thus by deduction arrive at the correct solution. Similarly, Sherlock Holmes, based on another medic, said, 'When you have eliminated the impossible, whatever remains, however improbable, must be the truth.'[3] Galen, a person of strongly held and aggressively defended opinions, did not allow alternatives other than his own. And the more his authority and reputation increased the less open he was to question. Although many of his ideas were completely wrong he was unchallenged. And, as Galen was expert in disputation, the chances of winning against him were small whatever the evidence.

His major contribution to medical thinking was in the development of humours. This concept was already ancient; the Chinese, the Indians and the Egyptians taught that the whole world and everything in it was made of four or five elements. The Greeks, such as Hippocrates and Galen (who like most Roman physicians was Greek), taught that life, the universe and everything was made up of four elements – fire, earth, water and air.

Each of these elements had two qualities or characteristics: fire was hot and dry; air was hot and moist; water was cold and moist; and earth was cold and dry. The qualities of the elements – hot, cold, dry and moist – were reflected in the four humours that went to make up a human being. The humours were blood (which was hot and moist); phlegm (which was cold and moist); yellow bile (which was hot and dry); and black bile (which was cold and dry).

Any illness was as a result of being 'out of humour', and caused by an imbalance between the humours. Health was restored by restoring balance or homeostasis. The humours related to the four temperaments or personality types (interestingly, much modern counselling is based on identifying personality types). Imbalance in any one direction caused the individual to be *sanguine* or dominated by blood – confident and optimistic; or *phlegmatic*, dominated by phlegm – calm and sluggishly indifferent; or *choleric*, hot and dry, dominated by yellow bile – angry and bad-tempered; or *melancholic*, dominated by black bile – surly and depressed. To restore the balance, the excessive quantity of the dominant humour was removed. For nearly fifteen hundred years medical treatment was blood-letting to reduce excessive blood, emetics to induce vomiting, purges and laxatives to cure depression, and hot baths and expectorants to bring up phlegm. The treatment promised wonders: blood-letting brought clear thought, continence and better hearing, aided digestion, sharpened the wit, eased the womb, improved sleep, restored the spirits and so on. But the dangers too were well recognized – in thirteenth-century Iceland doctors were exempt from laws regarding mayhem and murder![4] Isaac Judaeus decries the 'foolish and widespread custom' of blood-letting 'even if they need not'.[5]

The Roman Empire was the first in Europe with clean water, sewerage facilities, public lavatories and flushing toilets – about 1,500 years later than India. The Emperor Claudius built a harbour to ensure corn from Egypt whatever the weather and had a lake drained to prevent malaria. The Romans enjoyed public health unequalled throughout the world today. The expanding empire brought contact with new peoples resistant to disease unknown to the Romans. And vice versa. They encountered the new diseases of smallpox and measles, probably hastening the decline and fall of the Roman Empire.

By the second or third centuries medical schools were established, following Galen. His influence developed at the same time as the growth of organized Christianity which rapidly accepted his authority on all matters medical, an influence persisting until after the Reformation. To challenge the authority of this aggressive pagan doctor meant one challenged the authority of the Church, and therefore of God, making one liable to charges of heresy.

The early church considered healing as part of the Good News.

Jesus said to them, 'Go throughout the whole world and preach the gospel to the whole human race. Whoever believes and is baptized will be saved; whoever does not believe will be condemned. Believers will be given the power to perform miracles: they will drive out demons in my name; they will speak in strange tongues; if they pick up snakes or drink any poison, they will not be harmed; they will place their hands on sick people, who will get well.'

(Mark 16.15–18)

In the Acts of the Apostles healings and other works were evidence enough of God's authority, but by the time the Gospels were written down the Church needed Jesus' authority for practice. The longer ending of Mark is a kind of catechism, a list of resurrection appearances, probably culled from Luke and Matthew – though possibly reflecting a variant oral tradition. First, Jesus appeared to Mary of Magdala; next to two unnamed travellers on their way to the country (Emmaus, perhaps?); lastly to the eleven disciples, with the commandment given above; and then there is a creed-like 'After the Lord Jesus had talked with them, he was taken up to heaven and sat on the right hand of God.' It concludes by summarizing the disciples' work, preaching and performing miracles. Although not part of the original Gospel, it became associated with Mark soon after being composed, around 100 CE, adding a resurrection ending which supplanted or supplemented the shorter (also non-Marcan) ending.

It legitimates church practice at the end of the first century: believers are expected to do evangelism and miracles. The power to perform exorcism is given to them, and the gifts of speaking strange tongues, handling snakes, drinking poison and healing after laying on hands. The apostolic period was over and charismatic gifts were patently not just for apostles. The command to preach and the authority to heal are given to all. The Church continues as a charismatic community; gifts are to be exercised. In the early church healing was the norm.

> Is there anyone who is ill? They should send for the Church elders, who will pray for them and rub olive oil on them in the name of the Lord. This prayer made in faith will save the sick person; the Lord will raise them [the same word as is used of the resurrection of Jesus, and the raising of Jairus' daughter and the boy with epilepsy in Mark], and anyone who has committed sins will be forgiven.
>
> (James 5.14f.)

The early church saw human beings as a unity; body and soul were inseparable. If flesh and spirit had no close relationship, and both were inherently good, then the Word could not have become flesh and Christ not incarnated. Gnostics, however, believed spiritual equals good while physical equals evil; a spiritual God could not create evil matter. This meant two gods: the good God and an ignorant creator or *Demi-urge* (equated with the Old Testament God).' This then allowed two conflicting ideas about Jesus: either he only appeared to be human and was thus unsullied by the flesh; or Jesus was an ordinary man and 'the Christ' had come upon him in the form of a dove, but 'the Christ' and Jesus were totally separate entities. This 'Christ' left Jesus before the crucifixion as it could not suffer death.

Only those whose 'spiritual' nature was awakened by secret knowledge (*gnosis*) received salvation. This *gnosis* would be imparted by a God-sent redeemer, one of whom was Christ. And while some believed they were pure spiritual pearls who could do no sin and so lived exactly as they pleased, most Gnostics were rigorously ascetic. Most believed the more children born the more souls were in bondage. Thus women were the source of evil, so sexual restraint and even celibacy within marriage were practised. The Church stood against this dualism, teaching that the one God, who had created the spiritual, had created the physical too. An over-emphasis on ascetic denial of the body was to misuse the temple of the Holy Spirit. The whole person was saved and healed, not merely the spiritual. Clement of Alexandria wrote of 'Jesus who heals both our body and soul – the proper [person]'.

Irenaeus wrote to defend the Church against heresies, particularly Gnosticism. He claimed that the Gnostics were unable to duplicate Christian healings which included:

confer[ring] sight on the blind, [...] hearing on the deaf, chas[ing] away all sorts of demons; [...] cur[ing] the weak, [...] the lame, [...] the paralytic, or those who are distressed in any other part of the body, as has often been done in regard to bodily infirmity. [...] And so far are they [i.e. the Gnostics] from being able to raise the dead – as the Lord raised them and the Apostles did by means of prayer, and as has frequently been done in the brotherhood on account of some necessity, the entire Church in that particular locality entreating the boon [gift? favour?] with much fasting and prayer, the spirit of the dead man has returned, and he has been bestowed in answer to the prayers of the saints – that they do not even believe that this can possibly be done.'[6]

According to Irenaeus it is well known outside the faith community that such healings occur and such miracles are daily occurrences. The Church continued Jesus' and the apostles' ministry with healing as a mission tool, sharing the faith with healing. Evelyn Frost describes his clear picture of early church praxis:[7]

1. The laying on of hands.
2. Directing prayer to the Lord, [...] in a pure, sincere and straightforward spirit.
3. Using 'the name of our Lord Jesus Christ' – which name [...] cures thoroughly and effectively all who anywhere believe on him.
4. In raising the dead the entire church in that particular locality prayed with much prayer and fasting [...] 'on account of some special necessity'.
5. Twice Irenaeus mentions that no fee was ever expected for works of healing.

The healing ministry of the second and third century was not confined to slaves and commoners. Tertullian, a Christian writer living in North Africa around the turn of the third century, wrote, 'And how many men of rank (to say nothing of common people) have been delivered from devils, and healed of diseases! Even Severus himself [...] was graciously mindful of the Christians. For he sought out the Christian Proculus and in gratitude for his once having cured him by anointing, he kept him in his palace till the day of his death.'[8] Tertullian was showing how ludicrous persecuting Christians was, model citizens whose only crime was monotheism! The facts could easily be checked. This was the father of the present emperor, dead only a few years. It was well within living memory, five or ten years at the most. Christian healings, he declares, are not just fantastic stories current among the poor and uneducated, evidence can be checked in official sources. Tertullian also adds to Irenaeus' list anointing – pouring olive oil on to the affected area of the sick person, following James, the disciples (Mark 6.13) and probably Jesus (see the Good Samaritan). Tertullian also describes exorcism using the Name of Christ, breathing on the infested person, and using the sign of the cross.

The Church slowly expanded over the first three centuries, sporadically suffering persecution: 'the blood of the martyrs', wrote

Tertullian, 'is [the] seed [of the Church].' The few glimpses possible show a slow expansion of faith and influence. Persecution left the Church with a problem. Many Christians paid lip-service, sprinkling incense on the emperor's altar; more bought certificates showing conformity from sympathetic or crooked officials. What was to be done about those that repented? Apostasy was one of the three capital sins, with murder and adultery. Fierce debate raged over those that lapsed but later repented. Tertullian distinguished between the forgivable sin (*remissibilia*) and the unforgivable (*irremissibilia* or *inconcessibilia*), a distinction rooted in Scripture but developed in the early centuries. The mainstream Church allowed the penitent to rejoin the congregation after penance.

Liberalization allowed a more nominal Christianity, especially after Constantine. 'From then onwards,' Evelyn Frost wrote, 'the Church was not the assembly of saints but the body in which were to be found saints.'[9] The marks of the Spirit, the *charismata*, marked the saint. With an increasing conviction that the charismata were not for the ordinary Christian, the healing ministry became a mark of the saint. Thus first and second class Christianity was practised. With the shrinking of charismatic gifts and the converging relationship between Christian and secular power, the Church turned increasingly toward Galen. God continued to heal, but indirectly; Galen became his agent.

Saints, too, were consulted for healing, and undoubtedly successfully; creating professional jealousy between physician and saint. The desert mother, Thecla, was, according to legend, such a successful healer that her neighbouring physicians plotted to destroy her powers by rape. God, however, maintained her virginity by hiding her inside a rock.[10] After her death, her relics became objects of veneration because saints focused God's power.

During Diocletian's persecution hermits appeared in the deserts, fleeing Syria and Egypt where persecution was particularly harsh. By this time the numbers in the churches had swelled and at the same time commitment had lessened. As martyrdom passed a new spiritual elite was needed. The early hermits filled this gap. Among the hermits some were committed to love others; however, others chose deliberate isolation purely for their own spiritual purposes. Some were, to say the least, wildly eccentric. The movement led thousands to the deserts, some as tourists, others to swell the communities springing up. Pachomius, founder of the first Christian monastic community in about 320 CE, cared for seven thousand people at Tabennisi on the Nile. A further five thousand monks lived on Mount Nitria and Serapion of Arsinoë had over ten thousand souls in his care. One fourth-century traveller wrote that as many dwelt in the Syrian deserts as in all the towns together! 'Benjamin', wrote Palladius, '[...] lived uprightly and virtuously till his eightieth year. When he had reached the peak of virtuous living, he was considered worthy of the gift of healing, so that on whomsoever he laid hands or to whom he gave oil that he had blessed, were freed from every kind of sickness.'[11]

Abba Benjamin, as a saint, is given the gift of healing as a reward for a holy life, in direct contrast to the New Testament picture, where the gifts are given to the community. The pattern now becomes, the pilgrim goes to the saint whose personal holiness brings authority to heal. As the desert movement gained popularity it attracted the eccentric. The word 'asceticism' originally meant an athlete's training. The Desert Fathers probably thought of themselves as God's athletes. Some, however, were moved by a different motive. Macarius, according to Helen Waddell, 'seems to have been moved for a while by the ill spirit of competition'. He tried to outdo everyone else in austerity. When he heard of someone eating nothing cooked for the forty days of Lent, Macarius ate just raw vegetables for seven years. Pachomius sent him away with a flea in his ear.[12]

Others walled themselves up or lived on pillars forty feet up in the air, shouting down spiritual guidance to pilgrims and living like a 'squalid maniac'! They withdrew into the deserts to force their bodies into submission and then to neglect them entirely, their filthy, wasted, lice-infested bodies representing the peak of holiness. The Christian community changed from one where the sick were welcomed to one marked by self-imposed sickness through deliberate privation, mistaken for purity. Self-denial was reinterpreted into self-mutilation.

Basil the Great imposed order on to the monks' lives. He disapproved of extremists and the eccentric individual piety found in the fanatics, instead insisting on set times of prayer for the community. He founded a monastic hospital, the infirmary becoming a typical feature of medieval monasteries. Basil's ideas of poor relief ultimately led to the founding of almshouses and hospitals. Basil emphasized the 'official' Galenic approach while the saints and hermits were 'unofficial' – this pattern continued for much of the next thousand years. The establishment favoured the regularized, formally approved concept of homeostasis and anointing (once for healing, oil became for those *in extremis*, and the institutional Church lost the concept of anointing for healing).

Saints popped up sporadically. Even after dying saints had healings associated with them. The Roman church insisted on three miracles (generally miraculous healings) which were investigated carefully before canonization. After death saints became easier to control, so cults grew up around certain shrines like that of Becket at Canterbury and cumulative evidence suggests that some found healing at the shrines. Business interests inflated the spectacular successes – the thousands who went on pilgrimage visited successful saints, even if it was the medieval equivalent of a package tour!

The rising popularity of saints in folk-Christianity paralleled the increasing reliance of the establishment on the Galenic model. God still provided health and healing, but not exclusively. God and the saint shared the activity – on their own authority! God's authority came from being God and the saints had authority of their own, by virtue of their personal holiness. The Church became self-contradictory: a popular folk-religion centred on saints – the community of saints was now in heaven; on the other hand, anyone questioning Galen was defying the God-given authorities. In little more than two centuries the Church changed from a charismatic community into a community where the odd charismatic was to be found. The emphasis on the whole person, inseparable in body and soul, changed totally. Christianity was now concerned with the world to come. Physical bodies, once temples of the Holy Spirit, became merely vessels full of sin. The pearls of God were no longer words of wisdom, instead they were the lice that crawled on the aspiring saint. Eccentric, even psychopathic, behaviour became the example. Sanctity had become unattainable for the ordinary believer.

In the space of seventy-five years the Church became, first, a legitimate faith among many; then the dominant faith; then a faith that was dominating; then, finally, the only legitimate faith. In little under one hundred years the Church conquered the Roman Empire and Rome fell to the barbarians. In 313 Galerius issued an Edict of Toleration allowing Christianity to be practised legally, in

390 paganism was prohibited and in 410 Rome was sacked by the Goths.

Julian the Apostate, the nephew of Constantine, was born in 332 and exiled in his mid-teens to Athens. While there he was initiated into the Eleusinian mysteries, the oldest of the Greek mystery religions. When Julian became emperor in 361 he set about degrading the new and, he thought, morally lax Christian religion. His moral reforms included the paganizing of Imperial Schools, the re-establishment of worshipping the traditional gods, and rescinding all the privileges Christians had been allowed in the previous fifty years. He deliberately recalled all of the exiled bishops to cause conflict in the Church. He also actively persecuted Christians, inflicting 'barbarous sentences on persons guilty only of Christian faith and practice'. His writings attacked the Christians, among other things, for 'their habit of consorting with the diseased'.

Within thirty years of Julian's death even the emperor came under the bishops' authority. In 390 the military commander of Thessalonica was murdered by rioters. The emperor, Theodosius I, ordered as punishment a massacre of Thessalonians. Theodosius changed his mind but the orders arrived too late and seven thousand people were slaughtered. Ambrose, bishop of Milan, excommunicated the emperor until he had done public penance in the Church. The emperor was now in the Church and not above it. During the next century, this idea evolved and the emperor became subject to the Church – in particular, the bishop of Rome.

As the Church's power in the secular world increased, it emphasized intellect over spiritual gifts and the Church became a tool of social advancement. Less emphasis was placed upon Jesus' charismatic commands to heal the sick than upon the command to 'do this in remembrance of me'. The men – and by now the hierarchy was exclusively male – who entered the Church for ambition used their intellects to advance. The spiritual gifts were less easy to control for social advancement. As the emphasis on *charismata*, prophecy as well as healing, diminished, the emphasis on past revelation increased. So revelation became regarded as completed and, according to Louis Rose, 'there was hence a certain return to the fatalism of the old covenant that regarded all phenomena, including disease, as immediate expressions of God's will'.[13]

God's will might be changed by prayer but this might be blasphemy. If God had caused this disease, and if God is good, then the disease is for your good – however fatal! Illness was good for the immortal soul and to pray for healing would imperil the soul – bearing pain graciously saved the soul from eternal torment. Physical healing became seen as at best impious and at worst witchcraft. Even Galen was suspect. When physician to Emperor Commodius, he prescribed an engraved stone for dyspepsia. The use of spells and engraved stones were condemned by St John Chrysostom, who praises the woman who would rather see her husband or child die than try a magic amulet. 'Even if ten thousand who deal in [amulets] advance philosophical arguments, telling her "All we do is invoke God, nothing else" or similar stuff, the faithful old woman knows that this is idolatry.'[14]

Anointing was ritual practice evolving naturally from home medicine. Jesus' Good Samaritan pours oil mixed with wine on to the victim's wounds before bandaging them. Ritual anointing dated to the apostles, possibly to Jesus himself, as a lay practice. People brought oil to Holy Communion for the bishop to bless. Then they took it home again to use throughout the week, for cooking and lighting as well as for medicine. Food, light and health were necessities of life. There was no real distinction between the secular and the sacred – all life was life! In the Eucharist bread and wine were brought to the Lord's Table – so too were olives, cheese, milk, honey, olive oil and flour.

Gradually the ordinary oil evolved into something extraordinary. Even where the practice remained lay, oil was taken to recognized holy people such as hermits and saints to be sanctified. Abba Benjamin was so holy that if 'he gave [anyone] oil that he had blessed [they] were freed from every kind of sickness'.[15] Sulpicius Severus notes Martin of Tours curing two girls with oil that he had blessed and that 'the wife of the Count Avitian sent some oil to Martin that he might bless it (as is the custom) so as to be ready when needful to meet different causes of disease'.[16] Even living saints were not necessary! At the shrine of St Lawrence in Rome oil was poured through the saint's bones. The oil was collected, filtered and used for medicine. In an emergency even oil from a church lamp was better than ordinary oil from the market.

For the next four centuries there was little change in medical practice. The empire collapsed and fell to the barbarian invaders.

In the chaos, quality of life for people of the empire deteriorated. Life expectancy fell dramatically. The level of literacy and education dropped. Monasteries became outposts of learning and artistic endeavour. People's lives were suddenly filled with insecurity and instability. During this time the gospel travelled further. Clovis, a Frankish ruler from Germany, was baptized in about 500. A century later Pope Gregory sent Augustine to Ethelbert, the king of Kent. A century later Boniface went from Britain to the Germanic tribes in France and Germany. Converts were now baptized wholesale. Clovis made a bargain that if the Christian God was on his side in battle he would be baptized. He won his war, and he and three thousand of his followers were baptized.

Wholesale baptisms were a novel departure; previously a year's instruction preceded baptism. Baptism was so serious that Christians in certain occupations enrolled for instruction (as *catechumens*) but put off baptism until their death-beds. They believed certain sins were unforgivable if committed after baptism or, at least, involved lengthy reconciliation – baptism, however, gave you a clean sheet. A soldier – killing requiring up to twenty years' penance – put off baptism until after military service. Constantine put off baptism until his death-bed as political decisions leading to people's deaths made him blameworthy. Modern politicians take note! In practice those who underwent instruction before baptism understood the faith and practice of Christianity. Those involved in mass baptisms had none. Christ was simply added to the pantheon of gods and superficial Christianization meant little change in lifestyle.

When sick, people turned to various remedies. Magic and sorcery were used alongside prayers. Christian remedies were thought of as being neither better nor worse than others, morally or medically – they were simply alternatives. Anointing by lay people was only one method of healing in use but for this reason Church leaders felt it was being debased. To use oil blessed by a saint or a bishop alongside magic potentially brought Christianity into disrepute – but only if the patient recovered. If they recovered who caused the healing? God through the Church? Or the devil through the magician? Harry Edwards, a modern Spiritualist healer, has noted the contemporary use of this argument.[17]

The Frankish king Pepin began reforming the clergy and his son, Charlemagne, continued the reforms. Charlemagne was crowned

Holy Roman Emperor on Christmas Day 800 CE by Pope Leo III, indebting him to the papacy. However, by adroit political and economic manoeuvring, mostly through the ownership of clergy livings, he managed to achieve a great deal of power over the clergy. His friendship with his religious and educational adviser, Alcuin of York, led to a renaissance in learning and the religious life. Pepin and Charlemagne legislated to curb wine, women and song (and hunting!) among the clergy. They also dealt with the complaint that the clergy bore arms and brawled in taverns. Charlemagne and his reforming bishops issued a series of directives insisting that priests attend to spiritual duties and not waste time in secular pleasures. In particular, attention was drawn to the need for pastoral care of the sick and dying; they were instructed to bring them the sacraments, including unction – anointing.

In practice the system of penance for sin after baptism allowed reconciliation with God and the Church only once in a lifetime. So reconciliation was left until death was imminent. In 416 Pope Innocent I pointed out that penitents could be anointed only after reconciliation. This meant that anointing became a death-bed affair, now in the hands of the priesthood. Monastic hospitals became more interested in a 'godly' death than in recovery.

The reforms of Pepin and Charlemagne also included the injunction that a priest was not to shed blood. This allowed the Norman bishop, Odo of Bayeux, to ride into battle at Hastings with his 'mace of authority' instead of a sword. In the Bayeux Tapestry it looks like a big club – perhaps he merely beat his enemies to death without shedding blood. Much more in keeping with the pastoral office of bishop! But it also forbade priests to perform surgery. By 1123 the Lateran Council also ruled against priests as physicians – priests were becoming rich by selling medicine.

Death-bed reconciliations meant recovery after extreme unction made one 'dead to the world'. A recovered patient was unable to resume a normal occupation and worldly relationships were no longer considered possible. If married you were not allowed to live with your spouse. And neither was allowed to remarry either. A medieval ruling insisted, for this reason, that the spouse's permission be given before any anointing took place. The recovered patient had to become a monk or a nun, whether called to the cowl or not. It was almost punishment for recovery. Jesus' healing ministry restored the community. The official practice of the medieval church, if successful, destroyed families and caused a quasi-death.

By the eleventh century ritual anointing had become unbelievably complicated – anointing the injured part developed into anointing the head as representing the whole person. In a separate tradition fingers and toes were anointed. Sometimes the two traditions merged so the power infused the whole person. The Irish baptismal rite introduced, in the ninth century, anointing of the hands; from the same period came a symbolic anointing of the senses. Originally separate rituals, by the eleventh century they merged. A ritual attributed (wrongly) to Theodulf of Orleans suggests anointing of up to twenty parts of the body. 'Improbable as it may seem, this [...] in fact represented a simplification of a liturgy now going grotesquely to seed':

> After making his confession, the patient was washed, dressed in white and carried to church, where he was laid on sackcloth. Three priests assisted by sundry lesser ministers sprinkled and signed him with ashes while the seven penitential psalms were sung. Then, after the multiple anointings, the patient recited the Lord's Prayer and creed, received various commendations and farewells before receiving communion for the last time.[18]

It was obvious to patients that they were not expected to survive. Strangely, patients who underwent the official rite lay in the church until death, while at other shrines patients lay in church awaiting healing. This practice, incubation, was inherited from classical paganism. In the ancient world were many 'incubation temples' where patients slept and dreamt, anticipating the visitation of a god. The god would then pronounce the patient healed and they recovered. 'So popular' wrote Louis Rose, '– and apparently successful – were these that they were frequently the last centres of paganism to hold out against Christianity, and indeed the practice itself entered Christendom.'[19] George Gordon Dawson described incubation as an affective remedy, still widely practised in the Orthodox and Roman Catholic Church.

> When the ordinary Greek believes himself to be beyond the skill of the ordinary physician, he may appeal to the Madonna or local saint for a cure. He passes through practically the same course of treatment as obtained in the Æscepulian

*Life, the consulting room and everything!*

Temples. He performs certain rites, stays the night in the church, and, in sleep, may have a vision of a celestial being. In the morning, perchance, he awakes cured.[20]

Frequently the churches which practised incubation were dedicated to saints whose names relate to classical deities: for example, St Artemidos in Keos and St Dionysius in Naxos. In some medieval churches mattresses and even baths were provided for patients; 'a church in Cambridge [was] particularly renowned for its incubation cures'.[21] But the official liturgy promoted a godly death, not recovery.

With the Church more interested in death than healing other measures than unction were sought. Saints were asked to plead with God for those suffering anguish. And it was best to talk face to face, or at least face to relic. As an essential qualification for a saint was by now death, saints weren't mobile – they couldn't make house calls! So when spring arrived 'thanne longen folk to goon on pilgrimages'.[22] The shrine of Thomas à Becket at Canterbury had three arched recesses on each of its four sides for hopeful pilgrims to crouch or kneel while praying for healing. Folk-religion became more obsessed with saints and shrines as academic theology became more remote. 'On the eve of the Reformation the Church did not as an institution claim the power to work miracles. But it reaped prestige from the doings of those of its members to whom God was deemed to have extended miraculous gifts. It stressed that the saints were only intercessors whose entreaties might go unheeded, but it readily countenanced the innumerable prayers offered to them on more optimistic assumptions.'[23] And it was lucrative to a Church desperate for money.

The fantastical building schemes of the Middle Ages were wildly extravagant, so while officially church policy emphasized a 'godly' death with sacraments, more unscrupulous clerics encouraged a tourist industry and trade in holy relics. 'Thomas Aquinas, lying on his deathbed at Fossanova, thinking his last syllogism, can hardly have been unaware of eyes contemplating his body, minds thinking what a splendid relic he was about to become.'[24] Canterbury in 1420 drew some hundred thousand pilgrims to visit its relics – the resting place of Becket; the bed of the Blessed Virgin; fragments of the manger from Bethlehem; a piece of rock from Calvary; even Aaron's rod. Competition between townspeople

81

was so fierce that a bye-law was passed to prevent anyone calling out to advertise lodgings.

Walsingham was so highly regarded that it ranked equally with Rome, Jerusalem or Santiago de Compostella. Edward I visited ten times during his reign; Erasmus wrote that a man could not prosper unless he made an annual pilgrimage to Walsingham.

> Many seeking healing here [are] cured by our lady's might
> Dead again revived of this [there] is no doubt
> Lame made whole and blind given sight
> Mariners vexed with tempest safe to port brought.
> [Those with] Deadly wounds and lunatics
>     (that to here have fought their way)
> And also lepers [all] here have recovered
> By our lady's grace from their infirmities.

(Richard Pyson's description of Walsingham, 1465)

Some ordinary people went on pilgrimage, and it was easier to go to Norfolk than Spain or Italy or Palestine. Chaucer's pilgrims included ordinary working people – one was a ploughman (another, surprisingly, was a physician).

Throughout the Middle Ages appropriate saints were invoked for different ailments. St Blaise was especially called upon for his valuable prayers asking God's protection from throat infections. St Bridget, a visionary saint, was called to help those with eyesight problems. St Erasmus, killed by having his intestines wound on to a kind of capstan, was invoked for stomach complaints – he is also a patron saint of sailors because of that capstan! Prayers to St Dympna were used for mental illness and epilepsy. There is still a medieval foundation dedicated to her at Gheel near Antwerp. It is world famous for its practice of integrating patients into the community by placing them in private homes with families! St Lawrence who was roasted on a gridiron specializes in back pain. St Fiacre is patron of gardeners and helps sufferers from piles, which may or may not be connected; and so on.

At the same time less religious methods continued alongside those of the Church. While saints were invoked for healing, wise folk were also consulted. Well into the seventeenth century only unorthodox medicine was available to the majority of the populace. 'Sorcerers are too common; cunning men, wizards, and white witches, as they call them, in every village, which, if they be sought unto, will help almost all infirmities of body and mind.'[25] At the same time as demons were being chased away by saints, wise people chased away the fairies and hob-goblins. As Christian shrines were visited, so were other sacred places.

All over Britain country folk used to venerate certain standing stones for their properties of healing or bestowing fertility. Holed stones were regarded as the most efficacious, especially those through which children could be passed – such ceremonies being regarded by some as symbolic of rebirth. The most famous remaining holed stone is the Men-an-Tol which, standing between two ordinary stones, is to be found on Woon Gumpus Common east of Morvah in Cornwall. Children suffering from rickets, once such a universal childhood complaint, were squeezed through the smooth circular hole, and because it was be beneficial for a 'crick in the neck' it was also known as the Crick Stone.[26]

The Cerne Abbas giant was another: 'understandably with such a well endowed giant, fertility beliefs are associated with him, and it used to be the custom for a barren wife to sleep on the appropriate part of his anatomy in order to become pregnant'.[27]

In the Middle Ages people had four sources of healing and medicine, individually or in combination. The Church or saints were probably the first port of ·call, although pilgrimage was probably only a last resort. For preventative medicine, however, the Church won hands down. As late as 1620 the Bishop of Quimper threw an *Agnus Dei*, the stump of a wax candle impressed with an image of the Lamb of God, into a fire to put it out. St Mary's Church, Walthamstow, in London, has an *Agnus* carved into its tower to ward off lightning. It also has a lightning conductor – East Londoners are noted for hedging their bets! In 1591 John Allyn, a Roman Catholic in Oxford, claimed to possess some of Christ's blood which he sold for twenty pounds a drop – three times the annual salary of a master craftsman. He claimed the blood would free the bearer from all harm.

The second source of medical support was, of course, the medical profession. The physician had a peculiar relationship with the Church, a medieval Latin proverb suggesting that 'where there are three physicians there are two atheists'. Chaucer's physician is a miserly self-server more interested in prolonging his own life than his patients'. He uses natural magic and astrology to discover the right times to treat his patients, though as Chaucer implies these times are those most convenient for his pocket! The physician is in mutually profitable partnership with an apothecary, a chemist. This has an unfortunate contemporary ring about it, drugs companies having used marketing ploys and unwisely influenced certain doctors. Chaucer's physician understands 'the cause of every malady, whether it be hot or cold or wet or dry, and where they began, and of what humour'. If patients were continually sick it didn't unduly affect the physician's reputation, for full health was almost by definition unattainable.

A third source of medical assistance was, from even before the eleventh century, the monarch – treating scrofula, tuberculosis of the lymph glands in the neck. The sovereigns of France (from Clovis onwards) and England were 'invested with a royal touch, which by stroking the afflicted area of the sufferer was able to heal the glandular disease'.[28] Peter of Blois attributed the power of healing to the coronation anointing of his king, Henry II. 'It is a sacred duty to attend upon the lord king; for he is holy and the Lord's Anointed; nor has he received the sacrament of regal unction in vain, for if its efficacy be not known or be in doubt, the disappearance of bubonic plague and the cure of scrofula will beget the fullest belief.'[29] Curing the King's Evil was overtly political as well as religious. Sufferers were not cured by a usurper. Like King Arthur's sword in the stone, it marked the true-born king.[30]

Tudor monarchs all laid hands on the sick but the practice flourished, as liturgy and politically, under the Stuarts. Shakespeare mentions it in *Macbeth*, written during the reign of James I. Although set in the age of Edward the Confessor, the hidden political agenda declares James the legitimate king. Edward can heal the sick, unlike the murderous usurper Macbeth.

> ... here are a crew of wretched souls
> That stay his cure. Their malady convinces
> The great assay of art; but at his touch,
> such sanctity hath heaven given his hand,
> They presently amend.
>
> (Act IV, Scene 3:11.141–5)

James I was reluctant to touch his subjects for healing. His Puritan upbringing made it appear superstitious. 'Only when his advisers convinced him of its political expediency for enhancing the Divine Right, did the sceptical king consent.'[31] His Tudor predecessors made the sign of the cross over patients with a medal having the image of St Michael. James regarded this as superstition: he merely hung the coin, known as an *Angel*, around the neck of the patient.

Until the 1719 (Queen Anne) *Book of Common Prayer* an order of service was occasionally printed. 'At the healing' asks for God's blessing on those touched by the monarch, asking for their recovery. Charles II, legitimizing the Restoration, was prolific in his touching. His physician, John Browne, claimed Charles touched 92,107 people for scrofula during his reign. Many were, he claimed, cured. One eyewitness, the diarist John Evelyn, wrote on 28 March 1684 that 'six or seven were crushed to death by pressing at the chirurgeon's door for tickets'. In 1719 the last version of the occasional office was printed.

## AT THE HEALING

*Minister*:  Prevent us, O Lord, in all our doings with thy most gracious favour, and further us with thy continual help; that in all our works, begun, continued, and ended in Thee, we may glorify thy holy Name.

*The Gospel (for Ascension Day)* S. Mark xvi. 14–20

Let us pray.

*Minister*:  Lord, have mercy upon us.
*Response*:  Christ have mercy upon us.
*Minister*:  Lord, have mercy upon us.

Our Father, which art in heaven ...

*Then shall the infirm persons, one by one, be presented to the Queen upon their knees; and as every one is presented and while the Queen is laying her hands upon them, and putting the gold about their necks, the Chaplain that officiates, turning himself to her Majesty, shall say these words following*:

God give a blessing to this work; and grant that these sick

85

persons on whom the Queen lays her hands may recover, through Jesus Christ out Lord.

*After all have been presented, the chaplain shall say,*

*Minister*:  O Lord, save thy servants;
*Answer*:  That put their trust in thee.
*Minister*:  Send unto them help from above.
*Answer*:  And evermore mightily defend them.
*Minister*:  Help us, O God our Saviour.
*Answer*:  And for the glory of thy Name deliver us; be merciful to us sinners, for thy Name's sake.
*Minister*:  O Lord, hear our prayer.
*Answer*:  And let our cry come to thee.

Let us pray.

O Almighty God, who art the Giver of all health, and the aid of them that seek to thee for succour, we call upon thee for thy help and goodness mercifully to be showed upon these thy servants, that they being healed of their infirmities may give thanks unto thee in the holy Church, through Jesus Christ our Lord. Amen.

*Then the chaplain, standing with his face towards them that come to be healed, shall say:*

The almighty Lord, who is a most strong tower to all them that put their trust in him, to whom all things in heaven, in earth, and under the earth, do bow and obey, be now and evermore thy defence; and make thee know and feel, that there is none other Name under heaven given to man, in whom, thou mayest receive health and salvation, but only the Name of our Lord Jesus Christ. Amen.

The grace of our Lord Jesus Christ, and the love of God, and the fellowship of the Holy Ghost, be with us all evermore. Amen.

Monarchs were, by the end of the Middle Ages, enthroned by Divine Right. The Tudors, particularly, needed the Divine Right to legitimize their claim. They adopted some politically astute religious moves, one of which was healing, another the cult of Henry VI. This cult was vehemently anti-Yorkist and opposed the equally vehement anti-Lancastrian cult of Archbishop Scrope. Neither was canonized by the Church, though Henry VII began to promote his predecessor's cause at Rome, and built a magnificent relic chapel in Westminster Abbey. Henry VI's miracles 'include very overt political miracles, like the healing of a little girl afflicted with the "King's Evil", whose parents had refused to bring her to be "touched" by the "usurper", Richard III'.[32]

Finally, and for the poorest section of the population who were unable to go on pilgrimage or visit the royal court or pay the physician, there was more local treatment. At the same time as saints were invoked locally, home remedies were used and local dealers in herbal (and less savoury) medicines were consulted. The wise woman and the cunning man were approached for advice and for medication.

Much has been written on witchcraft in the late Middle Ages, some writers claiming an underground continuation of pre-Christian paganism. One of the Grimm brothers, Jacob, believed it an ancient Teutonic religion. In England, Margaret Murray influenced the neo-Pagan and parts of the women's movement, suggesting a continuation of pre-Christian religion. This, she claims, was interpreted as witchcraft. In fact, she suggests that the only explanation for the huge number of witches executed in Western Europe is the existence of a widely held religion.[33]

Dr Murray's research drew on the confessions of those convicted, particularly those extracted by Matthew Hopkins, the notorious seventeenth-century Witchfinder General. The confessions, however, are not easy to interpret. After being forbidden by a Parliamentary Commission to use torture he would 'walk' a suspect, walking them until exhausted and disoriented, and frequently managing to extort confessions. He claimed that 'when they did lie or sit in a chaire [...] immediately comes their Familiars into the room and scareth the watchers, and heartneth on the witch'[34] He was a hands-on psychologist of immense skill. By confessions and blatant plagiarism of earlier trials he gained convictions. He carefully used disputes and grudges to gain evidence. The vicar of Brandeston, Suffolk, was hanged for sinking ships, but in reality he was old, his sermons were long and rambling, and his congregation didn't get on with him.

Obviously, there are many pagan survivals: holy wells, especially those dedicated to St Bride, the Celtic goddess Imbolc,

Christianized; annual calendar customs such as May Day and Bonfire Night; fertility rites – throwing confetti over a new bride. But this did not mean a breach with Christianity: these superstitions were, and are, performed by people who continued as orthodox believers. Organized covens were fictions invented by witchfinders. Evidence was lifted wholesale from the compendium of witchcraft, *Malleus Malificarum*, the 'Hammer of the Witches'. However, pagan customs, regarded as witchcraft, certainly existed. The reformer Latimer wrote that when people are in trouble they 'run hither and thither to witches, or sorcerers, whom we call wise men'.[35]

It is impossible to distinguish the medical practice of wise men and women from that of physicians. Chaucer describes using horoscopes to discover the best time to treat a patient. Apothecaries used herbal remedies. Nicholas Culpepper, a physician-astrologer practising in London in the 1640s and 1650s (contemporary with Matthew Hopkins), published in 1653 his *The English Physician or Herball*. His description of plants includes a 'table showing the temperament of all the herbs', rating them in terms of the Galenic humours. Feverfew, for example, is strongly hot and very strongly dry. He also relates their astrological government. 'Venus governs this herb [feverfew], and hath commanded it to succour her sisters, women, and to be a general strengthener of their wombs, if the herb be boiled in white wine, and the decoction drunk. [...] It is an especial remedy against opium taken too liberally.'[36] Both the wise folk and the physician used urine to make a diagnosis – a cartoon by Hogarth dated 1736, called 'The Company of Undertakers', shows a physician tasting a patient's urine. Diagnosis was apparently done from a distance by this method, without the doctor even having to meet the patient at all. Eight hundred years earlier Isaac Judaeus had attacked 'fools who would base prophecies on it, without seeing the patient, and determine what disease is present, and whether the patient will die, and other foolishness'.[37]

The prescribing of ointments could, however, bring a charge of witchcraft. In England this was a civil offence, a crime against the person or property, and conviction depended on proof of malicious intent, and was punishable by hanging. One woman accused of witchcraft declared that 'she doth not use any charms, but that she doth use ointments and herbs to cure many diseases'.

Some cunning people used touch, often in imitation of the monarch. Charles I's jailers nicknamed him 'Stroker' because he laid hands on scrofula patients. One supposed seventh (actually fourth) son, James Leverett, in almost direct imitation, touched his patients declaring, 'God bless; I touch; God heals.' He was whipped and imprisoned for impertinence. Another seventh son, the boy of Godalming, insisted on fasting both for his patients and himself. One of the Irish gentry, an ex-Cromwellian soldier called Valentine Greatrakes, was the most famous healer of the seventeenth century; he too was nicknamed 'Stroker.'

> In 1662 the idea seized him that he had the power of curing the King's Evil (or scrofula). He kept it secret for some time but at last communicated it to his wife, who 'conceived it to be a strange imagination' and jokingly told him that he had an opportunity to test his power at once on a boy in the neighbourhood, William Maher or Meagher of Sallerbridge in the parish of Lismore. Greatrakes laid his hands on the affected parts with prayer, and within a month the boy was healed.[38]

By 1666, Greatrakes had cured the ague, a recurrent fever, and other diseases. His fame had spread and he was invited to Ragley Hall, near Alcester, to treat Anne, Vicountess Conway who suffered chronic headaches. He failed but attracted hundreds of people with a variety of ailments, some of whom were successfully treated. He was fêted everywhere (the Worcester city accounts record £10. 14s. for 'the charge of entertainment of Mr Gratrix'). He was championed by many of the famous people of the day, including the poet Marvell, the diarist Evelyn, and the 'sceptical chemist' Boyle. He came to London where he 'healed many members of the crowd who besieged his lodgings'.

Henry More, the Cambridge Platonist, and George Rust, the Dean of Connor, said his procedure resembled a religious ceremony. 'The form of words he used were, "God Almighty heal thee for his mercy's sake;" and if the patients professed to receive any benefits he bade them give God the praise.' His method was to drive the 'morbific matter' into an extremity such as the fingers, toes, nose or tongue. 'Into which parts when he had fixed it [...] would make them feel cold and insensible that the patient could not feel the deepest prick of a pin; but as soon as his hand touched those parts, or gently rub them, the whole distemper vanished, and life and sense immediately returned to those parts.' Another eyewitness said that 'there is something in it more than ordinary, but I am convinced it is not miraculous'. Greatrakes rarely received any payment, merely expenses. He believed he received the gift directly from God and that it had something to do with exorcism. In spite of his success, a number of 'cured' patients had pains which 'returned after they thought themselves well recovered'. By 1667 the Stroker's power began to diminish though he occasionally laid hands on people for the rest of his life. The short-lived Greatrakes episode is important: he had many carefully documented successes and claimed to have received a charismatic gift from God. That the age of miracles was not over flew in the face of theologians.

As the miraculous became the preserve of the saintly few and not 'the expectation of every Christian' theologians sought explanations, dividing theory and experience. St Augustine of Hippo began by writing that 'miracles are not allowed into our own time, lest the soul should always require things that can be seen.'[39] In the early chapters of the *City of God*, Augustine comments that those miracles that occur are not so famous nor so glorious as those found in Scripture. And why were contemporary miracles so inglorious? Because, he answers, they were necessary, before the world believed, to induce it to believe, but now that all the world believes, anyone seeking to be confirmed by wonders now is to be wondered at.

By the end of his life Augustine became convinced that some special miracles still happened. Someone brought a relative to him for healing. In a dream, a voice had said, 'Go to Bishop Augustine, that he may lay his hand on [the sick relation], and he will be healed!' Augustine, himself dying, said jokingly that if he himself was able to heal anyone he himself was first. Eventually, with poor grace, he agreed to lay hands on the patient. 'Immediately, the Lord caused the sick man to depart from him healed.'[40]

Augustine was thoroughly well armed philosophically against crude interpretations of the event, but had no defence against the event itself. The young Augustine had held that continually parading the miraculous made it commonplace; the universe itself was miraculous, harmonious and rational. In the last year of his life he experienced a number of local miracles which left 'the old Augustine' with a less secure attitude. However, his most influential writings were already written. Thus medieval theology became saddled with a philosophical and theological system that left little room for divine healing. Which is not to say that it didn't happen – it did! Augustine insisted that those healed made a written report called a *libellus*, read out publicly in church to check its accuracy. It was then stored in the bishop's library. Theology, however, concerned itself with more important matters – the eternal, with salvation and damnation, the nature of God and so on. The human body was small beer compared to the eternal destiny of the soul.

By the Middle Ages Augustine's philosophy was ousted by the Aristotelian philosophy of Thomas Aquinas. The 'angelic doctor' was the first post-classical Western thinker to distinguish systematically between the natural and the supernatural, reason and revelation, created and uncreated, essence and existence. Pope Leo XIII ruled that all Catholic philosophical institutions teach Thomism as the only right philosophy! According to Morton Kelsey Thomism 'was one of the factors that made possible the development of science in the western world'.[41] His *Summa Contra Gentiles* demonstrates the existence of God by deduction from nature. He describes God's natural revelation, defining healing in natural and remarkably modern terms. 'The body's healing proceeds sometimes entirely from within, as when a man is cured by his own natural forces; and when nature's efforts are assisted by external help of medicine.'[42]

Further, by 'the grace of healing [...] a benefit, namely bodily health, is conferred on man in addition to the common benefit bestowed in all miracles, namely the bringing of men to the knowledge of God'.[43] This profoundly affected both Protestantism and Catholicism – healing was God's self-revelation, physical benefits were a by-product.

Augustine, following Plato, taught that things are imperfect copies of an ideal, the *universal*. This allowed a reality beyond the senses. Aristotle, and Thomas, concentrated on the outer forms of things, which led to the adoption of a closed, naturalistic system with God outside. In the *Summa Theologica* God, nature and humanity inhabit two distinct worlds: that of reason, with everything having cause and effect; and that of faith. Aquinas distinguishes between philosophy, the knowable, and theology, the revealed. 'All we know of God is contained in what our reason learns by reflecting on the data of sense.'[44]

God's existence can be deduced from natural philosophy: everything has a cause, leading back eventually to a point where logically there must be something uncaused – a First Cause – that starts everything. The uncaused is God. So God is proven, and revelation takes over where reason finishes. 'Now, it is evident that to expect us to accept incomprehensible truths about God, [...] the surest means is to implant in us the knowledge of His incomprehensibleness.'[45] Miracles are only understood through faith, because they are to do with revelation. This distinction between reason and faith underlies the whole of modern, Western, white society. There is a distinction between the secular and the religious, in life, in thinking, and in morality. The soul and the body are separated.

Jesus, according to Aquinas, came primarily for souls to the exclusion of the body: 'consequently, He allowed the demons, that He cast out, to do man some harm, either in his body or his goods, for the salvation of man's soul'.[46] The body is irrelevant. Consequently, the functions of the Church and its sacraments are entirely spiritual. Unction was explicitly for the dying and not for physical healing. 'The thing signified here is the grace of the Holy Ghost: [...] whereby the sick being supported bears more easily the inconveniences and pains of his sickness.'[47]

The distinction between reason and faith led to a closed system where God's actions were always extraordinary: no longer natural but *super*natural. God could no longer share the activities of the cosmos. He was now entirely on the outside. Actions of God were seen as intervening rather than partaking in the ordinary, reasonable, world.

This, generally, meant that God could only be discovered intellectually. Thomas (following Gregory the Great) intellectualized the gifts of the Spirit. Paul's charismatic gifts became transformed into Thomas' more reasoned and reasonable ones.

It would seem that the seven gifts of the Holy Ghost are: for the apprehension of truth, the speculative reason is perfected by *Understanding*; the practical reason *Counsel*. In order to judge aright, the speculative reason is perfected by *Wisdom*; the practical reason by *Knowledge*: – the appetitive power, in matters touching man's relations to another, is perfected by *Piety*; in matters touching himself it is perfected by *Fortitude* against the fear of dangers and against inordinate lust for pleasures, by *Fear*, according to Prov. XV.27: 'By the fear of the Lord every one declineth from evil.'[48]

This list of seven is thought to come from the Latin Bible where piety is interposed between knowledge and fear in Isaiah 11.2. They continue in the Anglican Confirmation service where the bishop asks that 'the Spirit of wisdom and understanding; the Spirit of counsel and inward strength; the Spirit of knowledge and true godliness' rest upon the candidates, letting 'their delight be in the fear of the Lord'. In the Thomist world-view, in which God was experienced in the intellect, perhaps accompanied by a physical or sensory experience, these are more significant than Paul's charisms.

The Reformers accepted Aquinas' world-view unchallenged. To Luther important miracles were those of the Word; preaching and teaching were tools for soul saving. Other so-called miracles, like those of saints, are the devil's artifices. The Reformers restored emphasis on the preaching of the Word, claiming it was a return to the days of the apostles. Right teaching (that is, theirs) was its own justification; salvation doesn't need miracles – once the Word is preached there is no need to confirm it. Miracles were delusions of the devil anyway. For Luther, like Aquinas, the important gift of the Holy Spirit is intellectual. The Spirit gives *proper understanding* through the preaching and teaching of the Word. In the past there were, Luther admits, exceptional circumstances. The coming of the Spirit on the Day of Pentecost was an exception to the norm of Christian experience. But with the writings of the apostles, miracles become unnecessary.

Five years before Luther's death he experienced a change of mind, although, as with Augustine, his important works were already published.

When Luther arrived, he found Melanchthon apparently dying; his eyes were sunk, his sense gone, his speech stopped, his hearing closed, his face fallen in and hollow; and as Luther said '*Facies erat Hippocratica*'. He knew nobody, ate and drank nothing. When Luther saw him thus disfigured, he was frightened above measure and said to his companions, 'God forfend! How the devil has defaced this Organon!' He then turned forthwith to the window and

prayed fervently to God [...] Hereupon he grasped Philip
[Melanchthon] by the hand: 'Be of good courage, Philip,
thou shalt not die; give no place to the spirit of sorrow, and
be not thine own murderer, but trust in the Lord, who can slay
and make alive again, can wound and bind up, can smite and
heal again' [...] Then Philip by degrees became more cheerful,
and thus gained strength again.'[49]

In this tale both God and the devil are the agent of sickness; a 'spirit
of sorrow' (almost certainly Melanchthon's negative attitude) is
also blamed. Luther's advice seems half to have faith in God and
half to pull himself together. This doubt about the cause of illness is
not found in some of the other Reformers.

Martin Bucer had no such ambivalence. Bucer 'corrected'
Cranmer's *First English Prayer Book* (which formed the basis for
the *Book of Common Prayer*). God is the agent of sickness. But God
is blameless, for it is humanity's blind and rebellious nature that
impels us into sin and righteousness. This arouses God's righteous
wrath on us. We are to blame for our sicknesses, and death, and
eternal damnation. Illness is even a sign of favour.

Take therefore in good worth the chastisement of the Lord.
For whom the Lord loveth, he chastiseth. [...] What son
is he that the father chastiseth not? If ye be not under correc-
tion ... then ye are bastards and not true children. [...] I
require you to examine yourself, and your state, both
towards God and man: so that accusing and condemning
yourself for your own faults, you may find mercy at our
heavenly father's hand.'[50]

If you are healthy then perhaps you are not among God's dearest!
Good health is defined negatively as God's lack of interest.

Calvin typically maintained a more rigid attitude. While Luther
wrote to Pastor Severin Schulze about healing services, describing
his own practice in the last year of his life, Calvin held that 'they
make themselves ridiculous when they boast that they were
endowed with the gift of healing [...] for that was a temporary
gift and [it] quickly perished partly on account of men's ungrateful-
ness'. Luther, on the other hand, as Morton Kelsey says, 'seems in
his mellower years to value, rather than disregard this gift from
God'.[51]

Certain Protestant theologians have followed Calvin's stance. God did miracles then but the time of the apostles was special. God allowed the special to found the Church, but since then God has withdrawn his dispensation. Miracles are unnecessary, if not wrong – the Word is written down.[52] Sir Robert Anderson wrote that 'if signs and wonders were vouchsafed to us, as in Pentecostal days [then] faith would sink to a lower level'.

Two centuries later John Wesley condemned money-grubbing: 'And are they not partakers of the same guilt [...] whether surgeons, apothecaries or physicians, who play with the lives or health of men, to enlarge their own gain?'[53] He wrote a compendium of medicines called *Primitive Physick* which shows the state of medicine in the middle of the eighteenth century. Wesley died in 1791, the year Robert Knox, famous from horror films, was born. Knox taught anatomy, getting demonstration models from the 'resurrectionists' and murderers, Burke and Hare. It was another forty-one years before bodies were legally used for medical research.

Wesley died five years before Edward Jenner did his first experiments in vaccination against smallpox. Mary Wortly Montagu had pre-empted Jenner by using inoculation in 1718, a practice she had learned from people in Turkey. Inoculation used pus from a human smallpox sore to give a hopefully mild form of the disease. Vaccination (from the Latin *vacca*, cow) used pus from the related cow-pox. Vaccination was safer though people worried about turning into cows!

The seventeenth century physician was useless but decorative. Satin gilt-buttoned coat, buckskin breeches, silk stockings and buckled shoes, lace ruffles, frill-bottomed wig, swinging a long cane with a hollow gold head filled with an aromatic Marseilles vinegar. [...] It was repeatedly sniffed to afford the doctor security from infection and time to think.[54]

Eighteenth-century medicine was little better, with no anaesthetics, antiseptics or antibiotics. Surgery was crude and fast. The first European use of anaesthesia was more than fifty years after Wesley's death, performed by a surgeon who could remove a leg in two and a half minutes, start to finish. Speed reduced suffering and post-operative shock. The patient was conscious though probably half-drunk – often a scrap of leather was placed between the teeth to bite on, while assistants held the patient still. The surgeon in question, Robert Liston, held the knife between his teeth like a pirate and habitually notched up his score on the handle like a gunfighter!

In the seventeen century bacteria were first described. On 17 September 1683 Anthony van Leeuwenhoek cleaned his teeth and put the result under one of his 247 microscopes. To his surprise he discovered little animals 'more numerous than the population of the Netherlands, all moving about delightfully'. Nearly another two centuries passed before Pasteur discovered that they were bacteria. Bacteria were, he found, the cause of vinegary wine. The French wine industry hired Pasteur to prevent the ruin of their product. So he invented the subtly named 'pasteurization', a process which heats the product until the bacteria are destroyed. He then discovered that bacteria also caused disease in silkworms and, lastly, in humans. But broad-spectrum antibiotics had to wait until Alexander Fleming went on holiday.

Purges, emetics, hot baths and expectorants were used throughout Wesley's lifetime. According to Richard Gordon, 'bleeding, purging, puking and perspiring was the standard medical treatment which diminished only with the diminishing years of the nineteenth century'.[55] Fashions came and went in medicine, then as now, whether baths or enemas, leeches or quicksilver, and were reflected in contemporary literature. Jane Austen's *Northanger Abbey*, written in 1797, was set in Bath; Smollett practised as a physician at Bath and wrote that the waters caused 'the King's Evil, the scurvy, the cancer and the pox'. Enemas were fashionable among eighteenth-century courtesans, and a popular cartoon shows a fashionable woman about to be given an enema while a peeping tom peeks through the window! Alexander Pope wrote about enemas in his poem '*The Dunciad*' in 1728 with entertaining lavatorial humour. Colonic irrigation has recently revived in popularity.

'Leech' had long been a byword for 'physician'. Jesus' comment, 'Physician, heal thyself', became in one English version, 'Leech, leech thyself'. A contemporary of Wesley's, Dr Lettsom, apparently wore out three horses a day to earn his £12,000 a year (between two and three hundred times the income of an average curate). He did, however, treat needy clergy free of charge! A famous verse about him says:

*Life, the consulting room and everything!*

> When patients comes to I,
> I physics, bleeds and sweats 'em,
> Then – if they choose to die
> What's that to I? I Lettsom!

In the eighteenth century people quipped, 'A night of Venus and a lifetime of mercury.' Wesley offers this remedy for those suffering from *Lues Venerea*, as he calls it, in his *Primitive Physick*: '560. Take an ounce of Quicksilver every morning, and a spoonful of Aqua Sulphurata in a Glass of water at Five in the Afternoon. I have known a Person cured by this, when supposed to be at the Point of Death, who had been infected by a foul Nurse, before she was a year old.'[56] However, if you caught it in the usual way he had no sympathy – 'I insert this', he wrote, 'for the Sake of such innocent Sufferers.'

Another fashionable remedy of Wesley's time (appearing in later editions of of *Primitive Physick*) was electricity. Wesley lists forty-five cures of diseases ranging from St Anthony's Fire (erysipelas) to Menstrual Obstructions. John Yeoman, who tried electrical treatment in 1774, was not convinced!

> Then we was all Lactrified a Think is Imposable to describe. Its composed of a Mixture of cumbustables that if you Touch it the Fire flys out of it, besides You have Shuch Shudden Shock with it. We all hold hand in hand about 7 of us when I toucht it, and the Moment I was struck so hard in the Stomack that I could not stand, the Rest felt it as well as me, If there was 500 it would be all the same.[57]

Throughout the eighteenth century the number of physicians and surgeons increased. Hospitals were founded to care for the poor sick. This was not altruistic: it was dangerous for doctors to visit the appallingly insanitary living conditions of the poor. In London five hospitals were founded in just twenty-five years: the Westminster in 1720, Guy's in 1724, St George's in 1733, the London in 1740, and the Middlesex in 1745. After the Edinburgh Royal Infirmary was founded in 1729 other provincial towns followed suit. The hospitals had a double purpose: to treat the poor sick (the middle and upper classes were treated at home) and to provide guinea pigs. Trainee surgeons and physicians 'needed the poor to practise on'. Healing was not the unaided work of the

97

doctors as 'the London Hospital gave discharge certificates only to those patients who had attended chapel to give thanks for their recovery'. In the London hospital God was only acknowledged retrospectively – he was not allowed on the wards!

This was the world of John Wesley's *Primitive Physick*, 'an enormously popular book on practical medicine which helped many, many people in England'[58] and which had gone into nearly fifty editions and reprints by 1850. It explains that when humanity 'came out of the hands of the great Creator [...] there was no place for physick, or the art of healing'. But when they 'rebelled against the Sovereign of heaven and earth, how entirely the scene changed! [...] the seeds of weakness and pain, of sickness and death are now lodged in our inmost substance'. However, the fall, in cursing us to work by the sweat of our brow, conceals the blessing of exercise, 'both to preserve and restore health'. Wesley describes how medicines were orally transmitted in the 'first ages' and ''tis certain that this is the method wherein the art of healing is preserved among the Americans to this day'. 'And it is rare that the patient suffers long, those medicines being quick, as well as generally infallible.' Wesley implies that delay in medical efficacy is due to unscrupulous physicians not fallible medication (Sermon XLIV warns against money-minded doctors).

Wesley suggested 'a few plain easy rules, chiefly transcribed from Dr Cheyne': fresh air; avoiding the continuous company of unhealthy people; cleanliness; avoiding strong and spirituous liquors; remembering that 'Coffee and tea are extremely hurtful to persons who have weak nerves'; taking at least two or three hours of exercise a day. And of course he reminded his readers to 'above all add to the rest (for it is not labour lost) that old, unfashionable medicine, prayer', and to have faith in God, who 'killeth and maketh alive, who bringeth down to the grave and bringeth up'.

Wesley notes the remedies that he has tried and those which always work. It simply says '*Tried*' by those that he has tried or has the letter '*T*' by those which he has found infallible. For example:

Lunacy
561. Give Decoction of Agrimony four times a day:

562. Or, rub the Head several Times a Day with Vinegar, in which Ground-Ivy Leaves have been infused:
563. Or, boil Juice of Ground-ivy with sweet Oil and white Wine with an ointment. Shave the Head, anoint it therewith, and chafe it warm. Every other Day for three Weeks. Bruise also the Leaves and bind them on the Head, and give three Spoonfuls of the Juice warm every Morning. – This generally cures Melancholy.
564. Or, Electrify.

*Tried.*[59]

Wesley's father had 'Consumption' or tuberculosis. Wesley records: 'In the last Stage, *Suck a healthy woman daily. Tried by my Father.*' No comment! Another remedy that is recorded as tried concerns a Mr Masters of Evesham who 'was so far gone in a Consumption that he could not stand alone. I [Dr Dover] advised him to lose six Ounces of Blood, every Day for a Fortnight, if he lived so long; and then every other Day; then every third Day; then every fifth Day, for the same Time. In three Months he was well.' If he lived so long!

At the end of the book Wesley recommends cold bathing for everyone but particularly for children. He claimed that it cured them of:

Convulsions, coughs, Cutaneous Inflammation, Pimples and Scabs, Gravel, Inflammations of the Ears, Navel and Mouth, Rickets, Suppression of Urine, Vomiting, and Want of Sleep. It prevents the Growth of Hereditary Apoplexies, Asthma's, Blindness, Consumptions, Deafness, Deliria, Gout, King's Evil, Melancholy, Palsies, Rheumatism, and Stone?[60]

Wesley aimed to provide simple, cheap and easily procured ingredients for ordinary people. He describes the ailments in ordinary language for rural areas and the colonies (where physicians were not available) – America was still a colony when the 1770 edition was published. He recommends to those with 'plain unbiased reason, such remedies as air, water, milk, whey, honey, treacle, salt, vinegar, and common English herbs, with a few foreign medicines, almost equally cheap, safe and common. And this I have done on that principle, whereby I desire to be governed in all my actions, "Whatsoever ye would that men should do unto you, the same do unto them."'[61]

Like Augustine and Luther, Wesley experienced something he could not explain by natural reason. Normally one used Physic (medicine is part of creation) and prayer; but occasionally prayer alone was used. For example, on 16 October 1778:

> Immediately after a strange scene occurred. I was desired to visit one who had been eminently pious, but had now been confined to her bed for several months, and was utterly unable to raise herself up. She desired us to pray, that the chain might be broken. A few of us prayed in faith. Presently she rose up, dressed herself, came downstairs, and, I believe, had not any further complaint.[62]

Or on 24 April 1782.

> On Friday, I got to Halifax, where Mr. Floyd lay in a high fever, almost dead for want of sleep. This was prevented by the violent pain in one of his feet, which was much swelled, and so sore, it could not be touched. We joined in prayer that God would fulfil his word, and give his beloved sleep. Presently the swelling, the soreness, the pain were gone; and he had a good night's rest.[63]

Wesley's stated norm is physic with prayer, though it is expected that physic, or, *in extremis*, a God-fearing physician, is the normal operative in healing rather than any direct intervention of God. Experience seemed to Wesley to show that prayer works occasionally, though rarely, while physic can be infallible! Presumably as the scope of medicine increases the areas in which the natural is infallible also increases – while the supernatural is not so reliable. This would naturally increase reliance on the natural rather than the supernatural. In the Aristotelian philosophy of Aquinas there is logically no room for God. If a god exists then he/she/it is irrelevant because he/she/it cannot intervene. Therefore, religious healings cannot happen, though spontaneous healings of various kinds can occur by natural means – even if the mechanism is unknown.

Conservative theologians attempt to maintain a world in which God intervenes (or at least has done in the past), desiring to hold on to the Thomist categories of natural and revealed theologies, the natural and the supernatural. Liberal theology, on the other hand, largely sees the hand of God only in the processes built into the systems of the world during the creation. The 'indigenous weakness of liberalism ... [is that an] attention to the divine operation in the evolution of nature and man, while it had the merit of recovering a forgotten aspect of primitive theology, opened the way to a doctrine in which the uniformity of nature ousts the Biblical conception of a living God, and the certainty of human progress ousts the belief that God is judge.'[64]

The liberal view of the world takes the processes of history seriously. It ignores any experiences which do not fit such processes as meaningless. The conservative world-view allows such experiences to have happened in the past but has no theological tools to deal with them in the present. Healing is seen as a theological aberration and is thus pushed out to the fringes of Christian life. Both the liberal and the conservative rely entirely upon Aquinas.

The essential problem of theology is to make a relationship between experience – that is, how we see, feel, smell, taste and hear the world – and theory – how we intellectually arrange the world. One commonly used method, which is largely believed to be a liberal approach, though in reality is much more widespread than that, is to distinguish between the questions 'How?' and 'Why?' Science is concerned with the 'How?' questions. 'How does the universe work?' 'How is it made up?' 'How can I utilize the land that I have to feed my family?' 'How do diseases spread?' But as soon as we begin to ask, 'Why am I here?' 'Why do I die?' 'Why is there injustice?' 'Why was I born?' the questions become the realm of theological enquiry. Again we are enmeshed in the categories of Aquinas and Aristotle: 'How?' has to do with natural theology or nature and 'Why?' has to do with revelation or supernature.

Natural theology and revelation are categories with serious shortcomings. An argument about God from nature tells us nothing at all: 'observations made within the natural world can give us no information about anything beyond the natural world'.[65] And similarly, should any revelation occur, it is made to human beings and can only say things in terms of human experience: 'revelation [...] is always human at the point of delivery'.[66] New models are needed to view the world as experienced, because if the categories are right then the concept of God has no meaning. The Thomist world-view must be modified or discarded to fit the observed data. There is a commonality of the God-event in many people's experience, implying that it is more than subjective and must be allowed for in any theory of the cosmos.

The preoccupation with these categories has led to the idea of Christian healing, at the same time as it is becoming more widely practised in the Church, being marginalized theologically. Healing services are tacked on, perhaps once a month, often with little forethought or long-term pre-planning. Theologically it has been seen as the preserve of fringe elements, both Catholic and evangelical. One gets the impression that if healing occurs it is of marginal concern. It is, indeed, particularly to be identified with groups of fanatical extremists. Thus it is irrelevant to proper theological enquiry.

While the 'angelic doctor's' ideas were one philosophical approach among many the universe remained potentially open. Unfortunately Aquinas' teachings became the only prescribed philosophical model. The question of the work of the Holy Spirit has largely failed to be addressed. The sporadic outbursts of charismatic gifts which have occurred in history do not fit into this scheme of things. Therefore we shall shortly turn to God's Holy Spirit. First, however, a personal story of someone for whom the abuses of the medieval church are a present reality. The story will help us to be more aware of what is appropriate in a healing ministry. It is worth reflecting how easily people can be violated with the best of intentions.

## NOTES

1 Porter, R., *The Greatest Benefit to Mankind: a medical history from antiquity to the present.* HarperCollins, London, 1997, p. 61.

2 Gordon, R., *The Alarming History of Medicine.* Sinclair-Stevenson, London, 1993, p. 4.

3 Conan Doyle, A., *The Sign of Four.* Penguin, Harmondsworth, 1982.

4 McDougall, I., 'The Third Instrument of Medicine: Some Accounts of Surgery in Medieval Iceland', in Campbell, S., Hall, B. and Klausner, D. (eds), *Health, Disease and Healing in Medieval Culture*, cited in Rawcliffe, C., *Medicine and Society in Later Medieval England.* Alan Sutton, Stroud, 1995, p. 65.

5 Judaeus, I., *Guide for Physicians*, quoted in Rawcliffe, *Medicine and Society*, p. 65.

6 Irenaeus, *Against Heresies* II. xxxi. 2., cited in Frost, E., *Christian*

*Life, the consulting room and everything!*

*Healing: a consideration of the place of spirit healing in the Church today in the light of the doctrine and practice of the ante-Nicene Church.* Mowbray, London, 1949, pp. 194f.

7  Frost, *Christian Healing*, p. 65.

8  Tertullian, *To Scapula*, quoted in Kelsey, M., *Healing and Christianity*. SCM, London, 1973, p. 137.

9  Frost, *Christian Healing*, p. 181.

10  See Armstrong, K., 'The Acts of Paul and Thecla', in Loades, A., *Feminist Theology: a reader*. SPCK, London, 1990, p. 88.

11  Palladius, *Historia Lausiaca*, cited in Dudley, M. and Rowell, G., *The Oil of Gladness: anointing in the Christian tradition*. SPCK, London, 1993, p. 84.

12  Waddell, H., *The Desert Fathers: translations from the Latin with an introduction*. Constable, London, 1936, pp. 14f.

13  Rose, L., *Faith Healing*. Penguin, Harmondsworth, 1971, p. 31.

14  Barb, A. A., 'The Survival of Magic Arts', in Momigiano, A. (ed), *The Conflict between Paganism and Christianity in the Fourth Century*. Clarendon Press, Oxford, 1963, p. 116.

15  Dudley and Rowell, *Oil of Gladness*, p. 84.

16  Dudley and Rowell, *Oil of Gladness*, p. 85.

17  Edwards, H., *Spirit Healing*. Herbert Jenkins, London, 1960, p. 14.

18  Walsh, C. J., 'The History of the Rites', in Coyle, T. (ed), *Christian Ministry to the Sick*. Geoffrey Chapman, London, 1986, p. 12.

19  Rose, *Faith Healing*, p. 25.

20  Dawson, G., *Healing: Pagan and Christian*. SPCK, London, 1935, p. 59.

21  Rose, *Faith Healing*, p. 25.

22  Chaucer, G., *The Canterbury Tales: General Prologue*. Cambridge University Press, Cambridge, 1966, line 12.

23  Thomas, K., *Religion and the Decline of Magic*. Penguin, Harmondsworth, 1973, p. 28.

24  Brentano, R., *Two Churches*, cited in Finucaine, R. C., *Miracles and Pilgrims: popular beliefs in medieval England*. J. M. Dent & Sons, London, 1977, p. 28.

25  Burton, R., *Anatomy of Melancholy*, quoted in Thomas, *Decline of Magic*, p. 209.

26  Alexander, M., *British Folklore, Myths and Legends*. Weidenfeld & Nicholson, London, 1987, p. 43.

27  Alexander, *British Folklore*, p. 49.

28  Gusmer, C., *The Ministry of Healing in the Church of England: an ecumenical study*. Alcuin/Mayhew McCrimmon, Great Wakering, Essex, 1974, p. 86.

29  Gusmer, The Ministry of Healing, p. 87.

30 Duffy, E., *The Stripping of the Altars: traditional religion in England 1400–1580*. Yale University Press, New Haven, 1992, p. 164.

31 Thomas, *Decline of Magic*, p. 228.

32 Duffy, *Stripping of the Altars*, p. 164.

33 Murray, M., see Thomas, K., *Religion and the Decline of Magic*, pp. 614f.

34 M. Hopkins, *The Discovery of Witches: in answer to several queries lately delivered to the Judges of Assize for the County of Norfolk and now published by Matthew Hopkins, Witchfinder. For the benefit of the whole Kingdom*. R. Royston, at the Angell in Ivie Lane, London, 1647. Reprinted with an introduction by D. Ryan, Partizan Press, Leigh-on-Sea, Essex, 1992, Querie 9.

35 Thomas, *Decline of Magic*, p. 209.

36 Culpepper, N., *The English Physician or Herball*. Omega, Ware, Hertfordshire, 1985, p. 123.

37 Rawcliffe, *Medicine and Society*, p. 48.

38 'Valentine Greatrakes', *Dictionary of National Biography, Volume viii*. Smith, Elder & Co, London, 1908.

39 Augustine, *De Vera Religione*, quoted in Kelsey, *Healing and Christianity*, p. 185.

40 Possidius, *Life of St Augustine*, quoted in Kelsey, *Healing and Christianity*, pp. 187f.

41 Kelsey, *Healing and Christianity*, p. 213.

42 Aquinas, T., translated by the Fathers of the English Dominican Province, *Summa Contra Gentiles*. Burns, Oates and Washbourne, London, 1924, Vol. 4, Ch. LXXII.

43 Aquinas, T., translated by the Fathers of the English Dominican Province, *Summa Theologica*. Burns, Oates and Washbourne, London, 1920, Vol. II, Qu. CLXXVIII, Art. 1.

44 Gilson, E., *The Philosophy of St Thomas Aquinas*. Dorset, New York, undated reprint of the 1929 translation by E. Bullough, p. 355.

45 Gilson, *St Thomas Aquinas*, p. 43.

46 Aquinas, T., *Summa Theologica*, cited in Kelsey, *Healing and Christianity*, p. 216.

47 'The Dogmatic Decrees of the Council of Trent', *Dogmatic Canons and Decrees*. Devin-Adair, New York, 1912, p. 112.

48 Aquinas, *Summa Theologica* vol. II, Qu. LXVIII, Art. 4.

49 Seckendoff, V, L. von, *Ausfuhrliche Historie des Lutherthums*, cited in Dearmer, P., *Body and Soul: an enquiry into the effect of religion upon health, with a description of Christian works of healing from the New Testament to the present day*. Pitman, London, 1909, p. 355.

50 Cranmer, T., 'The Visitation of the Sick', *The Second Prayer Book of*

*Edward VI (1552)*, in *The First and Second Prayer Books of Edward VI*. J. M. Dent & Sons, London, 1952, pp. 418f.

51 Kelsey, *Healing and Christianity*, p. 233.
52 See for example Masters, P., *The Healing Epidemic*. Wakeman Trust, London, 1988.
53 Wesley, J., *Sermons on Several Occasions: forty-four sermons*. Epworth, London, 1944, p. 581.
54 Gordon, *Alarming History*, p. 93.
55 Gordon, *Alarming History*, p. 171.
56 Wesley, J., *Primitive Physick*. William Pine, Bristol, 1770, p. 97.
57 Cited in White, T. H., *The Age of Scandal*. Penguin, Harmondsworth, 1962, p. 32.
58 Kelsey, *Healing and Christianity*, p. 233.
59 Wesley, *Primitive Physick*, p. 97.
60 Wesley, *Primitive Physick*, pp. 150–3.
61 Wesley, *Primitive Physick*, pp. xxivf.
62 Wesley, J., *Journal*, cited in Dearmer, *Body and Soul*, p. 362.
63 Wesley, in Dearmer, *Body and Soul*, p. 362.
64 Abbott, E. S., Carpenter, H. J., Demant, V. A., Dix, G., Eliot, T. S., Farrer, A. M., Green, F. W., Hebert, A. G., Mortimer, R. C., Ramsey, A. M., Reeves, A., Smyth, C. H., The Bishop of Southampton, Thornton, L. S., *Catholicity: a study in the conflict of Christian traditions in the West; being a report presented to His Grace the Archbishop of Canterbury*. Dacre, Westminster, 1947, pp. 29f.
65 Freeman, A., *God in Us: a case for Christian humanism*. SCM, London, 1993, p. 19.
66 Freeman, *God in Us*, pp. 20f.

## FURTHER READING

Barr, N., *The Economics of the Welfare State*. Weidenfeld & Nicholson, London, 1987.
Lloyd, G. E. R. (ed), *Hippocratic Writings*. Penguin, Harmondsworth, 1978.
Illich, I., *Limits to Medicine – medical nemesis: the expropriation of health*. Penguin, Harmondsworth, 1977.
Payer, L., *Medicine and Culture: notions of health and sickness in Britain, the US, France and West Germany*. Gollancz, London, 1989.

# Intermezzo 1

## *Christine's story*

Another true story. Chris is a highly intelligent, articulate, professional woman. She is married with three children and is a talented musician. Coincidentally she also has *retinitis pigmentosa*, which progressively damages the retina. There is no cure. There are two forms: the centre fails and then, like ripples in a pond moving outward, more eyesight fails; alternatively, peripheral vision goes first. Christine has three per cent vision; it is like looking at the world through a pair of long, thin tubes. This is tunnel vision.

> I must have had tunnel vison from childhood but you're not aware that other people can see things, [...] in their field of vision. So it wasn't until I was married and went to an optician and he said, 'Oh, there's something very strange about you ...' And he got his little light, and he looked in the back of my eye, and he said, 'Oh,' he says, 'Oh yes, you've got about ten years' useful vision left.' And I went away and had six weeks off work with depression.

This was the first indication of anything wrong. At primary school she had an eye test. But her mother kept the results hidden which meant Chris went through school 'normal'. She wasn't much good at tennis but that was no problem – she was more interested in music anyway.

At university she started experiencing difficulties. She began having trouble travelling to and from college after dark. She could have completed her studies with the appropriate help but it wasn't until after university and marriage that she discovered the truth. After six weeks of depression and 'crying it out', Chris decided to dig her heels in and fight. She said to herself: 'I can

106

actually become very dependent on Chris [her husband] and make him do everything for me. And he can become very over-protective, just as my mother was. Or I can say to myself I want to really take a full part of life. And all that that means whether or not I can see. So I did [...] I do.' There are very few things that Chris doesn't do but she has one regret – she would love to drive a car.

In 1982, Chris became pregnant with her first son. Her sister-in-law, fearing that the gene might be passed on, took Chris to a church in Hereford. In a side chapel, the priest asked to pray for her. She knew that there was a relic there but thought no more about it. And the priest began to pray.

He began 'In the name of the Father, and of the Son and of the Holy Spirit' [...] I didn't go thinking I'm going to be healed, or this is going to be wonderful [...] because I didn't really believe in that sort of thing but my sister-in-law was so keen on my going. He got to a certain point in the prayers [...] much of which I don't remember because it was all so fast. And he got this thing [...] whatever it was. A hand [...] a leathery looking thing [...] and he slapped it on my eyes.

The hand was cold, not slimy but cold. Chris recoiled, shrieking, feeling repulsion, fear, hurt and anger; feeling violated, sick. The priest finished saying 'whatever it was and said all right you can go. And I was gone.'

The hand and arm are part of the Roman Catholic martyr, St John Kemble (alias Holland). He was born around 1600 in Herefordshire. In 1625 he was ordained priest at Douai. He returned secretly to a mission to Herefordshire and Monmouthshire. Unfounded rumours of a plot to replace Charles II with his Catholic brother James excused a general witch-hunt for Catholic recusants. Eighty-year-old Kemble was one victim. He was hanged, drawn and quartered in Hereford and canonized in 1970. After quartering, his arm was rescued by a woman at his execution. It was kept over the Lady Chapel altar in St Francis Xavier church, Hereford. Unfortunately, after three hundred years it has a fungal growth, and is now withdrawn from public display.

Christine had no warning; no permission was asked and no-one had told her what might happen. Suddenly, this mummified hand was on her face. Her revulsion can barely be imagined.

One of the things that you're told when you have an incurable disease is how very easily you can get sucked into that kind of thing. There's a clinic in Russia, for instance, that use chicken embryos and those kind of things [...] trying to plant them in your eye, and things like that. And you're told straight away there's no cure. There's no point in trying to find one. We will notify you when we find one. And there is no point in trying to find any kind of treatment, any kind of cure. And anyone who says that they can do that or offers you that is either, you know, a charlatan, a magician, just after your money [...] that kind of thing.

She had a nominal faith in some creative being but no thoughts about Christian healing. She went along with her sister-in-law's suggestion, completely unprepared. The natural repulsion was magnified by fear of the superstition where 'somebody's dead hand' had magical properties. She felt that the priest was indifferent and was only going through some cabalistic ritual. He had no idea of who she was or why she was there. She had already begun to use her blindness creatively, finding something positive in her vulnerability. Instead of a high-powered job and a sports car, she had to stop and think. 'It made me begin to question things ... to begin to value people and life.'

Her youngest son was born in 1988. Chris had high blood pressure and went to the doctor complaining of severe headaches and 'seeing things'. She was told to go to bed and not move. Ending what she describes as an awful pregnancy, she went into labour five days early.

'[...] they wired me up straight away. They didn't give me any painkillers. Nothing. Even gas and air I wasn't allowed. Then they turned me on my side and told me to stay there. It was Monday morning and I could hear the dustmen moving the bins and they said that they would get me ready for a caesarean. I was in such a state of agony [...] I just prayed to die. You know, God please take me now. I can't take any more. [...] And the next thing I knew I was absolutely bathed in warmth [...] this wonderful feeling [...] and the pain was taken away – I still felt uncomfortable but the excruciating pain was gone. And then there was a loud voice within me saying 'Chris, it's OK. You and the baby will be fine.' And I just felt really loved. [. . .] I felt absolutely loved and accepted as a person in my own right. And forgiven as well, you know everything you could ever feel was kind of all there in one go. And I can't say that I've ever felt the same since.

A doctor arrived and announced the obvious, the baby was stuck. He turned the baby and 'Tim was born about two minutes later, the cord was round his neck and chest and between his legs pulled tight.' And he should have been severely brain-damaged – but he wasn't. They were allowed to leave hospital six hours later. 'Whatever you call it, it was an experience. God saved me. I nearly did die because, you know, my blood pressure rocketed.'

Christine had two totally conflicting experiences. One of fear, horror, and violation and the other of warmth, love and acceptance. One touch was cold and dead, the other vibrant and alive. The theological categories, natural and supernatural, do not seem to fit. For both were natural experiences and gained a natural response. But neither were intellectual experiences. It argues for a theology of the right side of the brain.

# 4

# *The ghost in the machine*

'Organised religion has relied upon there being a gulf between heaven and earth to give it a purpose: the church's main reason for existing is to bridge this gap.'[1] For centuries the Church taught there was a vast gap between heaven and earth. There is a rift between God and creation, a deep chasm between nature and super-nature. The Church traditionally is the only line of communication between the two. God's edicts pass in one direction through the hierarchy, the people's prayers go in the other. The Church controls both the content and the means of communication. The eccentric saint, outside the institution, becomes institutionalized after death.

> Inspiration [...] becomes an institutionalized property of the religious establishment which, as the divinely appointed church, incarnates god: the inspired truth is then mediated to the masses through rituals performed by its duly accredited officers. In these circumstances individual possession experiences are discouraged and where necessary discredited. Possession in fact becomes an aberration, even a satanic heresy. This certainly is the pattern which is clearly and deeply inscribed in the long history of Christianity.[2]

Towards the end of the second century a strict apocalyptic sect emerged in Asia Minor. The leader, Montanus, came from Phrygia in modern Turkey. In either 156 or 172 he began to prophesy the end of the world. He claimed the New Jerusalem would descend from heaven to Phrygia and the Lord would reign for a thousand years on earth. He and two prophetesses, Priscilla and Maximilla, said they were seized by the Holy Spirit who spoke directly through their mouths. They expected their ecstatic utterances to be received as

God's very words. Like some Old Testament prophets their prophecies were in the first person singular. 'I am the Lord God Almighty, dwelling in man. It is neither angel nor ambassador, but I, God the Father, who am come,' prophesied Montanus. Priscilla had a vision in which 'Christ came to me in the likeness of a woman, clad in a bright robe, and he planted wisdom in me and revealed that [Pepuza, a town in Phrygia] is holy, and that here Jerusalem comes down from heaven.'

Hippolytus attacked them for heresy, particularly their possession by the Holy Spirit. He wrote that people 'have been captivated and deceived by wretched women, called a certain Priscilla and Maximilla, whom they supposed prophetesses'.[3] The three were condemned for adding novelties to the 'law and prophets and Gospels'. The Montanists magnified 'these wretched women above the Apostles and every gift of Grace, so that some of them presume to assert that there is something in them superior to Christ'.[4] A tiny percentage did, perhaps, but 'Catholic writers generally agree that the Montanists were orthodox except in their addiction to their prophets.'[5]

Tertullian, in later life a Montanist, taught of a developing relationship between God and humanity. 'Righteousness', he wrote, 'was at first rudimentary, when nature feared God; then by means of the Law and the Prophets it progressed to its infancy; thereafter through the Gospel it reached the fervour of adolescence; and now through the Paraclete it is being established in maturity.'[6] To the conservative Hippolytus this would depart from tradition. The reaction to the development of tradition was to project the supremacy of the past. The Gospels and the apostles' writings were held up as superior to present revelation. This began a process that closed the canon of Scripture and began the idea, fully developed in the Reformation era, that revelation ended with the apostles.

The Montanist crisis caused women to be treated with further suspicion, particularly in the West (the Eastern church has a continuing tradition of women as 'Spirit-bearers'). In much of the ancient world women led largely separate lives from men. In Christian circles this was modified and women were allowed freedom to mix and worship with men. Elizabeth Schüssler Fiorenza suggests that the Roman church was 'an association of equals. [...] Unlike their Athenian counterparts, Roman matrons were not sequestered in

111

the house. Women worked in trades, dined with their husbands, attended shows, games, parties, and even political gatherings, and were notorious for receiving preachers of strange cults into their homes.'[7] However, in Jewish circles this was not the case. To Jewish women who had been excluded from the synagogue the freedom permitted in the Christian meeting was freedom indeed, even though this relaxation did not extend to full equality.

The early church grew out of the synagogue with the community boundaries enlarged to include women, slaves, Gentiles and so on. Conflict between Jewish and Gentile Christians on boundaries is clearly part of the background to Mark's material. The woman with the haemorrhage pushing her way through the constraints of patriarchy to touch Christ shows women the struggle for equality. And, according to Mark, Jesus affirms her action. More freedom was available to women in certain of the mystery cults. Priestesses and prophetesses had a voice largely denied to women in other spheres. In certain fertility rites, ritual sex was practised; the cult of Cybele was 'orgiastic'.[8] The temple of Aphrodite Pandemos in Corinth (destroyed 146 BCE), and therefore Corinth generally, was a byword for immorality. The similarity between the freedom which women exercised in the cults and that in the emerging Christian church was potentially a problem. Pagan priestesses and prophetesses had a reputation for sexual licence; the Christian church too had prophetesses and so to avoid confusion Christian women needed to be squeaky clean. So St Paul wrote to the church in Corinth that 'it is disgraceful for a woman to speak in church'. But worse was to come.

I also want the women to be modest and sensible about their clothes and to dress properly; not with fancy hair styles or with gold ornaments or pearls or expensive dresses, but with good deeds, as is proper for women who claim to be religious. Women should learn in silence and all humility. I do not allow them to teach or to have authority over men; they must keep quiet. For Adam was created first, and then Eve. And it was not Adam who was deceived; it was the woman who was deceived and broke God's law. But a woman will be saved through having children, if she perseveres in faith and love and holiness, with modesty.

(1 Timothy 2.9–15)

If Paul was a misogynist then the writer to Timothy was worse. Men, following Adam, were not guilty of anything. It was the weak woman who was tempted and broke God's law. Men were obviously superior both in will-power and the ability to avoid temptation. Creation puts men first; women are God's after-thought. By including Timothy into the canon of Scripture the Catholic church justified stamping on the Montanists. St Paul wrote Timothy (he probably didn't but the author included enough Pauline references to make it appear Pauline!) – this then enabled the writer to assume Paul's apostolic authority, even though he was writing after Paul's lifetime. If the letter has apostolic authority, Priscilla and Maximilla are automatically wrong. End of argument. QED. Subject closed.

Extending the argument further, all women are automatically wrong. Pseudo-Paul states that 'a woman will be saved through having children': by the second century a woman has no salvation through Christ. She becomes a client of her children. The equality of those early heady days – 'in Christ there is neither male nor female' – is over. Church order takes precedence over the Holy Spirit.

Tertullian, a Montanist, must have been more tolerant of women than pseudo-Paul, though not exempt from the current patriarchal world-view: 'In the second century AD, a young man of the privileged classes of the Roman Empire grew up looking at the world from a position of unchallenged dominance. [. . .] Biologically, the doctors said, males were those foetuses who had realized their full potential [. . .] Women, by contrast, were failed males.'[9] Tertullian wrote that Adam 'down sunk in pit iniquitous did fall, By dragon-subdued virgin's suasion led'. Eve, presumed a virgin until expelled from paradise, was overpowered by the serpent. She, in turn, persuaded Adam to fall. And it was Adam that fell from grace because of her. If women, in Eve, had a major role in the fall, then equally women have a major role in the new creation. He equates Mary, Jesus' mother, with the new Eve, as Paul calls Jesus the new Adam: 'A virgin's debts a virgin, flesh's flesh, should pay.'[10]

The language describing the Spirit, frequently in a feminine form, became progressively defeminized. The Hebrew word *Ruach* – spirit, wind or breath – is a feminine noun, *Pneuma*, the Greek equivalent, is neuter. The word *Paracletos* used in John 15.26 is masculine and this trend continued with the transition to the Latin, *Spiritus* too being masculine. The Spirit underwent no gender change but the language, particularly in the West, underwent change. In the Syriac church the feminine pronoun and feminine attributes continued to be used of the Spirit.

I fashioned their members,
And my own breasts I prepared for them,
That they might drink my holy milk and live by it.[11]

The feminine was progressively seen as a lack of *maleness*. Born female meant born damaged: male was normal while female was abnormal. By the Middle Ages the feminine is an aberration, a mistake. Thomas Aquinas wrote that 'the active male seed intends to reproduce a perfect likeness of itself, and when females are conceived this is due to weak seed, or unsuitable material, or external influences like the dampness of the south wind'.[12] With the Latinization of the Holy Spirit and the loss of the feminine language of the Godhead, positive values of the feminine in theology largely disappeared. So much so that the rich feminine imagery used of God by such writers as Dame Julian of Norwich – 'Your tender mother Jesus [who] feeds us with his blessed breast' or 'You [who] on the bed of the cross [...] gave birth in a single day to the world'[13] – was abandoned.

For healing to become again the expectation of every Christian we need to rediscover a Spirit-theology, both feminine and masculine. For most of the Christian era the intellect and reason have been masculine while emotions have been feminine. 'For men must work, and women must weep,' wrote Charles Kingsley.[14] Men have to 'keep a stiff upper lip', wrote Phoebe Cary.[15] Women can show emotions while men show self-control. Men are intellectual, reasonable and powerful. Women are ignorant, emotional and weak. While one of the legs on which the Anglican Church rests, along with Scripture and Tradition, is Reason, any emotional understanding of God is relegated to the area of personal spirituality. The idea that reason and emotion are gender-related is a control mechanism: by using gender terms it conveys the message that only women are fit to waste time praying. Dividing reason from emotions led to a division between theology and spirituality, impoverishing both.

Historically, spirituality, a personal and therefore marginal concern, has been seen as appropriate for both sexes. Theology is about larger things and is almost exclusively male. 'The effect on women of being continually told that they are silly, frail and stupid, especially when coupled with an inadequate education that made it difficult to hold their own in reasoned argument, was that, inevitably, they took the denigration for truth and rapidly internalized it.'[16] The intellectualizing of God, theology, has largely marginalized women – not because of intellectual inferiority but because education was denied them.

Spirituality requires empathy, a characteristic of mind not gender. Empathy is a feature (in most people) of the right-hand side of the brain. The brain is divided into two cerebral hemispheres, two halves, joined by a mass of nervous tissue called the corpus callosum. The left hemisphere seems to be involved in speech and understanding language. Academic theology is an activity of the left cerebral hemisphere. If we are to love God with all our heart and all our mind, then the whole brain must be engaged. There can be no hierarchy of intellect over emotion. And both depend on humanness, not gender.

However, women are portrayed as being weak, emotional creatutes. In the Church historically women are a combination of Eve the temptress, Mary the virgin and Mary Magdalene the tart! The female is incomplete. She is weak Eve, too weak to resist temptation. She is virginal Mary, unfulfilled sexually. She is sexy Mary Magdalene, the prostitute and nymphomaniac (unsubstantiated male fantasy!) unable to control herself. However contradictory as a combination, the implication is clear. Women are defined negatively. Compared to the norm women are an aberration. Freud followed this premise, that women are incomplete men. He based his psycho-analytic philosophy on the fact that women *lack* a penis rather than that men lack a womb! Maleness reflects perfection, the Godhead. The female reflects the male – 'He for God only, she for God in him.'[17]

This has meant that the God of theology is both male and intellectual. However, does the Holy Spirit, in the Bible and in historical experience, fit this theology? This question is neither trivial nor academic. If the theology of the Holy Spirit misrepresents the Spirit of God, the mission of the Spirit that the Church shares will have become seriously impaired.

The Spirit is involved in creation. In the first creation narrative, the Spirit of God (or God's power or God's wind or an awesome wind) moves over the water (Genesis 1.2). Water is an image of the

115

primeval chaos from which order was going to be created. The Spirit moving – brooding is a better translation – is a maternal image. The Hebrew word *m*ᵉ*rachepteth* is found only here in Genesis, Jeremiah 23.9 (in a different form) and in Deuteronomy 32.11. In Deuteronomy the word refers to an eagle watching over her young, teaching them to fly, enabling them to take on adulthood – a new life of their own. The maternal image of creation, the idea that the Spirit of God is nurturing, protecting, bringing the potential into actuality, is a powerful one, not in crudely material terms but as empowering poetry. It celebrates the maternal in humanity; male and female alike share God's likeness. And the image of a Spirit who is both creative force and caring mother suggests God's continued involvement in creation. Creation is not manufactured and then left alone. Creation relates to God in a living way. And as a mother never ceases to be a mother, however the role changes, God's Spirit continues to nurture creation.

*Ruach*, the onomatopoeic, explosive snort of breath from the nostrils, is not breathed into Adam in Genesis 2.7. In this alternative creation story Adam becomes a living soul (*nephesh*) by God's breath (*n*ᵉ*shamah*). 'Whereas the animals are produced and brought to life simply, so to speak, by the universal divine breath blowing through the whole of Nature, and therefore partake of life only as a class of beings, Man receives his life by a special act of God, and is thus treated as a spiritual *I*, and accorded a closer association with God than the animals.'[18] However, according to the Psalmist, all living things share a common 'soul' with humanity, equally created and given life by God's *Ruach*:

> 'When you turn away, they are afraid;
> when you take away their breath (*Ruach*), they die
> and go back to the dust from which they came.
> But when you give them breath/or send out your spirit
> (*Ruach*) they are created [. . .]'
>
> (Psalm 104.29–30)

Humanity's being created from the soil implies more in Hebrew than in English. The word ʿ*adamah*, ground, is the feminine of ʿ*adam*, the word for man: humanity is a child of Mother Earth, of the ecostructure. Humanity's special relationship with God is because of God's act of breathing. It is not an innate quality of being human. God's Spirit creates the relationship.

## The ghost in the machine

The Spirit is involved in the redemption of the people. The prophet Ezekiel is shown by the Spirit a valley filled with old, dry bones.

> God said, 'Prophesy to the bones. Tell these dry bones to listen to the word of the Lord. Tell them that I, the Sovereign Lord, am saying to them: I am going to put breath into you and bring you back to life. I will give you sinews and muscles, and cover you with skin. I will put breath into you and bring you back to life. Then you will know that I am the Lord.'

(Ezekiel 37.4ff.)

While Ezekiel was prophesying he heard the bones begin to rattle and join together. Soon the bodies had internal organs and on the outside, skin. Everything was back in place. Like Frankenstein's creature, they were reconstructed but still dead. So God commanded Ezekiel to prophesy to the wind.

> 'Tell the wind that the Sovereign Lord commands it to come from every direction, to breathe into these dead bodies, and to bring them back to life.'

(Ezekiel 37.9)

As he obeyed, the wind or breath or Spirit blew into their lungs and, suddenly, a great army stood there.

> God said to me, 'Mortal man, the people of Israel are like these bones. They say that they are dried up, without any hope and with no future. So prophesy to my people Israel and tell them that I, the Sovereign Lord, am going to open their graves. [. . .] When I open the graves where my people are buried and bring them out, they will know that I am the Lord. I will put my breath/spirit in them, bring them back to life, and let them live in their own land. Then they will know that I am the Lord. I have promised that I would do this – and I will. I, the Lord, have spoken.'

(Ezekiel 37.11–14)

Life is more than existence – life is meaning. The people have no hope, they are exiles. The chosen people are severed from the promised land. Their lives are profoundly affected. The daily worship of God in the land has ceased. They are enslaved. 'How can they sing the Lord's song in a foreign land?' The creative Spirit brings hope to the hopeless and despairing. God will bring back the exiles and restore Israel's identity and worship. The dead nation will be revived! God's *Ruach* creates and restores, bringing the people back to life – not pathetic horror-film creatures – not living dead but living living!

The Spirit is involved in conferring power. In the book of Judges, the Spirit of the Lord gives Israelite heroes extraordinary physical power. Samson has the strength to tear a lion apart with his bare hands (Judges 14.6), kill thirty people (Judges 14.19), break ropes that tied him up, and kill a thousand men with the jaw-bone of a donkey (Judges 15.14f.). The Spirit put Gideon on like clothing (Judges 6.34); his inner force was the Spirit. In Joshua and Judges humans also have *Ruach*. It can be enhanced by additions of God's Spirit. *Ruach* is health and strength. As a person recovers from illness their *Ruach* increases but as they die their *Ruach* drains away. The necessary normal human spirit for life is a gift of God.

The normal human spirit can, on occasion, however, be enhanced, supercharged, filled and then added to. The Spirit gives the gifts necessary for leadership, as in the case of Othniel, for instance: 'The spirit of the Lord came upon him, and he became Israel's leader. Othniel went to war, and the Lord gave him victory over the king of Mesopotamia' (Judges 3.10). David was anointed as king while Saul was still ruling. 'Samuel took the olive oil and anointed David in front of his brothers. Immediately the spirit of the Lord took control of David and was with him from that day on. Then Samuel returned to Ramah. The Lord's spirit left Saul, and an evil spirit sent by the Lord tormented him' (1 Samuel 16.13–14f).

The Hebrew *Ruach* is the empowering Spirit that David was given, and which departs from Saul, and the evil spirit. The Spirit given to David as king *par excellence* and as God's divinely anointed has associations with the coming Messiah.

A new king will arise from among David's descendants. The spirit of the Lord will give him wisdom, and the knowledge and skill to rule his people. He will know the Lord's will and honour him, and find pleasure in obeying him. He will not judge by appearance or hearsay; he will judge the poor fairly and defend the rights of the helpless. At his command the people will be punished, and evil persons will die. He will rule his people with justice and integrity.

(Isaiah 11.2–5)

The divinely anointed king is given tools for the job. The wisdom and knowledge are gifts of God. The king is inspired and empowered by God's Spirit.

The Spirit informs the ethical and religious life of God's people. The Spirit brings ecstatic religious states – Saul, infected by the Spirit, 'danced and shouted all the way to Naioth. He took off his clothes and danced and shouted in Samuel's presence' (1 Samuel 19.23f). The Spirit is also supremely ethical: 'Here is my servant [...] I have filled him with my Spirit, and he will bring justice to every nation' (Isaiah 42.1). But the effects are personal as well as national:

> Create a pure heart in me, O God,
> and put a new and loyal spirit in me.
> Do not banish me from your presence;
> do not take your holy spirit away from me.

(Psalm 51.10–11)

The whole life of the people, individually and collectively, is changed by the impact of God's Spirit; intuitively they will know what is right.

> I shall [...] put a new spirit in them; I shall remove the heart of stone from their bodies and give them a heart of flesh, so that they will conform to my statutes and keep my laws.

(Ezekiel 11.19 REB).

God's Spirit brings permanent righteousness and intimate involvement in the ecology, in the very soil, of the land:

> But once more God will send us his spirit. The waste land will become fertile, and fields will produce rich crops. Everywhere in the land righteousness and justice will be done. Because everyone will do what is right, there will be peace and security for ever. God's people will be free from worries, and their homes peaceful and safe.

(Isaiah 32.15–18)

Justice, righteousness, peace, security, plenty, ecological healing and the right activity of the people are all equally of God's Holy Spirit.

The Spirit inspires prophets. Ezekiel has a vision of God's throne and is called to be a prophet. He hears a voice, records that 'God's

119

spirit entered me and raised me to my feet', and is commissioned to prophesy to Israel. Saul was overtaken by the Spirit and prophesied. Messengers sent to arrest David were also possessed. The prophetic manifestations of the Spirit appear mainly temporary. Nevertheless, this prophetic character underlies all the Spirit's interactions with humanity. The proclamation of God's will is the role of prophet and of king and of ordinary Israelite who follows the ethical demands of God's will. The prophets proclaimed God's righteousness because the people and their rulers were failing in their duties.

> The spirit of the Lord speaks through me;
> his message is on my lips.
> The God of Israel has spoken;
> the protector of Israel said to me:
> 'The king who rules with justice,
> who rules in obedience to God,
> is like the sun shining on a cloudless dawn,
> the sun that makes the grass sparkle after rain.'

(2 Samuel 23.2–4)

In the Old Testament the Spirit of God has a maternal image. The Spirit clothes himself with a human being, who is not always possessed willingly. The Spirit brings raw violence and destruction, maiming and killing. The same Spirit is life-restoring, renewing and recreating. The Spirit is equated with the activity of God. The Spirit is directly linked to the Covenant; the land where the Spirit dwells is the land of milk and honey. The people of the Old Testament seem to have been less interested in philosophical notions about God than in his activity. The Spirit is both the action and the mouth of God. The Spirit gives speech to the prophets. The Spirit brings judgement and justice. The Spirit gives life with restoration, power and strength, justice, righteousness and holiness.

The categories of the Old Testament are largely taken up and developed in the New. The Spirit continues to be involved in creation (or the new creation), in redemption, in the conferring of power, in ethical and religious life, and in prophecy. The Church is founded on the Holy Spirit. Jesus viewed his mission in terms of inspiration by the God's Spirit. In each of the Synoptic Gospels Jesus' ministry begins with the baptism of John where each insists that the Spirit is given him.

John's Jesus differs from all inspired prophets except perhaps Moses and Elijah. 'You will see the Spirit come down and stay on a man; he is the one who baptizes with the Holy Spirit,' God tells John the Baptist. 'I have seen it,' says John, 'and I tell you that he is the Son of God' (John 1.33–4). John stresses the importance of the Spirit's staying: the word, variously translated 'remain', 'stay', 'abide', 'dwell on', has a dual significance. It has the everyday meaning of permanence but in the Johannine community it seems to have also had overtones of mutual indwelling. The Spirit is given to the prophets for 'a time but [. . .] remains on Jesus'.[19] The crowds say to Jesus, 'Our Law tells us that the Messiah will live for ever.' For John, Jesus is Messiah and Son of God, therefore everything about him must remain for ever. The Spirit is not given to Jesus fleetingly, but remains on him. Jesus is not empowered for his mission as such, he is in permanently renewed life. In John, unlike the other Gospels, there is no evidence of Jesus being baptized. The Baptist describes his role as the one who baptizes with water and says that Jesus, in his turn, will baptize with the Spirit. Nowhere does it as much as imply that Jesus was baptized himself. There was no need: being Son of God and being permanently Spirit-filled are identical. One is not possible without the other.

The Spirit plays a greater part in John's Gospel than in the others. In John, Jesus is made God's *shaliach* by the Spirit's infilling. The community which formed the Gospel of John thought long and hard about what Jesus' life, death and resurrection meant. They saw Jesus in terms of the Isaianic 'servant': 'the spirit of Yahweh shall rest on the shoot from the stump of Jesse who is the Davidic king'. For John Jesus was that king; on him the Spirit rests in full measure.

The qualification – the *Holy* Spirit – occurs only three times in John. It is used once here, in the context of Jesus being the one who baptizes with the Holy Spirit. It is found a second time in John 14.25, looking towards the giving of the *Paraclete*, the Helper or Counsellor. Finally, John uses it, describing the giving of the Holy Spirit, in John 20.22. This has a probable liturgical significance, the conferring of the Holy Spirit relating to baptism. The images of death and resurrection, and the forgiveness of sins, are significant for baptismal liturgy. The Baptist himself has an obvious relationship with baptism.

121

The New Testament provides two distinct accounts of the coming of the Holy Spirit: John's account, and the Day of Pentecost.

> When the day of Pentecost came, all the believers were gathered together in one place. Suddenly there was a noise from the sky which sounded like a strong wind blowing, and it filled the whole house where they were sitting. Then they saw what looked like tongues of fire which spread out and touched each person there. They were all filled with the Holy Spirit and began to talk in other languages, as the Spirit enabled them to speak.
>
> (Acts 2.1–4)

Peter, thus enabled, preaches:

> God has raised this very Jesus from death, and we are all witnesses to this fact. He has been raised to the right-hand side of God, his Father, and has received from him the Holy Spirit, as he had promised. What you now see and hear is his gift that he has poured out on us.
>
> (Acts 2.32f.)

The Spirit's outpouring marks both a new beginning and a continuing sameness. In one sense the Church has already been founded; it remains the community that gathered round Jesus. So the mission of the Church is as it was. But Pentecost marks' the end of Jesus' ministry and a new beginning to the Spirit's involvement.

The spectacular events reported – rushing wind, a vision of fire, and the gift of speech – have obvious Old Testament parallels (for example Genesis 2.7; Ezekiel 1.13; Jeremiah 1.7). Luke's account uses traditional images for God's Spirit which add deeper meaning to present experience. Luke's account reflects the people's historic, present and continuing relationship with God. Pentecost marked the anniversary of God's gift of the Law at Sinai, according to the Book of Jubilees. Pentecost began a new epoch of the world. The Day of Pentecost was an appropriate day for the new age of the Spirit to begin.

> 'This is what I will do in the last days,' God says: 'I will pour out my Spirit on everyone. Your sons and daughters will proclaim my message; your young men will see visions, and your old men will have dreams. Yes, even on my servants,

both men and women, I will pour out my Spirit in those days, and they will proclaim my message.'

(Acts 2.17f.)

In Luke's church community these are the last days. The Day of the Lord, the *eschaton*, is here. 'Sometimes people sigh for, or pray for "another Pentecost". They might as well pray for "another crucifixion". Each represents a divine action which brooks no repetition. At Pentecost God gave the Spirit to the Church in full measure. The gift has never been withdrawn.'[20]

John's description of the giving of the Holy Spirit is less spectacular than Luke's. The sense of new mission is absent; it is comparatively prosaic:

Jesus breathed on them and said, 'Receive the Holy Spirit. If you forgive people's sins, they are forgiven; if you do not forgive them, they are not forgiven.'

(John 20.22–3)

Behind locked doors Jesus' disciples gather; they are in terror and shock. The Rabbi that they have followed is dead. Defeat has been snatched out of the jaws of triumph. The triumphal entry of Palm Sunday becomes the agony of Good Friday. Although John is looking back from beyond Easter, the disciples are still without this special knowledge. And suddenly, by the ordinary table and bench, next to the ordinary window and the positively dull door, Jesus comes among them. Nothing is ordinary any more. '*Mooreeffoc* is a fantastic word, but it could be seen written up in every town in this land. It is Coffee-room, viewed from the inside through a glass door, as it was seen by Dickens on a dark London day; and it was used by Chesterton to denote the queerness of things that have become trite, when they are suddenly seen from a new angle.'[21] With Jesus' appearance ordinary becomes sacramental. Bread and wine become *real bread* and *real wine*. The world is turned on its head. For John's church the Spirit is not explosive and sudden. John sees the Spirit bringing insight and discernment. He is the counsellor, the helper. The Holy Spirit is not passive but works in the Church.

In Luke the Spirit continues the earthly work of the earthly Jesus. Peter continues to teach the Good News – empowered by the Spirit just as Jesus was – and many are healed. The Spirit empowers the Church:

(1)  to preach, to speak God's word;
(2)  to baptize people so that sin can be forgiven; and,
(3)  to heal the sick.

The Church continues Jesus' work:

(1)  announcing Good News to the poor;
(2)  announcing release to the captives (Peter is set free from prison); and,
(3)  bringing health.

The new age is the old age. Luke emphasizes continuity.

Broadly, Luke's mission is earthly with heavenly implications. John's mission, on the other hand, is heavenly with earthly implications. Luke is missiological – to do with mission – and points outwards into the world. John is ecclesiological – to do with church – and points inwards to the community of faith. For Luke, forgiveness allows one to receive God's gift, the Holy Spirit. For John, forgiveness allows the believer to participate in the heavenly banquet here and now, feeding on Jesus the bread of life and the true vine. Luke and John together show the paradox of the Holy Spirit: in the explosion and in the quiet; in the fire and the water of baptism; both in the Church and outside. This is also the paradox of the Spirit in history. The Spirit identifies with the Church and with the eccentric saint. To over-emphasize either is an error. If Church and order are over-emphasized there is no power. If power is over-emphasized there is no Church order.

The Montanists were suppressed and the Spirit quieted. 'Where the church is, there too is the Spirit of God.'[22] The Orthodox Church developed a broader understanding of church than the West. Rome identified church with church hierarchy; the East identified church with the state. José Comblin has written that 'within the confines of the empire, everything is the church, and the Spirit is in everything. The world has been transformed by the Spirit. In this way, the world is never out of reach of the action of the Spirit.'[23] But in the West, church and state struggled for secular power, with the hierarchy claiming the Spirit's support. The Spirit, thus reduced, became seen only in the sacraments and the authority of the Pope. 'The theologian is really studying history considered in relation to God. Revelation is the word of God in history, in Scripture, in the Church where the Holy Spirit dwells.'[24]

Joachim of Fiore, described by Dante as 'richly endowed of the prophetic Spirit', was a twelfth-century mystic who viewed history and the Church quite differently.

He proclaimed the coming of a third age in the salvation of the world. The first had been the age of the Father in the Old Testament; the second the age of the Son with the coming of Jesus, and this was drawing to a close, to give way to the dawning of the age of the Holy Spirit [...] This would be a complete renewal of society, a complete change in history.[25]

The Fraticelli and the 'Spiritual' Franciscans saw themselves as Joachim's new order of monks who would rule the Church, for in this third age there would be no Pope. 'The final era was to be founded in 1260 [...] and the religion of S. Francis and the Holy Ghost was to supersede the Christian Church.'[26] These political radicals began preaching government based upon equality and freedom. 'One curious feature of the period was the appearance of numerous prophetical teachers [...] Many of their productions were inspired by the ideas of Joachim of Flora and the Spiritual Franciscans, especially their emphasis on Apostolic Poverty. They contained the inevitable mixture of politics and religion which called them forth.'[27]

The Church answered that the doctrine of the poverty of Christ and the apostles, which the 'Spirituals' held, was heretical. The idea that Christ might be poor threatened the status quo – including the Church's power and wealth. Charges of heresy excused persecution of the Spirituals, the Fraticelli and the like. Eventually a stricter order of Franciscans, the Osservanti, was founded; the Church recaptured the Spirit and lost the insight that the Spirit was not containable.

The Spirit, it seems, is found intuitively rather than intellectually: discovered in the Church and in the world; discovered in healing, in forgiveness, in justice, in the very soil. The Spirit is apprehended on the right side of the brain, in the empathic. The Spirit is a gift: the person with profound learning difficulties can be as much 'Spirit-bearer' as the philosopher. Both are fully human, equally the image of God. The Spirit cannot be quantified – even in those whose humanity is difficult to recognize the Spirit may be given in full measure.

In the twentieth century several movements have rediscovered both the Spirit and healing. All are in response to the nineteenth century. The Victorians had a secular philosophy of human progress. By the nineteenth century the division between heaven and earth was complete. 'God's in his heaven, all's right with the world.'[28] As long as God stayed where he was things would be all right! 'Progress, man's distinctive mark alone, Not God's, and not the beasts'.[29] Progress was everything. Marx's historical dialectic, inevitable progress, led unswervingly towards heaven on earth. The march was ever upwards towards perfection.

In nineteenth-century biblical scholarship the German Higher Criticism movement prevailed which, many thought, doubted the truth of Scripture. 'American seminaries exchanged professors with the German universities where liberal theology and higher criticism of the Bible were in vogue. It wasn't long until pulpits were being populated by literal apostles of unbelief.'[30] This created a fundamentalist backlash.

Popular theories of evolution made human beings the pinnacle of creation, spiritually, morally and physically. At the same time, many people felt offended by having the same ancestry as the great apes, especially since they frequently believed – as in the famous Punch cartoon of Darwin with an ape's body – that the Darwinists were saying that they descended *from* the apes. This was a common misconception. In a famous debate at the British Association in 1860, Bishop Samuel Wilberforce foolishly asked T. H. Huxley whether he was descended from an ape on his grandfather's or grandmother's side. As a naturalist himself he should have known better.

In industry and commerce, European and American goods flooded the world. The one-third world was the manufactory of the whole – the two-thirds world was viewed as an undeveloped market waiting for development. Mid-nineteenth-century missionaries went abroad to spread the triple gospels of Christianity, commerce and civilization. And commerce often led the way. Many missionaries were swept along with the tide of colonial empire-building.

The late nineteenth century saw an upsurge of revivalism. Moody and Sankey preached and sang across America and Europe. An eyewitness reported in 1873, 'I found the meeting on fire. The young men were speaking in tongues and prophesying.' Keswick Conventions in Britain and the Holiness movement in America searched for new meaning within religious life. In 1879 the eccentric Mary Baker Eddy began Christian Science services, which emphasized healing. She taught a quasi-Christian dualism where the mind controls the illusion of the body. Her writing obscures her ideas.

> The often-revised *Science and Health* remains an egotistical and at times paranoid and demonic book, alternating between the repetitive and the self-contradictory. Familiar words are used in a Pickwickian sense which a glossary does little to elucidate, and idiosyncratic and *ex cathedra* pronouncements of doctrines contrary to all experience are more frequently found than logical arguments.[31]

Mrs Eddy writes, 'You say a boil is painful – but that is impossible, for matter without mind is not painful. The boil simply manifests [...] a belief in pain, and this belief is called a boil.' If you don't believe in it the boil doesn't exist. And although 'the only effect produced by medicine is dependent on mental action', physic was not forbidden. Mrs Eddy herself used pain-killers but claimed the drugs were only necessary to counteract the 'malicious animal magnetism' of her enemies. Mrs Eddy did not claim to cure illness, she claimed neither illness nor the body had objective existence. She claimed to heal the illusion of the body. The active force had nothing to do with faith or anything supernatural. The therapeutic force was a gnostic-like understanding of 'the Science'. The name Christian Science was itself a reason for its expansion, capturing as it did both ideals, progress and respectability. Unfortunately it was neither Christian nor scientific; it was 'Christianity without tears'. Mrs Eddy 'regarded herself as the supreme healer and as infallible as Christ'.[32]

The Pentecostal movement too began at the end of the nineteenth century. The Guild of Health was founded in 1904 by, among others, Percy Dearmer, the author of a very influential book on Christian healing, *Body and Soul*. James Moore Hickson founded what later became the Divine Healing Mission in 1905. The Guild of St Raphael was founded in 1915. And other movements and organizations have followed in their wake. A. H. Purcell Fox saw three main causes of the revival of interest:

(a) 'The challenge presented by Christian Science and other cults which have attempted to make up for the neglect of the healing ministry by the Church.'
(b) 'The growth of psychological medicine with its revelation of the wonderful relationship between mind and body.'
(c) 'The re-awakening of large sections of the Christian world to the plain implications of the teaching of Our Lord in the Gospel.'[33]

Psychology was still in its infancy as the nineteenth century ended, and while Mary Baker Eddy was still alive the Christian Science movement expanded at an incredible rate. Fox's third element was fostered in an evangelical backlash against liberal theology and higher criticism. The introduction to Charles Grandison Finney's *Revivals of Religion* extols its virtues in 'inspiring simple-hearted evangelists, labouring to persuade the ungodly'.[34] And the psychological factor of a new century must be added into the boiling pot.

The first century theoretically began on January first, year one, and ended on the thirty-first of December, one hundred. Nineteen centuries later, 31 December 1900 was the very eve of the twentieth century. In anticipation of the twentieth century from the birth of Christ the air was filled with a steadily increasing expectancy. Nineteenth-century ideas of progress and optimism were bearing apocalyptic fruit. Just as humankind was the culmination of an evolving nature, so the twentieth century was to be the culmination of nineteen hundred years of progressive Christianity. As from midnight, things were not going to be the same. In the Bethel Bible School in Topeka, Kansas, the clock ticked away the seconds. The forty students and staff praying together began feeling more and more excited. As the emotional temperature rose the fervour of their prayer increased. As midnight came it reached boiling point; inhibitions were discarded. The Principal laid hands on some students and asked for a special blessing. As New Year's Eve became New Year's Day, one student, Agnes Ozman, began speaking in an unknown language. The phenomenon known as *glossolalia*, speaking in tongues, had returned to the Church after a gap of nineteen centuries. The modern Pentecostal movement had begun.

Although *glossolalia* was claimed as new it had probably never disappeared entirely from the Church. In the East it may have been

so commonplace as to excite little comment: 'a Patriarch of Con-
stantinople has been quoted as saying that tongues were a continuing experience among the Orthodox throughout the ages and that
there were provisions in their Church to govern the practice'.[35]
From Agnes Ozman the flame spread to Charles Parham, the
college principal, and twelve others over the next two days. Eventually thirty of the forty students spoke in tongues. Over the next
few years Parham and his followers held missions in which, as can
be seen from press reports, the participants were converted, sanctified, baptized with the Spirit and healed of sickness'. One typical
newspaper article read: 'Last week a woman arose during the
meeting and spoke for ten minutes, no one apparently in the
audience knowing what she said. An Indian, who had come from
the Pawnee Reservation in the territory that day to attend the
services stated that she was speaking in the language of his tribe
and that he could understand every word of the testimony.'[36]
Although there is a regrettable vagueness in the reports, their
mission obviously caught the mood of the time. Hundreds of con-
versions and healings were claimed.

One of Parham's students was the black pastor, W. J. Seymour,
who took the 'new Pentecost' to Los Angeles. The 1906 revival
began in 312 Azusa Street, which many believe to be the birthday
of Pentecostalism. Azusa Street was black-led and truly multi-
ethnic – nor was there discrimination on the grounds of age. The
first person to receive the gift of tongues was an eight-year-old
black boy. He and six others were baptized in the Holy Spirit and
received tongues on the same day, 9 April 1906. The reports of the
revival are couched in 'distinctly legendary form'. 'They shouted
three days and three nights. It was the Easter season. The people
came from everywhere. By the next morning there was no way of
getting near the house. As people came in they would fall under
God's power and the whole city was stirred. They shouted until the
foundations of the house gave way, but no one was hurt.'[37] 'The
noise of the glossolalia', writes Christie-Murray, 'drew curious
crowds. By the next morning there was no getting near the house,
those who approached it falling under the power, the sick being
healed and sinners saved as they entered.'[38]

In 1920 the Pentecostal Holiness Church in Georgia split over the
question of healing. One group led by Watson Sorrow and High
Bowling taught that it was no sin to use medicines to help heal

ailments. The other faction was led by F. M. Britton and G. F.
Taylor. They believed that it was not necessary to assist God in
effecting a cure. Britton refused medical aid for one of his sons, who
died 'without drugs'. His wife too died after 'refusing medicine'.
Britton was threatened with imprisonment for refusing medical
attention for his family but he 'never wavered in his views'.
Vincent Synan suggests that, rather than being the exception,
these cases were the rule for many early Pentecostals. The
Holiness churches tended to emphasize the 'fourfold gospel' of
salvation, sanctification, healing and the Second Coming. The
question of healing was discussed thoroughly by the National
Camp Meeting Association out of which the holiness churches
emerged. It was felt to be a side issue 'detrimental to a singular
promotion of Christian holiness'. Even if of secondary importance,
healing is still an important feature of holiness churches such as the
Church of the Nazarene.

The Anglican Church has as both its greatest strength and its
greatest weakness the ability to contain widely different views and
practices. While it contained Alexander Boddy and Pentecostals
within mainstream Anglicanism it also contained other healing ministries with different biases. The Guild of Health began as an
Anglican body but became ecumenical in 1915. The Guild of St
Raphael, founded that year, is Anglo-Catholic. On 10 October
1905, James Moore Hickson founded the more evangelically
minded 'Society of Emmanuel' (later the Divine Healing Mission).
Hickson was commissioned by the Archbishop of Canterbury to help
revive the Church's ministry of healing. He was told to go out 'like
the patrol of an army and come back and report'. The Archbishop,
Randall Davidson, would then 'lead the main body forward'.

Hickson had discovered his healing gift when he was fourteen. He
laid on hands and 'directed [... it], for the most part, to treating
minor aches and pains'.[39]

'We were sitting together one evening in the drawing room,' he
once related, 'and a little cousin was suffering acutely from
neuralgia; and in a simple way I was asking our Lord to help
her when it suddenly came into my mind, almost as though the
words had been spoken, "Lay your hands on her face." I did
so, with the result that the pain vanished. [...] After this I had
many cures and my mother told me that God was evidently

working through me in healing the sick and that we must pray about it, asking Him to guide me in the right exercise of this ministry.'[40]

He shared a belief with the emerging Pentecostal Church that the ministry of healing was in preparation for Jesus' Second Coming. He also believed that Jesus made this ministry for the rebuilding of relationships within the Church. Christ's healing presence, he felt, would bring about the healing of rifts in the Body of Christ. The Pentecostal movement, however, was divided on this issue. Boddy and others remained committed to their denominations but others felt that they were called out from the 'dead' churches.

The seventeen-year-old Dorothy Kerin experienced healing from a fatal illness. She had been an invalid for five years and was diagnosed as having tubercular peritonitis, phthisis, and meningitis. One evening in February 1912, when she had been deaf and blind and barely conscious for about two weeks, her relations gathered by her bedside. She stopped breathing. For about eight minutes her heart stopped and she didn't breathe. 'As I looked I saw One coming towards me, I thought he was coming for me, and held out my hand towards him, but he smiled and said, "No, Dorothy, you are not coming yet."' She said that she then saw 'a beautiful light' and heard an angel telling her, 'Dorothy, your sufferings are over. Get up and walk.' She sat up in bed and asked for her dressing gown. She then got up and asked for and fetched her supper.[41]

Dorothy's healing was acknowledged by a number of physicians including one specialist, a Dr Ash, with whom she stayed for about six weeks. She claimed that her healing came 'from God alone and that she had been entrusted with a message to the whole world, "a promise of healing to the sick, comfort to the sorrowing and faith to the faithless"'.[42] Miss Kerin founded a 'Home of Healing' in Ealing. During the Second World War she adopted nine bombed-out children and moved to Groombridge, near Tunbridge Wells. In a restored country house, she founded a new 'Home of Healing' called Burrswood, now 'the largest of all Christian healing homes and resource centres'. She is reported as having performed a number of healings, one of which (on the physicist George Searle[43]) reputedly occurred as a result of reading one of her books. Burrswood has a programme of orthodox medical treatment and regular healing services (every weekend) in close harmony. The undenominational church of Christ the Healer is the 'focus and inspiration of the life and work of the place'. Drugs are often used in combination with anointing with oil, medical staff and chaplains working alongside one another. The care of the whole person is emphasized, church and doctors and nurses complementing each other's work.

The international conferences of Anglican bishops, the Lambeth Conferences, are held about every ten years. In 1908 a committee looked at the subject of healing. In 1920, Resolution 63 asked for the appointment of a committee to investigate 'spiritual means of healing'. The next conference, 1930, adopted their report in 'its entirety [...] apparently without a dissentient voice'. The Report stated that 'the power to exercise spiritual healing is taught by Christ to be the natural heritage of Christian people who are living in fellowship with God, and is part of the ministry of Christ through His Body the Church'.[44]

'Every sort of curative treatment assumes, obviously, that disease is an evil to be combated,' says the Report 'Theologically stated this means that health, or an orderly condition of body, mind and spirit, is God's primary will for all his children, and that disease, as a specific violation or falling short of this orderly condition, is not only to be combated, but is to be combated in God's name, and as a way of carrying out His will.' Disease might be seen as coming from a misuse of free will or as a stimulus to scientific research or even as 'a means of spiritual discipline'. But disease is still an evil. 'Treatment [...] immediately directed to the complete restoration of the patient [...] may take the form of Unction (i.e. anointing with oil by a priest), or of Laying on of hands (either by a priest or a lay person), or of both.'[45] 'For the first time that I know of,' wrote Morton Kelsey, 'a modern mainline church acknowledged in an official pronouncement that unction and laying on of hands can have a direct effect on the body.'[46]

Although this report was accepted little happened until 1944 when Archbishop William Temple set up the Churches' Council for Health and Healing, an ecumenical body attempting to draw together the various healing movements and provide them with a common basis. On the Council are members of the British Medical Association, others from specialist training colleges, and representatives from the churches. In William Temple's words it was founded to 'clarify the message and to educate Christian people by various means to provide knowledge of spiritual healing and fuller co-operation and understanding between doctors and clergy and all those engaged in health in the full sense'.[47]

In 1953 the Archbishops of Canterbury and York set up a commission to 'consider the theological, medical, psychological and pastoral aspects of divine healing with a view to providing within two or three years a report designed to guide the church to clearer understanding of the subject'.[48] They failed miserably. The members met only seventeen times, took five years to report, and their findings were 'theologically [...] negative where not self-contradictory'.[49] The commission began by assuming lack of proficiency in the subject and expressed little interest anyway! Their findings expressed none of the confidence of the 1924 Report and saw the Church as alleviating anxiety, with a purely psychological and spiritual function. Almost apologetically they stated that 'many patients need above all else to be assured that in sickness as in health God's action, wholly personal, loving and creative, is working both in their innermost being and through those who are treating them'.[50]

The 1988 Report, *The Truth Shall Make You Free*, returns to the confidence of the 1924 Report. It stresses that 'the whole Communion [...] be involved in the ministry of healing by teaching about it, co-operating with the medical profession, and developing intercessory prayer groups in every parish'.[51] The 1988 Conference echoed Temple's key words: teaching, co-operation and prayer.

Paragraph 86 of the 'Mission and Ministry' section of the Report is important for all Christians:

86. We urge all Bishops to encourage, to oversee and to be themselves involved in the ministry of healing in their dioceses. The following are some ways of being obedient to our Lord's commission:
1. to declare that the ministry of healing should be a regular part of the ministry of every congregation;
2. to encourage intercessory prayer by members of every congregation, remembering our Lord's promise about agreeing together in prayer (Matthew 18.19);

133

3. to foster the use of the laying on of hands with prayer by the clergy and members of the congregation;
4. to bless and provide oil for the anointing of the sick and to encourage priests to make this anointing a regular part of their ministry;
5. to develop counselling ministries, concerned with inner healing and the healing of relationships, to provide for the ministry of absolution and the assurance of forgiveness;
6. to provide and oversee ministries of deliverance from demonic oppression where this is needed, and, where appropriate, with medical consultation;
7. to establish in each Province and/or diocese centres for the ministry of healing, both for ministry to the sick and for the teaching and support of those engaged in this ministry at the local level;
8. to work in partnership with doctors, nurses and all involved in the care of the sick, and to encourage medical research and the study of related ethical issues;
9. to ask for a fair distribution of resources and personnel so that all nations and all sections of the community may receive adequate health care;
10. to embrace the sick and impaired, for example, drug addicts and sufferers from AIDS, as part of the fellowship of the whole Church;
11. to support the Church's medical mission work throughout the world as a vital arm of its ministry and outreach;
12. to work for the establishment of hospices for the terminally ill and to provide appropriate ministry for the dying and their families; this will need to include counselling regarding the continuance or otherwise of life-support systems.[52]

The Roman Catholic Church claims a continual healing ministry from the time of the apostles, with saints healing both in life and death. One such was the Curé d'Ars. In France the Revolution meant the nineteenth-century ideology of progress flowered earlier, and so did the response. Jean-Marie-Baptiste Vianney became the parish priest of a remote village called Ars. From this obscure little village the Curé d'Ars became world famous and drew huge crowds (some 20,000 in 1855). He is credited, through the intercession of Saint Philomena with vast numbers of miracles.

'A nice thing happened to me today,' he related once. 'I was horribly ashamed. If I could have found a rat hole, I should have hidden in it [...] There's no getting away from it, God still works miracles. A woman brought me a child with a great tumour near one eye. She made me touch it, and it cleared away.'

'This time,' someone replied, 'you won't say it was St Philomena!'

'Ah! she probably had something to do with it.'[53]

Vianney knew, supposedly, who was going to be healed. In the chapel of St Philomena, 'his little saint', people with tuberculosis, those who were blind, those who had no speech, and those who were paralysed were supposed to have been healed. Before they went to the chapel Vianney went through the catechism with them and made certain of their faith. He 'showed them the obstacles that their own imperfection put in the way of grace. If he said, "It is impossible," or "You are unworthy of it," there was no cure.' However, Vianney was less interested in the body than the soul. 'This poor body,' he said, 'which must die, is not worth a great deal.' One day he met a child who was 'one open sore from head to foot'.[54] The Curé asked if he wanted to be healed and the child replied no. He explained he had been sinful before becoming ill and would rather continue suffering than be sinful. The saint said, 'Children so indwelt by the Holy Spirit put us to shame.'[55]

The middle of the nineteenth century was a period of social turmoil. In 1846 the potato crop failed and in 1847 the wheat harvest failed, causing widespread famine. Almost every European city with a population over 50,000 saw riots. Ten years later when William Booth began his preaching in the East End of London every fifth shop there was a gin-shop. Child chimney sweeps were protected only after Charles Kingsley's *Water Babies* (1863) caused an outcry. Slavery was finally abolished in the USA in 1866. In the north slavery continued until 1863, three years after the Civil War began. Whole areas of major cities like London were unpoliced and unpoliceable.

The brutality of the age, and devotion to a fictional martyr, explain why Vianney glorified suffering. The body was temporary, a refuge for the soul. The story of Philomena is 'one of the few stories worth telling [...]'. Unfortunately, it is almost complete fiction. Vianney meditated long on her legend. 'It is our duty to become saints,' he said, 'but let no-one know it. St Philomena points the way.' The martyr suffered in body to become a great soul, and the Curé d'Ars felt he was called to the cure of souls not bodies – a separation of soul and body found throughout Church history. Ghéon, Vianney's biographer, wrote dismissively that 'usually M. Vianney thought it useful – much more useful – to leave men in their diseases'.[56]

The year before Vianney died in 1859, a fourteen-year-old girl, Bernadette Soubirous, saw the Virgin eighteen times in six months. The apparition declared herself the Immaculate Conception (this title had been the subject of a Papal Bull in 1854). As she identified herself a spring appeared – the healing water of Lourdes. Since 1860 the number of visitors has increased until 'more than two million people go to Lourdes [...] each year'.[57] In 1882 the Bureau des Contestations Medicales was founded for people to register claims of healing – about 100,000 register annually.

> For a cure to be accepted the sufferer's medical state must have been certified by expert diagnosis before the visit, that the morbid condition concerned must be organic and have been regarded as incurable or at best as amenable only to very lengthy treatment, but that in fact an immediate recovery, which persisted at the time of the examination, took place when the shrine was visited.[58]

There is some evidence to support the claim that a small proportion of cases do fulfil these very stringent criteria. Between 1918 and 1957 'fifty-four specific healings had been accepted as miracles (i.e., impossible by any natural means)'.[59] This may be a small proportion of those claiming improvement either to physical condition or attitude, however, since the criteria are extremely rigorous. 'Certainly acute observers, including many non-Catholics and even non-Christians, have remarked that the place seems impregnated with a quality of well-being and that few leave it without some psychological improvement.'[60]

The Charismatic renewal began within the traditional mainstream denominations as an underground movement. In April

1960 an American Episcopalian minister, Dennis Bennett, told his congregation that he had begun to speak in tongues, leading to a wave of others, ordained and lay, 'coming out'! The extent of this spread of Pentecostal Christianity into the mainline Protestant churches during the 1950s only became apparent, notes Peter Hocken, after the news made the headlines, following Dennis Bennett's public profession of his receiving 'the fullness of the Spirit' and his subsequent resignation from his parish in Van Nuys, California.[61] While the Pentecostal movement largely became a separate denomination, the Charismatic movement was a surprising eruption of tongues and other charismatic gifts across the Protestant denominations. To the horror of Pentecostalists, who believed the Spirit to have led them out of the mainstream churches, tongues even erupted in the Roman Catholic Church.

In October 1985 a social anthropologist working for the Religious Experience Research Project at Nottingham University and the Alister Hardy Research Centre in Oxford affended a conference in Sheffield. The main speaker was one of the leaders of the American-based 'Vineyard' charismatic fellowship, the late John Wimber. Most of the 2,800 participants in the conference, to train people in the ministry of healing, were white, middle-class Anglicans. Wimber and his assistants would have a 'word of knowledge' about someone and a neighbour would be asked to pray for the person who responded to the 'word'. 'There is a woman here whose name begins with an L [...] She is thirty-two years old, has had a throat condition for eight years, and has taken medicine for it but it hasn't helped her.'[62] Dr Lewis, the social anthropologist, later managed to interview the woman believing herself to be the person described. Her name was Linda and while she was actually still some six months away from her thirty-second birthday, she apparently believed the description fitted her condition. Lewis suggests that the chances of Wimber successfully identifying one person out of a possible 2,800 were astronomical, and claims that the crowd needed to be 250 times larger for the description to have fitted one person so accurately.

Lewis points out that 'normally anthropologists study a small community over a long period of time but in this case I had a large crowd to study for only a few days'.[63] This being so, he appears not to have checked for medical corroboration of any existing throat problem. Nor does he seem to have followed the case up to see if the improvement, if any, was sustained. The difficulty of assessing any healing ministry is in these very points: prior existence of a condition, and permanence of healing. Anyone who believes themselves to be the one described is under intense pressure. Linda told Lewis that as Wimber began to speak she felt God talking to her. Her initial and approximate age were given; a throat condition was described. The naming of a condition suggests that God *is* going to heal it; there is increasing pressure for one's condition to match the description given in the 'word of knowledge'. The atmosphere in healing meetings is often highly charged with emotion. In a similar situation, not one in which Wimber was involved, I saw an artificial leg thrown across the room. People excitedly shouted, 'He's dancing for joy!' If so he was hopping on one leg.

At Wimber's conference the delegates were given a copy of *Healing* by Francis MacNutt, a handbook to the practice of Christian healing. He was the first Roman Catholic to attend one of Agnes Sandford's five Day Schools of Pastoral Care on healing. He 'immediately saw that the basic teachings on healing were very much in line with the Roman Catholic tradition. In fact, healing is probably easier for Catholics to understand than for most Protestants, since we have grown up with a tradition of saints blessed with extraordinary gifts, including healing, the one still used as a test for canonization.'[64]

MacNutt distinguishes between two kinds of suffering: one is like the cross which Jesus carried, a suffering imposed from outside, persecution – the cross which Jesus tells his followers to bear; the second is the suffering which Jesus removed, '*sickness*, the suffering that tears [people] apart from within, whether it be physical, emotional, or moral'.[65] He writes that while some saints have particularly prayed to share Jesus' suffering as a privilege, at times 'so much has been made of the redemptive value of suffering, that it has all but obscured the Good News of the gospel'.[66]

The Curé d'Ars prayed for the insider – unless someone was in a state of grace they could not be healed. 'It is impossible!' he would declare. In Wimber's conference the prayers were effectively for insiders. In churches where healing services take place the prayer is almost entirely for church members and their friends and families. Lourdes is, of course, open to all, Catholic and non-Catholic, believer and non-believer, but it is only about healing. The Jesus model has healing as part of the proclamation of the Good News. Healing is a mission tool not a pastoral one. Jesus' ministry was not pastoral, it was one of proclamation by word and action. And his healing ministry was almost entirely directed towards the outsider. It was more than 'a trick to bring in feeble souls'.[67] It was a sign of God's Kingdom arriving.

## NOTES

1 Freeman, A., *God in Us: a case for Christian humanism*. SCM, London, 1993, p. 45.
2 Lewis, I. M., *Ecstatic Religion*. Penguin, Harmondsworth, 1971, p. 132.
3 Hippolytus, *Refutiatio Omnium Heresium*, in Kidd. B. J., *Documents Illustrative of the History of the Church*. SPCK, London, 1920, Vol. 1, p. 169.
4 Kidd, *Documents*, p. 170.
5 Stevenson, J., revised by Frend, W. H. C., *A New Eusebius: documents illustrating the history of the Church to AD 337*. SPCK, London, 1987, p. 114.
6 Tertullian, *De Virginibus Velandis*, in Bettenson, H., *The Early Christian Fathers: a selection from the writings of the fathers from St Clement of Rome to St Athansius*. Oxford University Press, London, 1969, pp. 132f.
7 Schüssler Fiorenza, E., 'Missionaries, Apostles, Co-workers: Romans 16 and the reconstruction of women's early Christian history', in Loades, A. (ed.), *Feminist Theology: a reader*. SPCK, London, 1990, p. 71.
8 Frazer, J. G., *The Golden Bough*. Macmillan, London, 1920–3, p. 348.
9 Brown, P., *Body and Society: men, women and sexual renunciation in early Christianity*. Faber, London, 1987, pp. 9f.
10 Tertullian, 'Harmony of Old and New Laws', *Five Books in Reply to Marcion*, in Roberts, A. and Donaldson, J., (eds), *The ante-Nicene Fathers, translations from the writings of the Fathers down to 325*, Edinburgh, T. & T. Clark, 1868–70.
11 *Odes of Solomon* 42.8, in Charlesworth, J., ed., *Old Testament Pseudepigrapha*, London, Darton, Longman & Todd, 1983.
12 Aquinas, T., *Summa Theologica*, cited in Furlong, M., *A Dangerous Delight: women and power in the Church*. SPCK, London, 1991, p. 21.
13 Weisner, M., 'Luther and Women: the death of two Marys', in Loades (ed.), *Feminist Theology*, p. 132.
14 Kingsley, C., 'The Three Fishers', in *University of Toronto English Library Online*, Original Reference unspecified, dated 1851.
15 Cary, P., 'Keep a Stiff Upper Lip', *The Poems of Alice and Phoebe*

*Carey* (sic) 1850, quoted in *Oxford Dictionary of Quotations* (3rd edn) Oxford, OUP, 1979.

16 Furlong, *A Dangerous Delight*, p. 39.

17 Milton, J., *Paradise Lost*, 1. 299.

18 Eichrodt, W., *The Theology of the Old Testament*. SCM, London, 1961, p. 121.

19 Brown, R., *The Gospel According to John*. Doubleday, New York, 1966, p. 510.

20 Morris, L., *Spirit of the Living God*. IVP, London, 1960, p. 55.

21 Tolkien, J. R. R., 'On Fairy Stories', *Tree and Leaf, Smith of Wootton Major, and The Homecoming of Beorhtnoth Beorhthelm's Son*, Unwin, London, 1975, p. 59.

22 Irenaeus, *Adv. Haereses* III, xxiv, 1.

23 Comblin, J., *The Holy Spirit and Liberation*. Burns & Oates, Tunbridge Wells, 1989, p. 36.

24 Clark, M. T., *An Aquinas Reader*. Hodder & Stoughton, London, 1974, p. 392.

25 Comblin, *The Holy Spirit*, p. 37.

26 Deansly, M., *A History of the Medieval Church 590–1500*. Methuen, London, 1959, pp. 226f.

27 Elliott Binns, L., *The Decline and Fall of the Medieval Papacy*. Methuen, London, 1934, p. 152.

28 Browning, R., 'Pippa Passes', (1841) quoted in *Oxford Dictionary Quotations* (3rd edition) Oxford, OUP, 1979.

29 Browning, R., 'A Death in the Desert', *Dramatis Personae*, London, Chapman and Hall, 1864.

30 Zimmerman, T. F., 'The Reason for the Rise of the Pentecostal Movement', in Synan, V. (ed.), *Aspects of Pentecostal-Charismatic Origins*. Logos International, Plainfield, NJ, 1975, p. 8.

31 Rose, L., *Faith Healing*. Penguin, Harmondsworth, 1971, p. 64.

32 Rose, *Faith Healing*, p. 65.

33 Purcell Fox, A. H., *The Church's Ministry of Healing*. Longmans, London, 1959, pp. 13f.

34 Harding, W. H., 'Introduction', in Finney, C. G., *Revivals of Religion*. Morgan & Scott, London, 1910, p. xii.

35 Kelsey, M., *Tongue Speaking*, cited in Christie-Murray, D., *Voices from the Gods: speaking with tongues*. Routledge & Kegan Paul, London, 1978, p. 45.

36 Christie-Murray, *Voices from the Gods*, p. 93.

37 Hollenweger, W. J., *The Pentecostals*. SCM, London, 1972, p. 23.

38 Christie-Murray, *Voices from the Gods*, p. 95.

39 Rose, *Faith Healing*, p. 103.

40 Cited in Bennet, G., *The Heart of Healing: a handbook on healing.* Arthur James, Evesham, 1971, p. 37.

41 Kerin, D., *Fulfilling.* Hodder & Stoughton, London, 1963, pp. 13f.

42 Arnold, D. M., *Dorothy Kerin: called by Christ to heal,* cited in Maddocks, M., *The Christian Healing Ministry.* SPCK, London, 1981, p. 102.

43 Searle, G. F. C., 'A Testimony to "the Living Touch"', in Kerin, *Fulfilling,* pp. 18f.

44 *The Ministry of Healing: Report of the Committee Appointed in Accordance with Resolution 63 of the Lambeth Conference, 1920.* SPCK, London, 1924, p. 13.

45 *The Ministry of Healing,* p. 13.

46 Kelsey, M., *Healing and Christianity.* SCM, London, 1973, p. 117.

47 Maddocks, *Christian Healing Ministry,* p. 104.

48 Cited in Rose, *Faith Healing,* p. 108.

49 Rose, *Faith Healing,* pp. 108f.

50 Cited in Maddocks, *Christian Healing Ministry,* p. 106.

51 *The Truth Shall Make You Free: The Lambeth Conference 1988 – the reports, resolutions and pastoral letters from the bishops.* Anglican Consultative Council, London, 1988, MM 81, p. 47.

52 *The Truth Shall Make You Free,* MM 86, pp. 48f.

53 Ghéon, H., *The Secret of the Curé d'Ars.* Sheed & Ward, London, 1929, pp. 112f.

54 Ghéon, *Curé d'Ars,* p. 114.

55 Ghéon, *Curé d'Ars,* p. 115.

56 Ghéon, *Curé d'Ars,* p. 113.

57 Kelsey, *Healing and Christianity,* p. 237.

58 Rose, *Faith Healing,* p. 94.

59 Kelsey, *Healing and Christianity,* pp. 237f.

60 Rose, *Faith Healing,* p. 95.

61 Hocken, *Streams of Renewal: the origin and early development of the Charismatic Movement in Great Britain.* Paternoster, Exeter, 1986, p. 115.

62 Lewis, D. C., 'Signs and wonders in Sheffield: A Social Anthropologist's Analysis of Words of Knowledge, Manifestations of the Spirit, and the Effectiveness of Divine Healing', in Wimber, J. and Springer, K. (eds), *Power Healing.* Hodder & Stoughton, London, 1986, p. 252.

63 Lewis and Springer (eds), in Wimber, *Power Healing,* p. 253.

64 MacNutt, F., *Healing.* Ave Maria Press, Notre Dame, IN, 1974, p. 7.

65 MacNutt, *Healing,* p. 66.

66 MacNutt, *Healing,* p. 74.

67 Ghéon, *Curé d'Ars,* p. 115, 'Miracles of healing are no more than a trick to bring in feeble souls.'

# Intermezzo 2

# *Mel's story*

Mel has Friedreich's Ataxia but that would define her purely in terms of her impairment. She would probably go further and say that definition would actually disable her. For her disability is something that other people and the environment do to her. She is a person, she would say, with an impairment. Impairment and disability she defines as:

> *Impairment*: lacking in all or part of a limb, having altered or reduced function of a limb, organ or mechanism of the body.
>
> *Disability*: the reversible disadvantage or restriction of activity caused by contemporary social organization which takes little or no account of people with impairments and results in their exclusion from participation in the mainstream of social activities; disability is therefore a particular form of social oppression and discrimination.

Mel is an attractive, petite woman in her late twenties. She fights fiercely for disability rights. She is highly critical of the design of buildings and access to public utilities. Planners disable her by their thoughtlessness. Light switches are too often placed at the wrong height. Corridors are frequently too narrow. Stairs and escalators are too often installed in place of lifts. Too few buildings have access ramps. Attitudes, she suggests, disable people. She is very independent, articulate, intelligent and strong-willed. Mel is also a wheelchair user. Her wheelchair enables her to move around much as legs do for people who do not share her impairment. She is wheelchair *enabled* not wheelchair-*bound*.

Mel was first diagnosed as having Friedreich's Ataxia as a child of about eight and a half living in Portugal. She was noticeably losing her sense of balance, her muscles began to deteriorate and she was becoming unsteady on her feet. Her adoptive parents were obviously worried and took her to Lisbon for tests. Mel remembers being stuck full of needles! The specialist identified the condition but her parents were unwilling to accept his diagnosis.

It is always hard for parents to believe such diagnoses. It reflects on them. Not only need the child's impairment be accepted; there is nearly always guilt. Was it their fault? What if . . .? It was particularly hard for Mel's parents as they believed 'normality was synonymous with being able-bodied'. Perhaps because they lived in a country where they were outsiders complicated things. Unwilling to accept the findings of the Portuguese hospital, they took advantage of a family celebration, and brought her to Britain where the tests were repeated at Great Ormond Street. The diagnosis was confirmed.

Friedreich's Ataxia is a rare, inherited disease of the central nervous system, causing loss of balance and co-ordination, and causing difficulty in walking. The recessive gene has to be found in both parents to be transmitted to offspring. And even then the chances of inheriting the impairment are very small. It can affect some or all of the muscles and can begin at any time. Until the onset at eight, Mel had been able-bodied, 'running and jumping and everything', but progressively over the next three or four years the muscles deteriorated. Theoretically the disease can continue its progression with no remission, but over the last six years Mel has noticed no difference.

'I don't really remember very much about being taken to the first "healer". I was only little at the time. I remember being taken down a leafy green lane.' The green was a novelty for a child recently arrived from Portugal. 'I was taken into this big room and introduced to this guy [. . .] and he made me walk around, up and down.' At that time she could still walk 'albeit a little unsteadily'. 'My parents told me afterwards that I was walking better but I don't know. That may have been just their wishful thinking.' She remembers having to concentrate hard, which might have made a difference. Mel remembers little except the man was probably middle-aged ('when you're little everyone looks old!'). He said a few prayers and 'told me that if I believed in God I would be able to walk "normally" again'. Mel felt that it was her responsibility to have the necessary faith. However, the effects, if any, wore off very quickly.

When she was about ten, Mel's parents took her to another 'healer' near the village of Fatima in Portugal. Like Lourdes, Fatima is a place of pilgrimage with many claimed miracles. In 1916 and 1917 three children claimed to see a series of visions. In 1916 the children saw what appeared to be a boy of about thirteen. He was 'more dazzling than a glass of crystalline water penetrated by the rays of the most burning sun'.[1] This 'angel' appeared three times and the children, over-awed, kept their visions to themselves. Then for six months 'Our Lady of the Rosary' appeared to them at noon on the thirteenth of each month but one (when the children were detained by the civil authorities).

The lady was 'surrounded by a dazzling white light and she looked to be about fifteen years of age. She wore a long white gown tied at the neck by a golden cord. [...] A long, white veil covered her head and fell down to her waist and she held a rosary in her hands.'[2] When the children told their parents what they had seen rumours spread around the village. The next month sixty or so curious villagers accompanied them to the Cova da Iria. The third month about 6,000 people went with the children. By October between 70,000 and 100,000 people from all over war-torn Europe went to the shrine. Many claimed that the sun spun like a top, surrounded by a halo of cloud, and, bright as it was, eyewitnesses claimed they looked right at the light without hurting their eyes.

Mel was still walking, though only just and with assistance. She was quite interested in the story of Fatima, being a similar age to one of the children, Lucia dos Santos. They set off excitedly for the four-hour drive – it was like going on holiday! They stayed in a boarding house and drove to the 'healing centre' for half-hour sessions. Mel was looking forward to being able to walk and run and do ballet again. The man involved was a minor celebrity whose healings had been featured on Portuguese television. His work had so impressed some of the family's neighbours that they recommended him. Mel's family joined the 'healer's' long waiting-list. They paid the 'extortionate fees', waited their turn and, eventually, went to the 'clinic'.

They were ushered into a room and met the 'healer'. He was 'hugely fat and smelly'. And, to Mel's embarrassment, his flies were undone. He interviewed Mel and her parents for about ten minutes before they were shown into a large room with lots of tables. She never saw the 'healer' again. In this room were lots of people: the 'healer's' assistants, people hoping to be cured, and their families and friends. 'I had to get on this table [...] lie down on this table [...] which was not comfortable. This assistant or whatever, came up and started waving his hands over me slowly. He didn't touch me. The other guy, the "healer", I don't know if he came in the room [...] I was lying down. In theory he was saying prayers. After about half an hour of this we had to go away and come back the next day.'

This was a daily routine. 'And every day he charged God knows what. And if you missed a session you were in trouble.' The threat was never clearly stated but the implication was that if one missed a session the process wouldn't work. Mel was supposed to pray at the same time as the 'healer' and over a period of time 'it would happen [...] I would be able to walk again [...] to be normal'. Normal meant being able to walk again. The only people that Mel had ever seen in wheelchairs were elderly. In Portugal, she says, anyone with an impairment was hidden away for shame. It wasn't until she returned to England to do A levels that she met other young people in wheelchairs, some even younger than herself! That was a revelation.

Mel had few expectations of the encounter, however expensive. If a man was that fat and smelly, she remembers thinking, he can't be that good. But he had been on television so, she reasoned, there must have been something in it. After a week of the sessions there was no obvious improvement and, because of the financial burden on the family, they returned home. It had been a wonderful holiday but it ended with disappointment. Her muscles continued to deteriorate, she felt 'incomplete'.

Teenagers tend to be self-conscious about their bodies. There is much surreptitious comparison of one's development compared to one's classmates at school. Awareness of sexuality, of one's own and others' sexual development, becomes increasingly important. And having an impairment doesn't mean that one has no sexuality. People who use wheelchairs to aid their mobility have the same sexual hopes and fears and desires as other people.

When Mel was fifteen her hopes and fears were those of her classmates: 'boyfriends, my O levels and school'. She remembers a boy she 'really fancied' complimenting her, saying how nice she looked. She knew she wasn't unattractive – her parents had always said so but parents are biased. She looked at herself critically in the mirror. She was quite pretty – a little like a young Audrey Hepburn, elfin and dark. And the fact that this 'really nice guy' thought to say how good she looked still gives her obvious pleasure.

Mel and her family were still living in the Algarve when she was fifteen. Both she and her mum were being prepared for Confirmation by the priest from the Anglican Church there, Brother Douglas. The priest became a friend. He would pick Mel up from school once a week and come to tea, doing the confirmation class at her home. He was a 'brother, actually, [. . .] a kind of a monk as well [. . .] he was a character'.

> He had this [. . .] Brother Joseph [. . .] who was doing this healing. And I didn't know he was coming until he was in the Algarve. Brother Douglas had given us a few back copies of this other brother's magazine called *Healing Hands* [. . .] and I think my mum read them. The first thing I really knew about it [. . .] we were told we were going to another house one evening. This was where this chap had a room. Both of the brothers were staying there.

They were met at the door by the owner of the villa. She was full of enthusiasm about Brother Joseph's 'healing touch'. She'd had a pain in the shoulder and he'd touched it and was cured. 'And it was all wonderful.' As well as the hostess and the monks, someone else was in the lounge. He was, according to Mel, something of a colourful character who began to relate a story about how he was driving home from church one day. He claimed to have felt a sudden power surge, feeling suddenly filled with energy and strength, as though he could wrench the steering-wheel off. Luckily, he said, he had stopped the car safely. As he began to tell the story, Mel smelt a rat. It had obviously been pre-planned without her knowledge. She felt a bit miffed to say the least!

Brother Joseph wheeled Mel outside to a vine-covered patio and put his hands on her shoulders and then on her head. All this time he was praying. He was asking God to give Mel the strength to walk and be 'normal'. At this point she called him a creep; she thought that he had been 'slimy'. Before taking her out on to the patio he too had told a number of stories, including how he had discovered his healing gift and how lots of people had been helped through his work. He also told how he had once been caught on a barbed wire

146

fence by his sleeve. He fell back and caught the other sleeve and hung there as if crucified. He also said something about his mother's name being Mary too. The self-identification with Jesus bothered her, it was too strange.

There were no power surges, no effects whatsoever. She had been led to believe something wonderful would happen. She would be able to walk and dance and everything. The stories Brother Joseph had told were all very positive ones, with miraculous results. An expectant atmosphere was built up. Hands were laid on. Prayer was offered. But nothing happened. Nothing except one young girl losing her faith. Trustworthy people were no longer trustworthy. The promises that they had made for God were not kept. And Mel was left feeling that if she had done something she would have been healed. Nobody ever spelled out exactly what she was expected to do but it was, nevertheless, her fault.

Genes are the basic physical units of inheritance. Mel's parents passed on the genetic inheritance for hair colour. In the same way they passed on the colour of her eyes. Her sex was determined by the inherited genetic code. Each of these is characteristic of her. Her parents also passed on the gene causing Freidreich's Ataxia. It is not an illness. It has not attacked her from outside like a viral or a bacterial infection. She is not sick. She has Freidreich's Ataxia in precisely the same way that she is a woman. Both her gender and her impairment are to be found in every single cell of her body. To suggest that she might be healed of the one is as ridiculous as to suggest that she might be healed of the other. She is.

She has been hurt deeply by her experiences of 'healing'. They have, she once wrote, caused her 'untold misery and pain'. The expectations given by the 'healers' were neither caring nor sensitive. Nor were they, in any sense, realistic. The 'healers' did not ever suggest that her symptoms might be alleviated. Instead they each stressed that her impairment would be 'cured' and, in two cases, instantly. Mel is now suspicious of people involved in any 'healing ministry', wondering why her parents and the 'healers' so wanted her to be 'normal'. She says:

I now think that this was because people cannot accept disability. Christians tend to forget that disabled people are also 'made in God's image'. To me, this attitude shows a lack of 'wholeness' and [itself] needs to be healed. Healing is a change

147

of attitude [. . .] I've often thought, if I was suddenly made able bodied like those people wanted, I wouldn't know what to do with myself. I really wouldn't. I actually think it's dangerous of people [. . .] not only to expect that [. . .] but to make others expect it. God created me as a disabled person [. . .] when I came into his mind – in his great scheme of things – I was, I am a disabled person. And I always will be a disabled person. And I don't think that there's anything wrong with being a disabled person.

## NOTES

1 Jackson, B., *Places of Pilgrimage*. Geoffrey Chapman, London, 1989, p. 164.
2 Jackson, *Places of Pilgrimage*, pp. 165f.

# *Theodicy: playing dice with God!*

Medical decisions are not just about medicine. Bree Walker, an American journalist, has a congenital deformation of the hands and feet. When she decided to have a child a rival radio station discussed her pregnancy on air without her knowledge. Callers rang insisting on abortion. Genetic differences like syndactyly or Motor Neurone Disease (which Professor Stephen Hawking has) or Freidreich's Ataxia could disappear in one generation if everyone carrying the relevant gene was sterilized and suspect foetuses systematically genetically cleansed. This was the Nazi solution – the murder of those with disabilities.

Mass immunization requires social planning. The cost of medical care demands complex social, economic, political and ethical decisions. The cost of one simple operation would provide clean water for perhaps five hundred people in the two-thirds world. As Christiaan Barnard was performing the first heart transplant in Cape Town children elsewhere in South Africa were being vaccinated against measles by Oxfam. Health provision affects society. Preventative medicine requires social engineering. Models of healthcare are political models. All medical decisions are political.

By healing individuals of individual ailments, Jesus brought health to the community: a health more than physical – it was emotional, sexual, social, religious, and economic. Sickness and health affect the community: they are, therefore, political. Health and healing are individual and corporate. Those who have more resources have access to more facilities and medicine is generally less available to the poor. People with learning disabilities and others frequently receive less satisfactory healthcare because of communication difficulties. However, the politics of health is not just about haves and have-nots. Anyone sick is impoverished simply

because of their sickness. And society suffers from this marginalization.

The Jesus model shows the urgent task of restoring health. Jesus
restores *shalom*: 'People who are well do not need a doctor, but only
those who are sick. I have not come to call respectable people, but
outcasts' (Mark 2.17). Sickness needs turning round and making
good. J. R. R. Tolkien's word *eucatastrophe* – catastrophe made
well again – is the twist that becomes the happy ending. 'The birth
of Christ is the eucatastrophe of Man's history.'[1] The Good News
of Jesus' preaching is that there is a way to turn things around. All
life is affected – physical, moral, spiritual, social and psychological.
The imperfect is turned upside down and creation made anew.
Participating in Jesus restores health in the relationship with
God. *Shalom*, the proper condition of humanity – strength,
wholeness, peace, long life, salvation, soundness, well-being,
prosperity, completeness, and walking within the will of God, righteousness – is renewed.

The Christian community tries to walk the way of Christ with a
different understanding of health to that of Western society. Pope
John Paul II said in Southwark, in 1982:

> Today I make an urgent plea to this nation. Do not neglect
> your sick and elderly. Do not turn away from the handicapped
> and the dying. Do not push them to the margins of society.
> For if you do, you will fail to understand that they represent
> an important truth. The sick, the elderly, the handicapped and
> the dying teach us that weakness is a creative part of human
> living, and that suffering can be embraced with no loss of
> dignity. Without the presence of these people in your midst
> you might be tempted to think of health, strength and power
> as the only important values to be pursued in life. But the
> wisdom of Christ and the power of Christ are to be seen in
> the weakness of those who share his sufferings.[2]

This is revolutionary talk. People with impairments or who are sick
are centred in society, recognized as valuable. 'Let us keep the sick
and the handicapped at the centre of our lives.'[3] As Jesus demands,
outsiders are welcomed to the banquet. Those in 'the country roads
and lanes' (those outside the safe city wall) are invited into the
centre. Embracing the lessons of weakness means embracing the

teachers themselves – people with impairments and people who are sick!

In 1948 the World Health Organisation defined health as 'a state of complete physical, mental and social well-being and not merely the absence of illness'[4] – two ancient ideas, one positive and one negative.

> In classical Greek mythology, the positive and negative [...] were symbolized in the myths of Hygieia, the goddess of health, and her father Aesculapius, the god of healing. [...] Hygieia emphasized [...] health as a natural state of well-being. [...] Aesculapius, on the other hand, thought of health as the absence of disease, attained by treatment ...[5]

The WHO definition contains social well-being but the medical profession does not entirely concur. Michael Wilson notes of Orwell's *Nineteen Eighty-Four*, that while the Ministry of Peace deals with war, and the Ministry of Plenty with rationing, Orwell did not need to describe a Ministry of Health which deals with disease: we already have one.

Stephen Pattison suggests five distinct models of illness and treatment: Medical, Psychological, Epidemiological, Sociological, and Anthropological.[6] The *Medical Model* is most familiar. Illness is an enemy to be defeated. The enemies are bacteria, viruses, etc. The allies are the GP, the specialist, the laboratory and so on. The patient is the battleground in a war between good and evil. Patients have little responsibility for ailments affecting their bodies, alien invaders cause disease. Doctors must intervene to cure patients. The body is an individual biological mechanism, liable to invasion. Thus treatment is to repair the individual mechanism. The medical model regards the patient clinically, using the technological language. Samples are taken and analysed in a laboratory remote from the patient and a diagnosis made largely in isolation from the patient.

This can mean a patient being viewed as a case not a person – no more than a collection of symptoms. Research is curative, looking to cure a disease rather than prevent one, promoting the idea that science will always prevail. Preventative measures are only temporary and ephemeral. Efficient function is equated with well-being. Happiness depends on the physical state of the body. Other factors, such as effects on family and friends, and the impact of loss of income or of long-term care, are not relevant to the medical model.

The *Psychological Model* considers emotional and behavioural aspects of illness and treatment. While not denying that there are pathogenic factors such as viruses, the psychological model looks at such causative factors as stress. There is a direct relationship between the body and the mind, between one's physiology and one's psychology: extended and intense stress may make one more prone to ulcers; sexual fantasies have physical responses, etc.

Smoking, for example, affects health, but while in the medical model it is seen totally negatively as introducing carcinogenic substances and inviting lung cancer, psychologically it is a Displacement Activity.

> Smoking increases and decreases, not with any narcotic nicotine-need, but with the varying tensions of the day. [...] It is so much more than a question of inhaling smoke. There is the finding of the packet and the matches or lighter; the extraction of the cigarette from the pack; lighting-up; putting out the flame and getting rid of the lighter, match-box and cigarette packet; shifting the ashtray to a more convenient position; flicking a little imaginary ash from the front of the clothes; and blowing a little smoke thoughfully up into the air.[7]

Desmond Morris sees the smoker as having an advantage over a non-smoker in stress control. The fidgeting involved in smoking can be disguised as part of a pleasure routine. The smoker appears relaxed and calm under stress. The behaviour, smoking a cigarette, is a stress-control technique. It is not a simple 'Non-smoking good, smoking bad'!

The behaviourist teaches alternative coping strategies to the smoker who wishes to give up. The medical model suggests progressively reducing the intake of nicotine, treating the physical addiction. Smoking is treated both as a physical disorder and to prevent the onset of cancer. The psychological model treats the underlying psychological condition, stress, acting to reduce the incidence of such stress-related disorders as hypertension, asthma, ulcers, heart disease and cancer.

Psychological models emphasize character and behaviour rather than microbiological constitution. Individuals are responsible for their personal behaviour and behaviours likely to increase the chances of contracting illness are the patient's own fault, therefore one is to blame for illnesses. 'A large minority [of Americans] see AIDS as a deserved punishment for offensive and immoral behaviour.'[8] This 'victim blaming' may result in reduced healthcare provision. Do smokers deserve free NHS treatment for self-inflicted lung cancer?

The *Epidemiological Model* studies epidemics and the distribution of disease in whole populations. It is more about society than individuals and less about cure than prevention. The first Public Health Act was passed in Britain in 1848, the work of Edwin Chadwick, a man for whom 'there was hardly anything too bad to be said about him' because of his championing of the hated workhouse system. Public health became his responsibility when Shoreditch in London suffered an epidemic of typhus and influenza. The parish argued that people's living conditions were to blame and began to improve drainage, sewage and housing. The Poor Law Board argued that these were not their concern. Chadwick, the Secretary, agreed but appointed a committee to investigate. Drs James Phillips Kay and Neil Arnott went to Wapping and Stepney, while Dr Southwood Smith went to Bethnal Green and Whitechapel. Their *Report on the Sanitary Conditions of the Labouring Classes of Great Britain* 'made horrifying reading'.

> [...] plain descriptions of thousands of human beings living in the most disgusting conditions on the fringe of the greatest and most wealthy of the world's cities. Why did they do so? Because they couldn't help it; they had nowhere else to go, and besides they had to live near their places of work. Need it always remain so? No, declared Chadwick's doctors, and he echoed their claim; all these shocking evils could be prevented, by such simple remedies as light, fresh air, plenty of clean water, soap, refuse collection, street sweeping, house drainage.[9]

The 1848 Public Health Act failed by excluding London, balked by a 'hatred of any kind of interference with private property and deep mistrust of state control'.[10] Not until Dr Snow, 'one of the heroes of community medicine',[11] demonstrated that the cholera bacillus was transmitted in polluted water, was clean water conduited in from the countryside. This provision was not medical but political, cholera reminding MPs of their own mortality. It has been suggested that not until after the first Jack the Ripper murder in the East End did the middle classes begin to realise their vulnerability in the West End – not just to murder but also to disease. Political strategies for the prevention and treatment of disease created the Welfare State a century later. Beveridge said that it was necessary 'to use the powers of the State, so far as may be necessary without any limit whatsoever, in order to avoid the five giant evils': want, disease, ignorance, squalor and idleness. Disease was political; the power of the State was to fight disease!

Medicine may have had very little effect on general health. In Britain better diet has all but eradicated rickets; sewerage removal and clean water have successfully prevented outbreaks of typhoid and cholera. Large-scale immunization has controlled diphtheria and polio. Most of the great curative advances in modern medicine have had a very small effect while continuing poverty continues to affect health dramatically. 'Illness, therefore, has to be situated in a much wider social and moral horizon.'[12] Health provision is social provision. It cannot be divorced from housing and education. Healing in the epidemiological model involves changing society. Structural evils are combated rather than the individual's illness. Structures are to blame and not individuals, so individuals cannot be ultimately responsible. This is both a strength and a weakness. Individuals avoid guilt for their own ailments but they also avoid blame for those of their neighbours!

Pattison's *Sociological Model* distinguishes between disease, illness and sickness. '*Disease* [...] is taken to be the objective and observable existence of a pathological abnormality, *illness* [...] is taken to be the presence of symptoms of disorder which are perceived subjectively, and *sickness* [...] is held to be a socially sanctioned role.'[13] This model is about the perception of an ailment; distinguishing between the disease, the patient and society. It gives these three elements a function in the understanding of health and healing, demonstrating their relationship.

*Disease* is the bacteria or the cancer or whatever. Disease is separate from the person. *Illness* is subjective: the understanding of a person's disorder is in their individual perception. Mild stress can give the symptoms of a 'twenty-four hour bug' – the cure for both is the same, a day off work. *Sickness* is defined by culture and different cultures perceive sickness differently. In Soviet Russia dissidents were diagnosed as mentally ill and treated in mental hospitals. In Britain diagnosis of schizophrenia varies with ethnic origin – one is more likely to be labelled schizophrenic if Afro-Caribbean. The symptomatic 'deviant behaviour' is cultural, an attitude towards white authority, resulting from slavery. Women too are more likely to be diagnosed with mental illness: social alienation and loneliness treated with tranquillizers. Women, fifty-one per cent of the population, are regarded as different from the male norm. Female and black doctors compete in a traditionally white male world and to succeed tend to assume a white, male, middle-class perspective.

This model redefines sickness. Criminals would be treated differently if unwell. Certain crimes couldn't be perpetrated by someone like us. Therefore criminals must be insane. Child murderers are repugnant if sane but if they are sick they become less responsible for their actions. Sickness is behaviour deviant from the norm. The tendency of medical staff to adopt Western, patriarchal, middle-class viewpoints has meant that diagnoses have been on class, gender, race or intellectual lines. Stress in the articulate professional can be malingering in the less articulate.

The *Anthropological Model* is cross-cultural, looking at how different cultures define health and sickness, causes and treatments. Sickness is often caused by malevolent beings – in some societies these are witches, for Americans they are germs. Americans use disinfectant instead of incantations, declaring biological warfare on microbes. In the US dirt on vegetables is unhealthy while in France dirt shows freshness. Treatment and diagnosis too are different. Dr Jack Froom of the State University of New York watched English doctors examine their patients: 'a kid came in with an earache and the doctor looked at that ear. Here, we would at least have the patient undress to the waist ... and would have looked at the throat and lungs.' The information would probably make no difference, but the reflexes are different. In Germany antibiotics are restricted to severe bacterial infections, while in the USA they are commonly prescribed.

Jean Masamba ma Mpolo describes the traditional African understanding of illness as 'the result of wrong-doings. Thus, sin and its consequences are part of the same process whereby the individual is invaded by forces of death which are contained in the disobedience of agreed moral norms which also affect the

155

ecological balance.'[14] Sickness is the result of breaking the ethical code and so inviting the invasion of spirits – beings who cause someone to live in this world and the spirit world at the same time. And consequences are corporate. 'The sin of the individual can have consequences on the health of another person or the health of an entire community and family. Sin opens the doors for life-negating forces to disturb the health of the individual and to upset the ecological and the entire social equilibrium.'[15] The family, the community and the whole ecostructure are affected – illness is seen as taboo-breaking.

We can also distinguish an 'Economic Model' of healthcare, which emphasizes financial cost. Doctors are expensive commodities, more likely to be trained in an affluent society. Doctors are marketable and poorer people are unlikely to receive the same healthcare as richer ones. Poorer countries have fewer doctors per capita while in most developed countries the health bill has risen dramatically. The rising cost of medical care is of major concern in Britain. The increasing lifespan in the one-third world too demands that an increasingly smaller proportion of people fund healthcare.

The proportion of those incapacitated can impact catastrophically. The Plague pushed up labourers' wages and legislation was introduced to keep the economic status quo. In central Africa HIV has reached epidemic proportions; those most active sexually and at most risk are also the most productive economically. The World Bank estimated that in the late 1980s, in Tanzania, direct healthcare cost for each AIDS patient ranged between $104 and $631 – depending on whether the patient was nursed by relatives locally or with the best modern care available. Indirectly the cost is astronomical: the value of the healthy years of life AIDS steals from society is calculated at between $2500 and $5000 of lost income.[16]

The economic model sees health as a commodity to be bought and sold. The patient is viewed for cost effectiveness. An extreme example is 'triage' as used by mercenaries, when the wounded were sorted into three groups: those that would survive without treatment; those that would die anyway; and those who would recover if treated but not otherwise. Only the last were treated to preserve precious medical supplies.

The different perspectives show a range of attitudes towards health and sickness. We share paradigms across history and across the world, yet there are gender, class, regional, ethnic, educational and economic variations. Medicine is not mono-cultural. We are highly mechanized and technological yet maintain a continuity with traditional beliefs and practices that we would largely deny, notwithstanding the revival of interest in alternative treatments like herbalism and acupuncture.

Christian healing also exhibits a range of models, distinguishable by the locus of power. The healing power or gift can be located within an individual or in the corporate body, the community. In each of these models Christ is present, in four ways:

He is the sick man, the prisoner, the child, the stranger.
He is the giver of the cup of water, the clothes, the visitor.
He is the one who preaches the Gospel.
He is the one who receives those who preach the Gospel.[17]

In Christian healing it is Christ who is encountered, whichever the model. The individual models might be described as the Functional Model, the Institutional Saintly Model, the Charismatic Healer Model, and the Pastoral Care Model. The corporate models are the Sacramental Model, the Fellowship Model, and the Creation Model.

In the *Functional Model* the individual leader of a congregation, such as a priest or minister, is the instrument of healing on behalf of the community. This is an institutional model, the function of the minister or priest as called by God into the institution of a denominational church being the important consideration. The formalized community of a church have healing done for them, on their behalf, but without their active involvement. The ordained person can effect healing because she or he is an ordained priest or minister called by God and legitimized by the church, wherein is sited the power. Without examining cases too closely, one can see that there is an expectation of the miraculous among people with whom the priest comes into contact. People expect the person with the cure of souls to be involved in healing the body too, though to a lesser extent. In the Church of England the parish priest is frequently installed into a parish with the requirement to 'come among us as a healer' and is given a symbolic flagon of oil.

A similar model, in some ways, might be the *Institutional Saintly Model*. However, here the personal holiness of the 'saint', a sanctity largely irrelevant in the functional model, effects the healing. Cults such as that of the Blessed Virgin at Lourdes or Fatima, which are more or less part of the institution, are the focus. But the saint is the instrument through which God works. The saint is adopted by the institution and becomes, as a result, institutionalized. However, the saint is empowered as a healer by virtue of personal holiness rather than by representing the institution. Popularly it is frequently considered to be the saint who effects the cure rather than God; thus prayers are often addressed to a saint instead of the saint's being asked to add his or her prayers to our own.

The third individual model is that of *Charismatic Healer*. In this model the healer is someone who believes God has specifically given them an individual gift. Thus it is the touch and prayer of that individual through which God heals. It is a role that stands outside the institutional models. The healer is empowered neither by personal holiness nor by accreditation by human institutions. The healer has a direct relationship with God and has a divine mission. This model is more often found, though not invariably, among Protestant denominations.

The final individual model is that of the *Pastoral Care Model*. This is really an interloper in many ways, as it is both individual and collective. Individuals such as priests and pastors may qualify as individuals but pastoral teams certainly do not, even when they fulfil the same role! This is also an interloper in that it has more to do with general healthcare than with spiritual healing as such. However, many Christians are involved in caring for the sick both as professionals and as family or friends. In many ways their care is indistinguishable from that of people who do the same things who are not Christian, but it involves a specific spiritual dimension. 'It is a doing of what God did when he visited his people.'[18] Indeed, for Christians sick visiting is being Christ, taking Christ out into the community and meeting Christ in the person visited. 'Koinonia, visiting the sick and giving a cup of [...] water in the remembrance of Christ, and mission, are therefore but different aspects of the same reality, the Whole Christ.'[19]

The alternative to the individual focus is the focus on the community. So Michael Wilson's book *The Church is Healing* or Bob Lambourne's *Community, Church and Healing* both emphasize the role of the whole Church in healing. Community models may be sacramental or not but share common ground by involving the whole church community.

The *Sacramental Model* is similar to the Functional Model but enacted in the context of the community. Sacraments are performed by a recognized and authorized representative of the community, the pastor or priest. The locus of healing power is the sacrament, the Eucharist or anointing. The body of Christ in the Eucharist is healing for the body of Christ that is the community. The oil of healing is used for anointing with the prayer of the community. God works through the symbol recognized in the context of the church. As the outward sign – the bread, wine, oil – is eaten, drunk or poured on, the inward reality of healing is discovered.

In the *Fellowship Model* prayer, perhaps with the laying on of hands, is practised by the community. The imposition of hands is not done by an individual charismatically empowered by God. The hands, even if those of one person, represent those of the whole community. The locus of power is not in the individual charismatic but in the community as a whole.

The *Creation Model* of healing and healthcare describes God's work through natural causes. Healing occurs through the natural order – medicines are part of creation. Human beings, as part of that creation, can effect healing and affect health. Healing comes from God as part of the continual process of creation. In this model energies are to be funnelled into the 'non-religious' models of healthcare. The locus of power is outside the church. It is better to concentrate on preventing all illness or healing all people irrespective of belief than the alternative. From this viewpoint the church models may perhaps be seen as, at best insular and at worst introverted and selfish.

The spectrum of Christian healing has at its heart an essentially divided view of God that reflects the wider Church. On the one hand, some people regard the Christian God as one who personally intervenes in history. 'If I have the power to help a friend when I see him hurt, I use all my powers to help him,' wrote Francis MacNutt. 'The most tangible sign that God loves us is that he stoops, as Jesus did, to heal the wounded.'[20] Other people regard God as being involved in the processes of the world. In this view God cannot intervene but does bring healing through those processes. Michael Wilson, for example, seems to suggest that God does not intervene in miraculous ways but is involved in the process of creation, and that healing is located there.[21] Dietrich Bonhoeffer writes 'that since man has come of age and can understand and manage the physical world so efficiently, he no longer needs a God who works directly in the physical world to help him in his helplessness'.[22]

From the theological point of view health and sickness require meaning. They are the concern of *theodicy* – the problem of evil. And the problem of evil affects our whole view of God. Our understanding of health and sickness are fundamental to our view of the world. It is not enough merely to acknowledge the existence of sickness or health – they need to be interpreted as part of the human experience. Is there meaning in this experience? If God exists, how does God fit into human suffering? If God is loving, how can God allow pain? If God is forgiving, why does God inflict suffering? The very nature of God is at stake.

'*Gott würfelt nicht*' – God does not play dice – was Einstein's reaction to the quantum theory. The reality is, whatever Einstein said, it certainly feels like it! Good things happen to bad people. Bad things happen to good people. God apparently finds time to answer some prayers but not others. Some Christians regularly pray for healing for a slight headache. And God, they claim, acts. A mother calling on God for her child's life is left unanswered in an uncaring universe. It feels as though God is playing with loaded dice. And they are loaded in favour of a tiny minority!

Suffering is a fact of life. None of the explanations given by the Bible or by philosophers or theologians feel completely satisfactory. The biblical creation story is a story of a fall from innocence into suffering caused by disobedience. The Ten Commandments agree with the Buddha that desire causes suffering: desiring the rightful property of another, divine or human, is wrong. Worship, for example, belongs to God alone. To worship another object or creature takes God's property, worship, away from him. Property belongs to someone, including their own person, which is why slavery and rape and murder are evil acts. Seizing someone else's property causes suffering. Ultimately, the suffering is to thief as well as to victim. By stealing, we damage relationships with others. By damaging our relationships we become isolated in the community and, thereby, suffer.

Jesus took the idea further and declared that anticipation was the act.

You have heard that it was said, "Do not commit adultery.' But now I tell you: anyone who looks at a woman and wants

160

to possess her is guilty of committing adultery with her in his heart.

(Matthew 5.27–8)

This is truth but not the whole truth. In African tradition suffering can be caused by taboo breaking, breaking the community's rules. Breaking taboos can even cause damage to the environment.

Denial of the commandment to love one's neighbour can cause ecological harm. A polluted environment can only be tolerated if those who live and work there are undervalued. For example, the intolerable conditions of workers in the Industrial Revolution were a direct result of their employers' lack of love. Workers continue in similarly horrific conditions in areas presently duplicating the Industrial Revolution. Their pollution, over-crowding and disease are a legacy to succeeding generations.

One need only think of Chernobyl to realize the direct link between pollution and undervaluing the individual. The priority of the state over the individuals, as in the previous USSR, meant the leak received less attention than it deserved. The sins of the fathers have been visited on the children even to the umpteenth generation indeed. The exploitation of people and the exploitation of the planet are equally caused by a desire to own that which belongs to another and are so inter-related as to be inextricable. There is little difference in result between exploitation by the state or exploitation by a multi-national business interest. The whole of creation continues to groan.

We cannot interpret suffering as neutral observers. The sufferer cannot be unmoved by the suffering, and cannot merely observe impassively. Neither can we observe suffering in the abstract – we only observe our own and others' reactions to it. In reality suffering is ever-present as our experience. We cannot become divorced from the experience of suffering – it is programmed into our very existence. In our discussion of God we must recognize, as it has been recognized in physics, that observers are involved.

We have learnt that man cannot describe the physical world as if his own investigations had no effect upon it. The classical physicist who could sit, as it were, on one side of a translucent screen with his thoughts and experiences, viewing the world he studied on the other, is now the impossible spectator. For much of physics the dividing screen is lost, and cannot be

161

replaced. [...] It is not [...] that his emotions bias his results, but rather that his act of observation participates in forming the world.[23]

Observation *is* participation. Our interpretation of events is bounded by our experience. This does not imply that God or the universe are wholly subjective, but our interpretations are. The idea of wholly objective truth is no longer tenable. Nonetheless, shared experiences of both the universe and the God-event make both more than subjective. And of this shared experience our predecessors left signposts.

> The believer's exploration into truth does not involve setting out into uncharted territory to explore matters which have never before been encountered – rather it involves encountering the detailed accounts of others who have made the journey before. [...] The believer's exploration into truth thus consists not so much in pioneering as in attempting to evaluate a long stream of tradition which expresses the faith to which the believer and tradition alike are committed.[24]

Isaac Newton acknowledged his debt to the shared tradition of science: 'If I have seen further it is by standing on the shoulders of giants.'[25] The scientific community now recognize themselves as a community with common values and, in common with theology, acknowledge this as a faith community. Michael Polyani wrote, '[W]e must now recognize belief once more as the source of all knowledge. [...] the sharing of an idiom and a cultural heritage, affiliation to a like-minded community: such are the impulses which shape our vision of the nature of things.'[26] In theology, as in science, there is shared language and framework. As human beings we share common experiences but can view the world neither from the experience of being God nor from the experience of being another creature. We may empathize with God and our fellow creature but we cannot enter into their experience. We are only able to look from our own viewpoint and by looking we affect the results of our observation. It is impossible to remain dispassionate – to live is to suffer.

> We wonder at ourselves like men betrayed,
> Suffering is permanent, obscure and dark,
> And shares the nature of infinity.[27]

Whatever the rational explanation, life feels unfair. And this sense of unfairness must be taken seriously. Any pastoral theology must begin in suffering and unfairness. We cannot afford a theology that 'smells of the lamp'.

Our world has no fair play. Every day new horrors clamour for attention. Children murder other children. Mothers, pushed beyond their limit, batter babies. Men beat women. In the last century millions of people have been slaughtered systematically. The sub-Saharan belt of Africa has seen hunger and starvation on an unnerving scale. There have been earthquakes, tidal waves and volcanic eruptions. And this is not the whole story. Ignored by the media, people by the thousand have died from road traffic accidents and other undramatic causes. Suffering is the one ever-present and ever-visible reality. We are perpetually bombarded with images of suffering, on a hitherto unimaginable scale. The media are not to blame for our compassion fatigue. The images simply reflect the needs and desires of our society. We share a sense that if God exists, he or she is uncaring. If God is love that love is capricious, meted out to favourites. If God exists then he or she seems unable to help. Worse still perhaps – God is unwilling to help. The nightmare we fear is that it will turn out to be reality and God will be the nightmare. Somehow, we all feel, God is to blame.

Pastoral theology must take into account people's experience. It must start where we are. 'Ideas and expectations of salvation and human happiness are invariably projected from within concrete experience and the pondered fact of calamity, pain, misery and alienation [...] there eventually emerges an anthropological projection, a vision of what is held to be the true, good and happy mode of human life.'[28] We can only stand in our own shoes.

God's relationship with evil is crucial to our thinking about God and healing. Is God good? Can he do anything about suffering and sickness? 'If God is perfectly good, He must want to abolish all evil: but evil exists; therefore either God is not perfectly good or He is not unlimitedly powerful.'[29] For the atheist this is the perfect proof of God's non-existence – 'The only excuse for God is that he does not exist.'[30]

There are two classical 'excuses' for God: the 'free will solution', usually identified with the thinking of St Augustine, has been important in the development of Western Christianity; in the East there are echoes of Irenaeus' 'greater good solution'.

163

The 'free will solution' argues that God, infinitely good and powerful, gave his creatures free will. This free will is necessary to experience the gift of love. Without free will one is coerced into serving a dictatorial monster, God. God, however, wants to be loved willingly. Therefore he gives the choice to love or not to love, to serve or not to serve, and there is no coercion.

Augustine grew up in a world of neo-Platonic philosophy. It taught that without evil there was nothing with which to compare goodness. This view gives evil its own reality. However, Augustine taught evil as an absence of true reality. Evil and suffering are the result of choosing not to serve God. The act of turning – '*aversio a Deo, conversio ad creaturas*', turning away from God, toward creatureliness – causes evil. Not that creatureliness is evil; evil comes from turning from God, 'not because that is evil to which it turns but because the turning itself is wicked'. Adam's free will allowed disobedience and we suffer the results of his fall. The fall changed the human condition irretrievably. Adam's proximity to God is now distance. Free will is therefore the cause 'of our doing evil', and, God's 'just judgement is the cause of our having to suffer from its consequences'.

Augustine's God remains impassive, untouched by any responsibility. Suffering is the human condition because of the free choice. And through complicity in Adam we all stand condemned. God remains all-good, all-powerful, unchanging and unchangeable.

In the 'greater good solution' human beings are changing from the 'image of God' into the 'likeness of God'. when created, human beings are an *imago*, a chrysalis which metamorphoses into God's likeness. Adam was created immature, like a child. His fall is not the catastrophe of Augustine but an inevitable part of learning maturity. Adam was like a child touching a cake left out to cool. Correcting the errant child teaches responsibility. 'And instead of the Augustinian view of life's trials as a divine punishment for Adam's sin, Irenaeus sees our world of mingled good and evil as a divinely appointed environment for man's development towards the perfection that represents the fulfilment of God's good purpose for him.'[31] Suffering is ultimately good, moulding us into better people. We mature through experiencing life. A life including both goodness and suffering turns the imago into the butterfly. God is perfectly good because ultimately suffering and evil are good things. There is no need for God to take responsibility because evil is, in the end, essentially good.

Both of these arguments contain truth, but does a God who is above responsibility fit our experience? Schleiermacher suggested that God was the author of evil because evil is necessary for redemption – 'everywhere human evil exists only as attached to good, and sin only as attached to grace'.[32] God wills evil to exist and recognized potential evil since before creation. God must have designed creation complete with evil. God cannot be absolved of responsibility.

Classical theology attempts to exonerate God but experience suggests that God is to blame. Schleiermacher echoes our experience and theology must reflect this shared sickness and death. It must address Hitler and the Holocaust; the Khmer Rouge and the killing fields; Sharpeville and Soweto; Hillsboro'; Biafra and Rwanda. The horror seems endless but defines our age. Theology must take into account the fact of the unimaginable evil in the world.

It would be easy to shrug responsibility for evil on to a devil. If I am demon-infested then I am no longer responsible. 'It was the voices in my head made me do it!' We can all breathe more easily if the devil is to blame. The possessed individual acted alone but it was the demon's fault. The community need not share responsibility. It would equally be easy to claim the world had gone mad – mental illness too reduces responsibility. The condition is to blame, individuals are not responsible for their actions. Illness too takes responsibility out of the human sphere, the community remains unbesmirched. Marx suggested that the structures of society are evil. Theologians have further suggested the existence of institutional demons. It is true that the institutions are at fault. But institutions and systems do not exist in isolation. Multi-national companies may perpetuate poverty or sickness, and Institutions perpetuate discrimination, but I, too, am to blame for I use their products or support the infra-structures and thus share in the abuse of the poor and marginalized.

We have a peculiar attitude towards suffering and death. Incredible suffering is often preferable to death, particularly from the perspective of medical staff. Doctors fight the ultimate enemy, often going to obscene lengths which merely prolong the agony for patient and family alike. We comfort others with the thought that 'At least she didn't suffer much', but put off death for as long as possible. The comedian Woody Allen once commented, 'I'm not afraid of dying, I just don't want to be there when it happens.'

We show little eagerness to be 'promoted to glory'. The rush to join the heavenly banquet is conspicuously absent. We actually don't really trust God to deliver his promises. We are not sure whether God is as loving and forgiving as he claims. St Paul asked the church in Rome, 'If God is for us, who can be against us?' Unfortunately, the evidence of our senses acts against God.

Medieval theology, remote from reality, argued how many angels could dance on the head of a pin. Modern theology too has removed God from ordinary people and made him unable to intervene in history. Aristotle's world-view places God outside of nature. 'Aristotle's God was supposed to be purely self-absorbed self-thinking thought. [...] The idea is as empty as St Thomas' doctrine that God is his own existence because *what* God is is merely *that* God is.'[33] The world-view discarded in physical science in the light of the Enlightenment continues in theology. Theologians persist in a patently absurd world-view. While science no longer requires a closed system, the queen of sciences clings to it. Classical theodicies leave God untouched by suffering or responsibility and do not answer pastoral need.

Human beings are natural creatures and can only appreciate something in a natural way. If God is supernatural, and we can only experience the natural, then we cannot experience God. The conclusion can be either: God is natural, for human beings claim experience of a reality they call God; or the categories are wrong. So either to experience that which we call God is impossible, or the distinction between God and creation is not between natural and supernatural but something else.

If the categories are correct, God is a human construction, wholly and entirely subjective. However, we encounter God in a way suggesting objective existence. These God-experiences are not continuous or predictable. But they are not uncommon. The experience of God we share is many-faceted. We experience an aesthetic God, the artist whose brush colours the dawn or the sunset; a creator, who looked at creation and saw that it was good; a loving parent experienced as a comforter; a capricious monster, a God of wrath – one who gives or withdraws care on a whim. And we experience the participation of and in the Christ, the God who brings forgiveness and the power to change oneself.

If God has a more than subjective existence, then the problem of evil has only two logically consistent solutions: monism and dualism. 'Unfortunately neither of them is compatible with the basic claims of Christian theology.'[34] In monism creation is a harmonious unity. God allows evil for his own purposes, as in *The Book of Common Prayer*'s 'take [...] in good part the chastisement of the Lord'. Evil can become the domestic servant of God instead of a deadly enemy. And we find ourselves calling evil good.

The Gnostics suggested dualism, two gods. One is a superior god, the father of the Christ. The other is the *Demi-urge*, the God of the Old Testament. The first is Spirit, the good God. The other one is Job's capricious God gambling with Satan. The Gnostics recognized the essential dualism of experience.

If God is to be one then we need to address this perceived duality. Christianity is aggressively monotheistic but we experience both overwhelming good and evil. We are devastated by suffering, whether of bereavement or by violence. Equally, we are robbed of words by kindness. Paradoxically monism and dualism both contain truth.

The book of Job is a fictional debate about the nature of God: of the three statements made about God and Job, only two can be true.

(1) God is all-powerful;
(2) God is just and good; and,
(3) Job is a good person.

If God is all-powerful and just then Job cannot be a good person because God does not give him the justice due to a good person. Therefore, if statements (1) and (2) are true then statement (3) is false. If, on the other hand, Job is a good individual and God is just and good then God cannot be all-powerful. He is unable to prevent evil things happening to Job and his family. Therefore, (1) cannot be true if (2) and (3) are. Finally, if God is all-powerful and Job is a good person then God cannot be just and good, otherwise why does he allow Job's sufferings? Harold S. Kushner suggests the best solution is to assume that 'God is all-powerful'[35] is mistaken, thus allowing God to be on the side of the suffering human.

167

However, we do not quite feel that God is on our side – except for those individuals among us whose certainty is itself frightening.

In the concentration camps of World War II, the Jewish people suffered unimaginable losses. They lost family, friends, whole communities. And in the post-Holocaust world there has been, as a result, a loss of hope and a loss of faith. How could a God of love and justice allow such cruelty to exist?

> *1 June 1942*
> When the two women caught sight of the Germans they began to flee, but were overtaken and arrested. They intended shooting them on the spot in the village, but the mayor wouldn't allow it. They then went into the woods and shot them there. [...] When the cart returned it was full of blood. Who ...[36]

The above is the last entry in the diary of Dawid Rubinowicz, a fourteen-year-old Polish Jewish boy. The diary breaks off suddenly and Dawid almost certainly died in Treblinka. To step into his shoes is impossible but his story needs to be addressed.

In one concentration camp a group of learned prisoners put God on trial. In Jewish law God has a legal status. A synagogue is not owned by the worshippers but is run by a manager, legally differentiated from the owner. God is the owner and can be taken to court! Technically, one can have a 'legal disputation with the Lord'. Job's disputation ends with him condemning God's actions. 'Sincere criticism of God is never rebuked,' says the *Encyclopaedia Judaica*. 'God reproaches Job's friends, who were on His side; but Job is rewarded despite his searing indictment of God's actions.'

In this slave-labour camp the Jewish labourers were brutally mistreated and forced to work for six and a half days each week. One Sunday afternoon they decided to bring God to justice. The charge was neglect: God had not cared for his chosen people properly. Witnesses were brought for the prosecution. God allowed the destruction of his people. The evidence was all too visible. There were the death camps. There was the destruction of the Warsaw ghetto, the systematic desecration of graves and looting of synagogues. Whole families had been murdered as political policy. If God was good, how could he allow this to happen?

The bench of rabbis sitting in judgement had little trouble in coming to a decision. God was guilty as charged. God had not cared for his people properly. There was a sense of desolation. There could be no future hope. Silence fell. Finally, one of the inmates stood. 'So God is guilty,' he said uncertainly. 'But now the sun is setting. It is time for evening prayers.'

This story seems bleak. It echoes our experience. God is guilty. The story moves me profoundly but I am not sure quite how. There is even some hope, bleak indeed, but hope nevertheless. It echoes the hope on a wall of the Warsaw ghetto:

> I believe in the sun even when it does not shine.
> I believe in love, even when I cannot feel it.
> I believe in God, even when I do not see him.[37]

There is a sense of duty in adversity, a heroic last-stand hope. There is glory forged in pain and suffering. This glory, this heroism, is still not quite enough. It is reminiscent of Tevyeh the milkman in the musical *Fiddler on the Roof*, 'Lord, I know that we're the chosen people. But, just for once, couldn't you choose someone else?'

Blaming God is the same as blaming the devil. It takes away the responsibility for one's actions. This is comforting but we have the gut-feeling that somehow we participate in the same humanity as Caligula or Pol Pot. And, therefore, have the same potential for evil. God's crime is not one of action but of inaction, neglect. God is guilty of allowing pointless agony, whether in Belsen or Biafra or Bangladesh or to the baby in the maternity ward. Or on Calvary.

> At three o'clock Jesus cried out with a loud shout, *'Eloi, Eloi, lema sabachthani?'* which means, 'My God, my God, why did you abandon me?'
>
> (Mark 15.34)

The prisoners in the concentration camp spoke from their experience of God. God had deserted them at their hour of greatest need. Jesus cried out from his experience. God had deserted him, too, in his hour of need. The author of Job spoke of his experience of suffering through his fictional character.

> Though I am innocent, all I can do
>   Is beg for mercy from God my judge.
> Yet even then, if he lets me speak,
>   I can't believe he would listen to me.
> He sends storms to batter and bruise me

169

without any reason at all.
He won't let me get my breath;
    he has filled my life with bitterness.
Should I try force? Try force on God?
    Should I take him to court? Could anyone make him go?
I am innocent and faithful, but my words sound guilty,
    and everything I say seems to condemn me.
I am innocent, but I no longer care.
    I am sick of living. Nothing matters;
    innocent or guilty, God will destroy us.
When an innocent person suddenly dies,
    God laughs.
God gave the world to the wicked.
    He made all the judges blind.
    And if God didn't do it, who did?

                           (Job 9.15–24)

Job's voice is the authentic voice of suffering. His is the voice of the sick, the marginalized and the poor. He knows the horror of God laughing. Has God 'left undone those things which [he] ought to have done'? Does God indeed share our guilt?

A nurse told me that she and her mother went to visit a dying friend. The friend was riddled with disease and in searing, constant pain. The nurse was wildly angry. Partly at her own profession. Partly at herself, at her guilt for being part of such an uncaring profession. She had seen some horrific things in her career – but this was unimaginable. It seemed as though God had forgotten the dying woman. She was lingering in agony until God, like a child with a discarded toy, finally got round to her.

The nurse stepped away from the bed and began to scream silently at God. The strength of her anger and the violence of her language shocked her. She shouted silent, obscene curses at God. She needed to remind God of what he *ought* to be doing. She cried to God to let her friend die. Finally she left the room, still hurt and angry. God was not absent – he was merely absent-minded. A few minutes later her friend died. God had been reminded of his duty and had eventually done what was required.

This experience still haunts her. At various times she has different explanations for its meaning. What she wasn't prepared for was the strength of her feelings. She feels somewhat guilty for the violence of them but still feels that they were justified. It was as though God had simply forgotten his duty. Her experience reflects that of the Psalmist:

> Wake up, Lord! Why are you asleep?
> Rouse yourself! Don't reject us for ever!
> Why are you hiding from us?
> Don't forget our suffering and trouble!
>
> (Psalm 44.23f.)

This strand of the biblical material we have edited out of the Christian tradition. The idea that we can argue with God and fight with God and complain to God about his shortcomings seem to us impious. But a strand within Scripture outspokenly blames God. 'The harsh reality of life has forced the community to ask probing questions about faith, and to these questions there are no immediate or easy answers.'[38] Ancient Israel had room for screams of pain from the oppressed, room to doubt God's goodness. More than one third of the Psalms are laments. Anger is expressed towards God and humanity. The Psalms and Lamentations are in the Bible because they are the religious experience of people. Cries of 'How long?' and 'Why?' are not new, they were 'repeatedly discovered to be as authentic as cries of "Hallelujah"'. In the Jewish tradition God can be prevailed upon to listen and even to change his mind.

> At last the Lord woke up as though from sleep;
> he was like a strong man excited by wine.
>
> (Psalm 78.65)

An impassive, unchanging God comes from Greek philosophy not the Judeo-Christian tradition. Jesus talks of 'my father'. This is a personal, not a universal, fatherhood. God as the Father of all created beings is alien to the Bible. It comes more from Greek philosophy and mythology than from the Jewish setting of Jesus. The idea of creation/fatherhood is biological. Zeus may have had sexual relationships with human beings but the Judeo-Christian God does not. Mary, the *Theotokos* – the God-bearer – has no sexual relationship with God. She is not Leda and Jesus is not a demi-god.

The biblical concept of God's fatherhood is of relationship. We tend to view the story of the prodigal son through a tradition that makes the prodigal the hero of the drama. The narrative follows him to a far country and charts his eventual return. In first-century Palestine he was the villain. The real hero is the son who stays behind and continues to do the father's will. He is prepared to continue in the right relationship of son to father, a subordinate position. His father remains the head of the household. The prodigal is welcomed back to demonstrate the father's love and forgiveness, but the story still stresses the relationship of right activity: 'Whoever does what God wants him to do', said Jesus, 'is my brother, my sister and my mother.' God is father because he is obeyed like a father. And God the father allows, indeed causes, suffering. To the Lamentations poet, God was actively to blame.

I am one who knows what it is to be punished by God.
He drove me deeper and deeper into darkness
And beat me again and again with merciless blows.

He has left my flesh open and raw, and has broken my bones.
He has shut me in a prison of misery and anguish.
He has forced me to live in the stagnant darkness of death.

He has bound me in chains; I am a prisoner with no hope of
   escape.
I cry aloud for help, but God refuses to listen;
I stagger as I walk; stone walls block me wherever I turn.

He waited for me like a bear; he pounced on me like a lion.
He chased me off the road, tore me to pieces, and left me.
He drew his bow and made me the target for his arrows.
He shot his arrows deep into my body.
People laugh at me all day long; I am a joke to them all.
Bitter suffering is all he has given me for food and drink.

He rubbed my face in the ground and broke my teeth on the
   gravel.
I have forgotten what health and peace and happiness are.
I have not much longer to live; my hope in the Lord is gone.

The thought of my pain, my homelessness, is bitter poison;
I think of it constantly and my spirit is depressed.
Yet hope returns when I remember this one thing.'

(Lamentations 3.1–21)

*Theodicy: playing dice with God!*

But in anger there is dialogue, allowing the possibility of reconciliation. With indifference dialogue ceases and relationship is severed. For too many people anger faded because anger against God is frowned upon in the Church (many others have maintained their anger and abandoned the Church). In this attitude the Church ignores an important element of the scriptural tradition, the anger and pain of the Old Testament poetry. The Church has driven the hurtful side of experience either into obscure corners of faith practice or completely out of Christian worship, but 'the *pain at the centre of praise* has theological warrant in Israel in the cries of hurt, rage, doubt, vengeance, and isolation'.[39]

But in anger is continuing relationship. God is shouted at, screamed at, argued with, sworn at, but not denied. 'Even in Auschwitz countless Jews and also some Christians believed in the God who despite all the terrors was nevertheless hiddenly present. [...] They trusted and – this is often overlooked – prayed even in the hell of Auschwitz.'[40] The prayer and the shouting and the imprecations and the angry fists shaken at the empty sky keep communication between human and God open. To ask 'Why me?' is not wrong. To scream to God to wake up is not wrong. These reactions are in an odd way hopeful. God is still there for us to shout at even if he is 'hiddenly present'. The relationship persists. The poet of the Lamentations, even in his anger and pain, still holds on to the relationship.

> The Lord's unfailing love and mercy still continue,
> Fresh as the morning, as sure as the sunrise.
> The Lord is all I have, and so I put my hope in him.
>
> (Lamentations 3.22ff.)

God cannot be condemned for the actions of human beings but neither can he be wholly absolved. If he is indeed the creator he set the ground rules in which human beings can create such suffering as happened in the destruction of Jerusalem in 586 BCE. And indeed as happened in the Nazi death camps. The Nazis are responsible. But so is the wartime British government which refused to acknowledge the rumours of the death camps when they first leaked out of Nazi Germany. The sin of omission, not doing anything about it, is no less real than the sin of commission.

'God is guilty. It is time for evening prayers.' God is guilty but he remains the only hope. He is all that remains.

It is into this sense of bleakness and guilt, which we feel we somehow share with God, that Jesus comes to us as the incarnate God. Jesus comes, not as sinless, spotless and dehumanized, but as someone who participates in our guilt by partaking in our humanity. And he bears what seems like God's guilt by participating in his deity. In the cross, God can no longer be seen as shirking his responsibility. In the cross, Jesus freely chooses to accept responsibility. The obedience even to the cross is not then to an undeserved punishment. It is a partaking of and a participating with. Jesus suffers for and with us because he shares our very humanness.

This does not allow us to push our responsibility off on to God. By sharing responsibility, moral problems become harder not easier. Guilt is shared but not avoided. And God shares the moral dilemmas by partaking in them. The responsibility for the evil actions of an individual is not avoided, it too is shared. By sharing our humanness, we share the responsibility for all of the activity of the community. Indeed, we share responsibility for the whole world through its inter-relatedness. As we become aware of distant events, they can no longer be ignored. So Hitler does not bear all of the blame for the Holocaust. He did not exist in isolation. All humanity shares the responsibility for the Holocaust. Every single human shares in the responsibility for the hungry child. Every single person participates in the responsibility for the victim.

In the same way, God shares responsibility by appearing not to intervene. If anything, his guilt seems worse. Those times when we perceive God intervening appear irrational. There is the story of the atheist at Lourdes who challenges God, if there is a God, to heal the desperately damaged child kneeling next to him. The atheist stands, healed. The child is carried away unchanged. The Spirit might, like the wind, blow where he wishes, but why in such an irrational way?

On the cross, Jesus became the means by which we could be forgiven. In Mark's Gospel, as we saw, Jesus continually extends the boundaries: between ethnic groups, Jew and Gentile; between ethical groups, those under the Law and those who weren't. He reaches out across the gender boundaries. He even transcends the boundary between the living and the dead. And he becomes the gate

174

in the boundary between the human and the divine. In him the categories of natural and supernatural no longer work. By participating in Christ and his cross, we are not restrained by boundaries.

On the cross, Jesus also becomes the means by which God can be forgiven. The boundary is transcended in both directions at once. Movement becomes possible between divine and human, and between human and divine. The Lord's Prayer talks of reciprocal forgiveness. 'Forgive us our debts, as we forgive our debtors.' We can now forgive God for we feel the need to forgive God for what he has put us through. Jesus' cross rebuilds the bridge between earth and heaven. The earthly Jesus and the risen Christ are one and the same. We now look from beyond the events of Easter. The author of Mark's Gospel recognized the continuity. His Jesus is continually seen through the experience of a church that knows the living Lord, the Christ.

We can forgive God those things that have happened to us through the cross. But we can only forgive those things that have happened to us. We cannot – we have no right – to forgive on behalf of someone else. We cannot forgive on behalf of, say, the Holocaust victims. We were not the victims. The Lord's Prayer talks of us asking God's forgiveness for those who have sinned against us. It does not ask God's forgiveness for the sins our neighbours commit against each other. On the cross, according to Luke's Gospel, Jesus asked for God's forgiveness to be expressed to those who were crucifying him. The suffering of God has become a reality because he suffers and participates fully in the cross. For the healing of ourselves, we need to forgive God. And for the healing of the suffering, crucified God we too need to reach out in forgiveness.

There is resentment against God for allowing us to suffer. By forgiving God, this sense of resentment and anger can be dealt with. If God seems, to us, to be capricious and negligent then this needs to be addressed by forgiving him. The God who finds parking spaces for Charismatics but is not concerned about the agony of a suffering world needs to be addressed. In the cross, God can find our forgiveness too.

In the worship of the Church there is a sense of incomplete reconciliation. This is not merely because of the unfinished nature of creation. It is not just because the eschaton is not yet fully here. In the liturgy of the Eucharist, there is a space for confessing one's sin to God. This allows for God's forgiveness to be sought and obtained. Confessing and willingly turning away from one's misdeeds allows for God's forgiveness to be experienced. This allows for partial reconciliation between the worshipper and God. The exchange of the peace allows forgiveness and reconciliation to occur between people. Theoretically, at this point one can go to another person and sort out a problem that exists before joining the heavenly feast.

There is, however, no space for the worshipper to acknowledge the experience that God has allowed evil to happen. Therefore the worshipper is not given the opportunity to express their anger and hurt and grief against God. There is no provision for forgiving God. There remains a barrier. It might be subjective but the resentment remains. And this needs to be dealt with. While the worshipper is resentful of God there can be no full reconciliation. So any reconciliation between heaven and earth remains partial. God has reached out to forgive us but we do not respond and reach back. By not acknowledging what we perceive of as God's guilt we allow the resentment to fester and damage our whole relationship. By extension, our whole life is marred.

On the cross Jesus acknowledged that he felt that God had abandoned him. Through the cross we can echo that acknowledgement and forgive God for our similar experience. The cross is a bridge and the traffic is not just one way! God is the one who forgives. God is the one who receives forgiveness. And God is the means by which forgiveness is made possible. God is discovered in his self-offering. He is discovered in the humanity of Jesus, God's self-communication.

Classical theodicy has to remain largely irrelevant. Our relationship to the unfairness of it all continues to some extent to be one of bewilderment. But in this bewilderment we find God. He shares the responsibility. There can be no logical explanation for the sense of injustice. In the end we stand, as Job did, as Jesus did, railing at an apparently uncaring universe. But we stand at the foot of the cross looking up at the true face of God. A twisted agonized face. A face that shows the reality of human suffering. And we hear a voice that is full of pain. The dying Jesus is asking for forgiveness for those who roll dice at the foot of the cross. In his death he makes the forgiveness real both for the dice-players below him and for the dice-player of the universe. God and humanity meet in forgiveness at the cross.

*Theodicy: playing dice with God!*

## NOTES

1 Tolkien, J. R. R., 'On Fairy Stories', *Tree and Leaf, Smith of Wootton Major, and The Homecoming of Beorhtnoth Beorhthelm's Son*, Unwin, London, 1975 p. 71.

2 John Paul II, 'On Sickness and Suffering', text of an address given at a service for the sick in St George's Cathedral, Southwark on 28 May 1982, in Coyle, T. (ed.), *Christian Ministry to the Sick*. Geoffrey Chapman, London, 1986, p. xvii.

3 John Paul II in Coyle, *Christian Ministry*, pp. xviif.

4 Duncan, D., *Health and Healing: a ministry to wholeness*. St Andrew Press, Edinburgh, 1988, p. 57.

5 Wilkinson, J., in a paper to the Standing Committee on Health and Healing of the General Assembly of the Church of Scotland, cited Duncan, *Health and Healing*, pp. 56f.

6 See Pattison, S., *Alive and Kicking: towards a practical theology of health and healing*. SCM, London, 1989, pp. 21–45.

7 Morris, D., *The Pocket Guide to Manwatching: a field guide to human behaviour*. Jonathan Cape, London, 1977, p. 279.

8 Connor, S. and Kingman, S, *The Search for the Virus*. Penguin, Harmondsworth, 1989, p. 257.

9 Royston Pike, E., 'Edwin Chadwick', in Canning, J., ed., *One Hundred Great Nineteenth Century Lives*. Century, London, 1983, p. 387.

10 Wood, A., *Nineteenth Century Britain 1815–1914*. Longmans, London, 1960, p. 121.

11 Pattison, *Alive and Kicking*, p. 27.

12 Pattison, *Alive and Kicking*, p. 28.

13 Pattison, *Alive and Kicking*, p. 28.

14 Masamba Ma Mpolo, J., 'Spirituality and Counselling for Health and Liberation', in Lartey, E., Nwachuku, D. and Wa Kasonga, K. (eds), *The Church and Healing: echoes from Africa*. Peter Lang, Frankfurt am Main, 1994, p. 23.

15 Masamba Ma Mpolo, in Lartey *et al.* (eds), *Church and Healing*, p. 23.

16 Connor and Kingman, *Search for the Virus*, pp. 224f.

17 Lambourne, R. A., *Community, Church and Healing: a study of some of the corporate aspects of the Church's ministry to the sick*. DLT, London, 1963, p. 48.

18 Lambourne, *Community, Church and Healing*, p. 120.

19 Lambourne, *Community, Church and Healing*, p. 123.

20 MacNutt, F., *Healing*. Ave Maria Press, Notre Dame, IN, 1974, p. 92.

21 See, for example, Wilson, M., *The Church is Healing*. SCM, London, 1966.

22 Bonhoeffer, D., *Letters from Prison*, cited in Kelsey, M., *Healing and Christianity*. SCM, London, 1973, p. 225.

177

23 Shegel, R., 'The Impossible Spectator', *Sixth Centennial Lecture at Michigan State University* (1975).
24 McGrath, A., *The Enigma of the Cross*. Hodder & Stoughton, London, 1987, p. 52.
25 Newton, I., letter to Robert Hooke dated 5 February 1675/6, quoted in *Oxford Dictionary of Quotations* (3rd edn), Oxford, OUP.
26 Polyani, M., quoted in McGrath, *Enigma of the Cross*, p. 53.
27 Wordsworth, W., 'The Borderers', *The Complete Poetical Works of William Wordsworth*, Macmillan, London, 1888.
28 Schillebeeckx, E., *Jesus: an experiment in Christology*. Collins, London, 1979, p. 19.
29 Hick, J., *Evil and the God of Love*. Macmillan, London, 1966, p. 5.
30 Stendahl, quoted in Hick, *Evil*, p. xi.
31 Hick, *Evil*, p. 221.
32 Schleiermacher, F., *The Christian Faith*, cited in Hick, *Evil*, p. 234.
33 Cupitt, D., *Taking Leave of God*. SPCK, London, 1980, p. 89.
34 Hick, *Evil*, p. 21.
35 see Kushner, H., *When Bad Things Happen to Good People*. Pan, London, 1981.
36 Rubinowicz, D., trans. D. Bowman, *The Diary of Dawid Rubinowicz*. William Blackwood, Edinburgh, 1981, p. 87.
37 quoted in Küng, H., *Judaism: the religious situation of our time*. SCM, London, 1992, p. 608.
38 Davidson, R., *The Courage to Doubt: exploring an Old Testament theme*. SCM, London, 1983, p. 8.
39 Brueggermann, W., *Israel's Praise: doxology against idolatry and ideology*. Fortress Press, Philadelphia, 1989, p. 133.
40 Küng, *Judaism*, p. 607.

# 6

# *The end and the beginning: fitting the jigsaw together*

To go back to the beginning, David's behaviour was suddenly changed. He was healed of an obsessive ritual. He was no longer besieged by drumming for twenty per cent of his waking life. But his learning difficulties remain. This sums up the problem with Christian healing. It seems to have no logic, no justice, no sense. If God can heal, why doesn't he do it properly? Although the drumming is largely a thing of the past, David remains a withdrawn young man needing twenty-four-hour care. There is, however, an incredible degree of improvement; his quality of life is much improved.

Christine has recently been diagnosed with Multiple Sclerosis and her eyesight continues to deteriorate. Yet she continues to claim the experience of being healed by God during the birth of her youngest son. And this experience of partial or inner healing while the disease or impairment remains unchecked is not uncommon. The shared sense of a compelling presence or even, perhaps, of a compelling absence at the moment of greatest despair points to the reality of the experience. There is a commonality in experience, pointing to objective reality. The shared participation and observation make the nature of the observation more than just subjective.

Mel was hurt by Christians who, she feels, gave her unrealistic expectations. To be told her lack of faith keeps her in the wheelchair is itself disabling, stigmatizing her for her impairment. The Church has a peculiar knack of disabling people with impairments. Full access for wheelchair users to both sides of the Communion table, and large-print hymn books and Bibles, are only a beginning. Loop systems work for hearing-aid users but not for someone who is profoundly deaf. For worship to be sign-assisted is ambitious but not unrealistic. People with learning difficulties

179

need more than just a few colouring books to keep them quiet! Access is external. People with impairments are disabled by human environment and attitude. To stigmatize people with impairments is an attitude. We need a change of direction, of heart. Mel is not an incomplete human, she is whole as she is! She has an image of herself that is positive – she is as God planned her to be.

> You it was who fashioned my inward parts;
> You knitted me together in my mother's womb. [. . .]
> You know me through and through:
> My body was no mystery to you.
>
> (Psalm 139.13f. REB)

A Mel who has not shared her life – including Friedreich's Ataxia – is not Mel. God consciously chose to pattern her as he has. She is not a failed creation, not abnormal; she is an ordinary, complete human being.

The difference between diseases which can broadly be termed 'functional' and those which are 'organic' has been long recognized. *Malleus Maleficarum*, the fifteenth-century encyclopedia of witchcraft, distinguished 'subjective' and 'objective' causation. Spiritual healing seems to have positive benefit in functional illnesses. Symptoms are alleviated in some organic diseases. Some cancers can be affected by will-power or faith-healing or Christian healing and occasionally cancer patients recover spontaneously. There is a link between physical sickness and mental process and spirituality but the mechanics of the links remain elusive. Partial or symptomatic healing is not uncommon, while complete healing is rare.

John A. T. Robinson suggested that *complete* healing can be only possible when the Kingdom we pray for comes. 'Usually, [Jesus] speaks of the Kingdom as merely having "drawn near". [. . .] in his acts of healing the kingdom of God has "come upon" or overtaken those he is addressing – and the Greek word [used in Luke 11.20] contains within it the idea of something that has come before its time.'[1] Although Easter changes the world utterly, all creation still groans in labour. Everything is different while everything remains the same.

It is most important to remember that this is the perspective in which the whole of the New Testament's teaching on health is set. [...] It is quite evidently not God's will that death shall be done away with within this age. Even those whom Jesus raises from the dead have to die again – and they must die of something. Jesus shows that he is even now the resurrection and the life – for body as well as for soul – as he is even now healer of all our diseases. But he does not go around raising men from the dead for its own sake or even for their sakes.[2]

Lazarus will die again. Disease and death are defeated by the cross but not yet. They continue. But the Kingdom still comes upon some people and they experience healing here and now.

God heals as a sign of his coming Kingdom but this seems the work of a callous and capricious God. If healings are signs of God's promise then why is God-healing so random? At Lourdes only a tiny, almost insignificant proportion is systemically healed. Thousands sense relief but the percentage organically healed seem an insult to those who are not. However, many of those who seek healing at Lourdes are like Mel, Christine and David, and not ill. They cannot be cured of being themselves. Children are taken by parents as Mel was to Fatima, parents wanting the best for children, thinking that impairment is illness.

The healings recorded by Mark are representative signs. The man with paralysis, whose friends show a pattern for faith and care, has the microcosm of society healed as he is healed, showing illness as not directly caused by sin. The person, unemployable because of his withered hand, returns to full economic health, showing how suffering's urgency overrides ritual. The man possessed by the mob, a Gentile with chronic mental illness, returns to family and friends empowered with Good News. The woman, once ritually unclean, is restored to health, to full social, ritual, sexual and economic life, showing Jesus' accessibility to male and female equally – even if women have to fight through a patriarchal society to achieve it! The girl is restored to her family from the jaws of death, baptized and communicant. The boy's story shows the value of faith that has honest doubts and the need for continuous and passionate prayer. In Mark the Kingdom reaches out to include marginalized people, but their stories are included to make specific teaching points, not because they are biographical details of Jesus' life. Carers are praised for faith and included. The unemployed are restored to employment and included. Gentiles are given status.

181

Women are shown that equality is worth struggling for. The girl and the boy show the importance of children in God's people. For some the Kingdom has come upon them now. For others the Kingdom is drawing near. Healing in Mark is the fulfilment of God's eschatological promise in history.

The Christian Church has for centuries offered an abusive ministry of healing. It has neither offered truth nor delivered good news. It has been at once both arrogant and timid. To put the hand of a centuries-dead saint on to the face of someone with partial sight or to tell someone that if they had enough faith they could get out of the wheelchair are just other examples of the abuse of the power that the able-bodied continually exert over the disabled person. In the same way, prayer without the expectation of God's action is an insulting abuse of God's grace. Week by week churches pray for the sick in the same breath as praying for world peace or an end to world poverty, and with as little expectation. They are gestures made for the sake of form. The Roman emperor Julian the Apostate accused Christians of being odd because they were forever consorting with the sick. But nowadays people who are sick or who have an impairment are marginalized as much by Christians as by society generally. Francis of Assisi may have embraced a person with leprosy but this Christian approach to people with illness or impairments no longer distinguishes the Church!

The Church has forgotten to engage in the struggle with the injustice of sickness. Churches in the one-third world have begun to re-engage with bringing Good News to the poor as having meaning beyond mere words. The Christian community claims to be biased towards the marginalized but leaves the struggle with the injustice of illness to medical practitioners who mistakenly see the battle as one against death not injustice. When we ignore the struggle we ignore the insights of those who would share the struggle with us.[3]

I had another pupil whom I shall call Luke, who appeared to be continually bewildered. He was diagnosed as extremely violent and kept heavily sedated. Occasionally I would take pupils into local churches to sit quietly. Peace and quiet was rare for these young people, residential schools for pupils with challenging behaviour being frequently chaotic. Sleep is broken by screaming. Tantrums go on all night. People run up and down corridors shouting.

Rhythmic rocking, possible to ignore during the day, seems louder at night. And disturbed nights affect everyone. Sleepy, irritable pupils are roused, bathed and dressed by irritable, exhausted night-care staff. Days beginning like this continue to go downhill.

One day I took Luke and Dennis, another pupil, to church in a nearby town for the mid-week Eucharist. We slid into a back pew, sat quietly and watched. It was a hot summer's day and the cool was welcome. We began to relax. The building was too large to be oppressive, yet still safely enclosed. The sense of quiet was almost tangible. Then the priest began to pray for the mentally ill. As he prayed Luke began to wail in a strange, high-pitched ululating voice akin to a police siren. As he wailed people turned round to give us angry looks. I became embarrassed and tried to shuffle Luke out. His wail became louder, now signalling distress. The congregation projected a mixture of aggression and fear. I picked up their feelings and transferred them on to Luke. He responded with extraordinary stubbornness and even louder wailing. At the moment when the priest prayed for the mentally ill, Luke began his unearthly ululation. Luke has severe learning difficulties, he did not understand what the priest said. He just chose exactly the right moment to wail.

Luke has learning difficulties and is mentally ill. The two must not be confused. People with learning difficulties are not ill but anyone *can* become mentally ill. People with learning disabilities have the same chance of mental illness as anyone else. We went out. Luke was, by now, distressed. He wanted to stay and I had forced him outside. I transferred my embarrassment to Luke. I was exasperated and I was angry. I felt excluded from the Eucharist. It was OK to pray for the mentally ill but quite another to let them in. Luke's distress came from my hurt. I used my power and made him powerless. My attempt to give him a sense of self, of peace and quiet, had backfired. I felt marginalized, excommunicated, excluded from the presence of Christ. In my turn, I used physical strength to expel Luke from Christ. What for me was metaphorical exclusion was for him reality.

The congregation must have thought we were poking fun at them. We were three scruffy men sitting in the back and locally there was fear of 'hippies' or 'New Age travellers' following a major music festival. Travellers were blamed for spreading disease, leaving syringes around and stealing sheep. In an area dependent on wool since the Middle Ages, the last was most heinous! Local feeling was running high. Anyone looking, dressing and acting 'differently' was shunned.

Saint Simeon el Salo is the patron saint of puppeteers and a particular favourite. Dictionaries usually describe saints as mystics or abbots or bishops, but Simeon is described as eccentric. He 'devoted himself to caring for the most wretched and neglected among the people, especially harlots. To share the contempt in which social outcasts were held, he behaved in such strange ways that he was nicknamed "the crazy" (*salus*). So outrageous did his behaviour become, if it was reported correctly, that it seems likely that he was at times really out of his mind.'[4]

Since the abortive visit to the Priory Luke has been there again. Informal links have been made between some residential staff and the church. Luke went to a wedding there and the church is perhaps a little more accepting of strange behaviours. Was Luke's peculiar cry prophetic? Did Luke become a 'fool for Christ's sake', changing life in the Priory? Simeon el Salo was variously seen as both a hypocritical rascal and a prophetic, holy monk. The line between prophecy and lunacy might not be easy to draw.

The church in Corinth believed that physical and mental wholeness was a sign of God's favour. Paul comes to them with some kind of impairment – *asthenia*, sickness or weakness or a disability. 'The literal meaning of asthenia as a physical sickness has particular force in the Corinthian context. In the eyes of a community, which recognized healing as a sign of God's presence (1 Corinthians 12.9f., 29f.), the existence of a sick apostle can only suggest the lack of spiritual power.'[5] Paul denies spiritual weakness and continues: '[. . .] on the contrary, much rather those members of the body that seem to be naturally (*huparchein*) somewhat feeble are necessary'.[6] The members of the body that seem naturally weaker are, in reality, indispensable. These members are weaker because of nature, how the world is. It is not a judgement. There is no condemnation – in fact, the opposite is true.

Paul likens Christ's body to a human body. Paul is, as commentators point out, referring to the genitals by the 'naturally weaker' parts. Paul is using *asthenia* in its usual sense of bodily weakness or impairment. It is not shameful to be weak or impaired; on the contrary, this is natural and a specific gift of God. 'God has constructed the body in the way that he has to give more abundant honour to the parts that are impaired' (my translation). The genitals[7] are not clothed because they are shameful. They are clothed to denote special status, just as crowns denote royalty. And in the same way as the genitals are honoured by clothing, the person with a physical weakness is honoured by God with special status. The impaired person, the sick person and the weak person have been chosen by God to have special status in the community.

There is status for people who have impairment or illness. Theirs is the centre. This is not something allowed by the able-bodied – God alone appoints to the place of honour. The person who is sick or who has a disability is, according to Paul, God's chosen cohesion in the church. The centre is denied to the able-bodied! The person who is weak or the person who is sick or the person who has an impairment is the very ikon of God's presence, the very image of God. In the Kingdom the world's values are turned upside down – the first last and the last first.

God has chosen to be identified with the person who is broken and impaired. In Jesus the person whipped by the scourge of illness is healed. Jesus released the woman with the haemorrhage from her scourging, taking the blows himself (Isaiah 53.5, Mark 15.15). He took the image and reality of impairment upon himself at the cross. In Jesus on the cross, the person who is broken is recognized as God's child (Mark 15.39). On the cross Jesus is mocked for impairment (Mark 15.31). He is unable to save himself. He is no longer able-bodied – if he ever saw himself as such – Jesus' self-identification is with Isaiah's physically impaired suffering servant, 'so disfigured that he hardly looked human'. Jesus is impaired, disabled by the nails that hold him on the cross, preventing movement. He is quadriplegic, all limbs paralysed. He is disabled by the mockery he receives. So a person who is sick or a person with an impairment is welcomed as being the image of Christ in the Kingdom.

Thus a person with impairment or illness is a prophetic voice in the Church. People who are ill are sent to the fringes of society, particularly those with mental illness. 'Odd' behaviours cause a person to be shunned and isolated in the community. But the Church is the community in which Christ, the one who has the single ministry of healer and proclaimer, is made real. In this community, the body of Christ, God has placed the person with a weakness, an impairment, an illness. And God has chosen this person as his own instrument of cohesion for the community. The person with *asthenia* is the glue that holds Christ's body together.

Mark stresses the importance of community: Jesus goes to the edge of society to include the outsider. Jesus' healing affects every sphere of existence: it has social effects, people returned to families and friends; economic effects, people able to take financial responsibility for themselves; physical effects, strength and health returned; and, spiritual effects; relationship with God restored. The cosmic powers felt to oppress humanity were exorcized.

Healing is of primary importance to the Jesus portrayed in Scripture – forty per cent of Mark's Gospel, almost certainly the earliest, is taken up with healing stories. The Passion narrative aside (a quarter of the Gospel), Mark's major concern is Jesus and health. Mark's risen Lord, the Christ, is healer. In Irenaeus' time health was still considered of first importance, and in his *Adversus Haereses* he describes the practice of his day.

- The authority for performing any miracles is *His Name* (i.e. the name of Jesus Christ).
- The mechanism by which miracles are performed is *grace from Him*.
- The aim is to *promote the welfare of others*.
- Different people receive different gifts. *Some [...] drive out devils [...] Others [...] heal the sick.*
- The result is sometimes conversion: *those [...] frequently both believe in Christ and join themselves to the Church* (i.e. healing and exorcism are mission activities).
- The *dead are raised.*
- The practice of *laying on hands* is for making the sick whole.
- The gifts are *for the benefit of nations*. They are not for insiders.
- It is all to be open and above board, without *any deception*.
- No money is to change hands, *no-one takes any reward [...] For as she has freely received from God, freely does she minister.*[8]

Irenaeus points to 'the gifts which all over the world the Church has received from the Lord, and put into action day by day, in the name of Christ Jesus'. Healing is one of the charismatic gifts visible in the Church every day. In the experience of this highly educated, intelligent and critical writer the Church is a community of faith expressed in action. While, at a later date, Abba Benjamin healed by virtue of personal holiness, Irenaeus describes the gifts as directly from the Lord, mediated through the Church rather than individuals. While individuals receive gifts, their use proceeds out of the community of faith.

In the first century a person's name invoked their authority. Jesus' authority was used both with permission and without – power/authority could be hijacked. The woman with the haemorrhage *steals* Jesus' power. But any infringement of rules is waived because of the emergency, she has no time to waste. But, as Irenaeus stresses, the mechanism for healing is God's grace; and, as Paul discovered, God's grace is enough.

> To keep me from being puffed up with pride because of the many wonderful things I saw, I was given a painful physical ailment, which acts as Satan's messenger to beat me and keep me from being proud. Three times I prayed to the Lord about this and asked him to take it away. But his answer was: 'My grace is all you need, for my power is greatest when you are weak.'

> (2 Corinthians 12.7ff.)

Paul had a disability, a weakness, an *asthenia* – his thorn in the flesh, a periodically painful condition. Three times he prays specifically for healing and even a saint such as Paul is not healed. Neither is Jesus released from his disability – the cross. Prayer does not guarantee physical healing, nor can the medical profession. Prayer, however, demands an answer!

The Church uses Jesus' name daily in worship, acknowledging that 'at the name of Jesus every knee shall bow'. Jesus' name is invoked for healing or in intercession, but without the sense that the name invokes the person names are no more than a set of phonemes, the sounds by which we are called. In our culture we have no sense that a person's virtue is intimately involved in their name. Shakespeare's Juliet asks Romeo to change his name. "Tis but thy name that is my enemy. [...] What's in a name? that which we call a rose by any other name would smell as sweet. [...] Romeo, doff thy name; And for thy name, which is no part of thee, Take all myself.' Biblical writers, though, thought the name as much a part of a person as their body or their personality. 'In the Bible a person's name was his being, not just his label, so when his life changed, his name changed too. After wrestling with the angel, Jacob (which means "heel", possibly in the modern sense too) became Israel (someone who struggles with God).'[9] When Saul becomes Paul it is more than a change of heart, it is a change of person, a new creation in Christ. Jesus *is* saviour because he is called saviour. His name, 'Yahweh saves', means that, through him, God brings salvation. In the same way God's name – Yahweh, *I am that I am*, is more than a word, it is the very essence of God distilled into sound. So it is with the name Jesus. In New Testament usage, the very salvation of God comes when his name is invoked.

In our world a name is just a word. So by invoking the name of Jesus, we invoke no more than the word, the sound alone, and not Jesus himself. The immanent physical, material person of the Christ has been replaced by the word 'Jesus'. By divorcing the name from the person the living heart has been torn from the liturgy.

We think of the liturgy as those stilted words said by priests. Nothing could be farther from the truth! Liturgy is the work (*ergon*) of the laity (*laos*). It is the common work of the community. In ancient Greece, *leitourgia* was civic duty. It was a responsibility to perform public works, like providing arms to defend the city. In its original secular sense liturgy was the social equivalent of the department of public works. And the liturgy – the sharing of material bread and material wine – is the most materialist thing that the Church does. The people *did* liturgy, they did not *say* it!

The things of all God's people became progressively professionalized throughout Church history. Saints were once all of the ordinary Christians. Miracles were expected by every Christian and church community. Saints then withdrew to the desert and miracles went with them. The signs of God's Kingdom became the business of the super-Christian, the extraordinary and the eccentric. So rare did miracles become that they were symbolic of sanctity and not of God's Kingdom. So Vianney's fictitious Philomena was credited with miracles. Vianney even gave the credit to the saint, and only incidentally to God. For Augustine and Luther and Wesley and Vianney physical healing was not expected. It came as a complete surprise. My own experience confirms this. I 'went along' with the prompting of the Spirit. I had no expectations. What happened came as a total shock. My negative experiences with Christian healing in the early house church movement had left me suspicious of healing. But I cannot remain untouched by the temporary *charism* that I experienced then and occasionally since. But, generally, the eccentric and the extra-ordinary became institutionalized. With institutionalization, the imputed powers of the saints were adopted and absorbed. The institution increased its power both in the secular world and in the spiritual. The people were disenfranchised, their power slowly and subtly drawn into the structure.

The oil of the sick too became clericalized. Polycarp said that the clergy had a duty to look after the sick. In the third century deacons were asked to tell the bishop who was sick and arrange a visit, 'for it is a great comfort to the sick person that the chief priest should remember him'. But the bishop did not anoint.

> Despite what we might have expected from the letter of St James, anointing does not seem to have been part of this clerical ministry. Instead people took their own oil along to the Eucharist for it to be formally blessed by the bishop, according to Hippolytus, at the end of the Eucharistic prayer. They took it home again and kept it by them for use when they or any of their household or neighbours took ill [...] this use in sickness was utterly unstructured and open-ended: the oil could be applied externally by oneself or another, or taken internally, and its application could be repeated as a course of treatment until the condition improved. There was no ceremony, and it was not considered to have anything to do with dying or the danger of death, as we see from the fact that it was used for all sorts of con-ditions – blindness, boils, cuts and bruises, as much as for serious organic disorders. [10]

While anointing was a ministry of the people it was part of the very ordinary things of life. Food was taken to be blessed by the bishop; bread, wine, milk, honey, cheese, olives and olive oil were all used in the Eucharist. The ordinary things of life show the physicality that the Eucharist then enjoyed.

Anointing too is a materialistic practice – it uses the same oil for cooking and lighting and medication. Necessities of life were brought to the communal Eucharistic celebration to be blessed and taken home for use. The same oil was used for lighting and cooking and healing because God's healing was not magic – it was normal. Later, the oil itself became regarded as holy and anointing was reserved to the clergy. Professional Christians – priests and bishops – visited the sick, and this soon became the official visit of the Body of Christ. Then the visit of the Church. This continues – some people will not accept a visit from the lay ministry team instead of a visit from the vicar! There was nothing left for ordinary Christians to do!

For the Christian life is to be one of continual prayer. 'Pray without ceasing', Paul wrote, echoing Jesus' 'Always pray' – a general command to all Christians. But even prayer has been professionalized. It didn't take long before the early Christian communities followed the pattern of the Jerusalem Temple. Acts 3.1 implies that the disciples continued the Temple's threefold daily prayer tradition: morning, afternoon and evening. Rabbinical tradition suggested that to exceed this was to bother God: 'God must not be wearied with incessant prayer. A man ought not to pray more than three times a day. Hourly prayer is forbidden.'[11] But Jesus had challenged this tradition by suggesting that prayer be continual, and Paul echoed this. But as the Christian Church became more formalized, so did prayer. When the monastic communities began in the fourth century, prayer became more the job of the 'religious' than the laity. 'By the middle of the fifth century the basilica churches of Rome began to have attached to them religious communities which were responsible for singing the full round of daily offices there, and thus monasticism came to exercise a strong influence on the worship of the city.'[12] This 'full round' was probably – *Nocturnes* (the night office, originally at midnight); *Matins* (which followed on directly from Nocturnes); *Prime* (at the first hour, 6 a.m.); *Terce* (at the third hour, 9 a.m.); *Sext* (at the sixth hour, Noon); *None* (at the ninth hour, 3 p.m.); *Vespers* (at sunset); and *Compline* (before bed). This pattern was impossible for the ordinary Christian.

The idea of unceasing prayer became a professional calling. And continual prayer became a ritual cycle of prayers. The nine-times-a-day prayer of monastic tradition became the universal standard. Human nature tends to routinize what was once spontaneous and the routine was impossible for ordinary people with work to do. So the lay people became slowly content to leave prayer to the religious communities and the religious professionals. Formalized, routine prayer took the place of personal interaction with God. Instead of 'everything you do or say, then, should be done in the name of

190

the Lord Jesus, as you give thanks through him to God the Father' (Colossians 3.17), prayer became a formal, routine hour on a Sunday morning; and it became the job of the vicar to do the praying – with the added superstition that the vicar's prayers are more powerful.

This professionalized prayer has been heavily edited. Formal prayer does not include the anguish of the marginalized. It does not cry out 'Oh God, why?' on behalf of the mother whose child is dying. It does not groan 'My God, my God, why have you deserted me?' on behalf of the dying. It does not include the angry 'How long, O God?' of the disenfranchised, the slave, the poor. It does not make, with the person with disabilities, the outraged and outrageous comment that 'When an innocent person dies, God laughs'. Prayer has been disembowelled.

For prayer to have any meaning it has to cause God to act, for as Karl Barth notes, he 'does not act in the same way whether we pray or not'.[13] Jesus' insistence on unceasing prayer is because prayer moves, indeed enables, God to act. 'Forgive them, Father! They don't know what they are doing,' presupposes that without his pleading God would not forgive. Intercession is about getting God to change his mind – in the shocking words of the Revised Standard Version, to '*repent of the evil he thought to do*' (Exodus 32.14 RSV). It is an anti-Christian fatalism that says 'Thy will be done' without a struggle. Jesus wrestled with God in the Garden of Gethsemane and only after long and passionate dialogue did he accept the cup of suffering – it was no simple acceptance, no 'whatever will be will be', or even 'whatever God wills so be it'.

The idea of passionate disputation with God has been lost from our tradition and needs to be recaptured. Disputation is not magic, there is no coercion involved. Argument is not magic; magic is 'understood among [modern] pagans to be the "art and science of changing reality (or consciousness) according to the Will"'.[14] Prayer is not using art or science or imposing our will on that of God, but rather getting God to change his mind. This is not done through force but through relationship and dialogue. Jesus told the parable of the widow and the unjust judge to illustrate this (Luke 18.1–8). The widow does not force the judge to give her justice – force and violence are if anything against her, a widow is defenceless. She has no power, no authority, no rich resources to draw upon. What she has is irritation value. Like the dripping of a water torture, her constant presence wears away at the judge until his eyes are heavy and dark with sleeplessness and finally he gives her justice. She has a relationship with the judge, not perhaps a happy one but nonetheless a relationship, she is always there! The moral of the story, Jesus tells his disciples, is that 'God will judge in favour of his own people who cry to him day and night for help. Will he be slow to help them? I tell you, he will judge in their favour and do it quickly.'

We pray so that God is able to change things. We faithfully engage with God in the creation and salvation and healing of our world. But God is caught in the 'surprise' that paralysed Jesus in Nazareth (Mark 6.6). By the blasphemous insertion of the phrase 'if it be thy will' we paralyse God. We make an idol of him, a god 'formed by human hands' like the idols who 'have mouths, but cannot speak, and eyes, but cannot see' (Psalm 115) – and our prayer that God should change his will becomes self-contradictory. 'If it be thy will' presupposes that God's will is unchangeable and that, unlike the people of God in the Bible, we cannot enter into negotiation with God. The Christian God is one who has a relationship with his people and Christian prayer must be for God's reign to come on earth; this is confident prayer, demanding prayer. As Walter Wink puts it, 'That is why the phrases of the Lord's prayer are not indicative but imperative – we are ordering God to bring the Kingdom near. It will not do to implore. We must command. We are commanded to command. We are required by God to haggle with God for the sake of the sick, the obsessed, the weak, and to conform our lives to our intercessions.'[15]

It is the year AD 67. The might of Imperial Rome is at its mightiest. The fires of Imperial Rome are at their fieriest. The horror that is Nero the emperor of Imperial Rome is at its most horrible. And the whole place smells pretty bad too!

In the back rooms and cellars of mighty Rome the persecuted Christians hold their secret meetings. There are Priscilla and Aquila, good, middle-class, Jewish Pharisee people. They were friends of St Paul, you know, and they don't let you forget it. They name-drop Paul into every argument. Let's listen in.

'Slavery is wrong.' This is Ampliatus. 'If Jesus brings freedom, then why am I still a slave? Why can't I demand freedom? I'm a Christian, aren't I? Didn't his message of freedom from oppression include me?'

'Paul told me that slaves should do their work as slaves cheerfully' – that's Priscilla. 'As though they served the Lord and not merely human beings. Paul has spoken!'

'Paul says *this*. Paul says *that*,' Ampliatus mutters. 'I sometimes wish Paul had kept his great big mouth shut.'

It seems that the poor are always being told to keep their noses out of politics. Jesus isn't about action is he? No, of course not, he is about faith, isn't he? Listen to the voice of reason, don't make waves. There are other people here too. Over there is Phoebe – you know, people say she is a *prostasis*! A *prostasis*? In her home church. She is a leader, a patron, a chief, a bishop maybe! She is hot on women's rights. She knows her stuff too!

'According to this letter God made man in his own image', muses Urbanus. 'That is why women only reflect the glory of man. Didn't God make Adam the man first? Women were made out of man.'

'Women were made second because they were God's *final* word in creation!' says Phoebe. 'Just watch, the last one always takes precedence in processions! Woman is the crown of God's creation.'

'God is male though,' Urbanus persists. 'Father and all that.'

'You'll be saying he has tes ... There *is* a feminine·nature in God, you know, don't try and pretend there's not! Wisdom, Sophia, is the feminine nature of God. You just can't make the heavenly God in your own image. And don't try to bring Jesus into it. Jesus takes sides with us as oppressed and silenced women. He is our lover, our comrade and our servant in suffering.'

There is someone over there who is obviously bursting to tell us something. This is Rufus and this must be his mum.

'Did you know my dad carried Jesus' cross for him? He was there, you know.'

It plays on his mind. He tells everyone. I think he feels sort of half proud, sort of half guilty. I mean, as if it wouldn't have happened anyway, even if Simon of Cyrene hadn't been there. The soldiers would've just chosen someone else, wouldn't they? Still, 'I was only following orders' is not really a very good excuse, is it? Over in that corner is Miriam. She has come to the meeting for the first time with her friend Claudia. She doesn't seem to know the routine like everyone else. She seems to be praying.

'Lord, listen to me. Lord, listen to me. Lord, rouse yourself and listen to me.'

She has been praying like this, loudly and continuously, for about an hour. People are beginning to get fed up with it.

'Lord, listen to me. Lord, listen to me. Lord, rouse yourself and listen to me.'

'Hold your peace!' – that's Justus. 'Enough, woman. You're driving me crazy. Leave the Lord alone. He obviously doesn't want to listen to you.'

'Lord, listen to me. Lord, listen to me. Lord, rouse yourself and listen to me.'

'Please Miriam, leave off now,' says Nereus. 'You'll get us all into trouble. Look around you. Most of the church are already in heaven. They've already been martyred. Like Paul, yes, Priscilla, of course, and Peter and all the others. Please. If you must pray keep your voice down.'

Whatever they say or do she carries on calling out and crying and praying aloud. She has more important things to think about than Nero's soldiers. Her mother is dying. But the small church, hiding in the darkened and echoing house, in the flickering torchlight, is frightened. They might be able to face martyrdom out there. In the arena. In the light of day. But not here, in the shadows. Not at night among the whistling ghosts. Fear ripples through the air like a poisonous snake slithering silently through tall grass. It spreads from person to person. Face to face. Still the loud and persistent voice, crying out loud. *For crying out loud, stop!*

Eventually they call for Mark. Let him talk to them all and tell them a story about Jesus to quell their fears. Mark is a small nervy man who doesn't normally push himself forward. But he spent a lot of time with Peter, Jesus' disciple – you know, the one that Nero had crucified upside down. Yes, that's the one. Well, he told Mark everything that he saw and heard. Mark is the community's memory of Jesus. Some people say he even met Jesus. He is like a book on legs! Did Jesus do anything or say anything that might help us. Is there any comfort?

'Peter told me about the time they went to Jericho,' he muses. 'As Jesus left with his disciples and a large crowd, they came up to a man who was blind, sitting by the side of the road. He is very poor, he has been abandoned by his family and he is unable to survive from one day to the next except by begging. His name is Bar Timaeus. When he hears all the kerfuffle of the crowd coming up the road he calls out and asks people what's going on.

'"It's Jesus of Nazareth," someone tells him.

'"Jesus! Hey, Jesus!" Bar Timaeus shouts. "Jesus! Son of David! Over here! Hoi! Help me!"

'Now, lots of people start telling him to be quiet. They start telling him off, to keep his beggarly nose out of the affairs of his betters. The Messiah's got nothing for a blind beggar. Get back to his blind business and beg properly and quietly. This just makes him more determined. He keeps on shouting.

'"Jesus of Nazareth! Hey, Jesus! Hoi! Son of David! Take pity on me!"

'Eventually, Jesus hears him. He stops dead in his tracks which makes everyone stop suddenly and fall over themselves. I remember we thought it funny, all these people just tripping over their own feet in the rush to stand still. They were all waving their cloaks and shouting "Messiah! David's son! King!" It was the road up to Jerusalem, you know, that last week. And then Jesus stops. Middle of a triumphant procession and he stops.

'"Who is shouting?" Well, everyone was. The crowd looked at each other. What did he mean, "Who's shouting?" Everyone, I mean there we were all singing 'Going to Jerusalem, Going to Jerusalem, na na na na, na na na na.' And then while they're all looking round at each other the voice comes again, hoarse with shouting.

'"Jesus of Nazareth! Hey, Jesus! Hoi! Son of David! Take pity on me!"

'"Bring him over to me," says Jesus. So the crowd look for the source of the voice and find Bar Timaeus sitting in the dust.

'"Get up, he wants you," they tell him. Well, according to Peter he just threw off the rags that were round him and stood up. He held out his arm and demanded that someone guide him. Now he was no longer frightened. He no longer flinched away from every sound in case it was accompanying a kick or a punch. He came up to Jesus, head high, carefully but proudly.

'"What do you want me to do for you?" Jesus asked him.

'"Teacher," Bar Timaeus answered, losing a bit of his bravado now it came to the point, "I want to see again."

'"Go," said Jesus. "your faith has made you well." And as Jesus and the disciples and the crowd went on to Jerusalem, Bar Timaeus went too. He followed Jesus from that moment.'

Mark finished the story and his eyes lost the dreamy faraway look that they always had when he retold the stories of Jesus. He looked round at the congregation.

'Well, what is that supposed to mean?' demanded Aquila. 'What has that all to do with us sitting here with that deranged woman shouting loud enough for the soldiers to hear?'

'Yes,' agreed Priscilla. 'Paul put up with his sufferings and so should we. He prayed three times to be healed and each time was told no. God's grace is enough for us, that's what he always said. Our sufferings are an offering that we can make to the Lord.'

'Wait,' said Junia quietly. She is an apostle, Paul's own words. When she speaks in the meeting, people listen. 'I think that Mark was inspired by the Spirit to tell us this story. It is about someone having the courage to go against the crowd. It is about calling out to Jesus in prayer even when you don't know if he can hear. It is about being healed and getting dignity and it's about the responsibility of the people to take others to Jesus. Thank you, Mark.'

She goes across to Miriam and kneels beside her and puts an arm round her shoulder. The two women raise their voices together.

'Lord, listen to us. Lord, listen to us. Lord, rouse yourself and listen to us.'

Slowly more and more voices join in the prayer and the fear of the soldiers is lost in the act of praying. The only important thing is to pray. Miriam is no longer an outsider. She has been a prophet for the whole church. Her message is to keep on calling to Jesus. Bar Timaeus tells us the same. Pray continuously.

God is not static in our prayer but dynamic. It is God himself who calls us to pray and even supplies us the wherewithal to pray with:

In the same way the Spirit also comes to help us, weak as we are. For we do not know how we ought to pray; the Spirit himself pleads with God for us in groans that words cannot express. And God, who sees into our hearts, knows what the thought of the Spirit is; because the Spirit pleads with God on behalf of his people and in accordance with his will.

(Romans 8.26–7)

We do not free God from the 'surprise' of inactivity on our own initiative. God reaches out to us first and only then do we pray. The Spirit of God, untamed and untameable, reaches into us, trapped in inactivity, and inspires us to prayer. This is not, however, the formal prayer of the hour on a Sunday morning – the Spirit's groans are inarticulate, they are not set prayers argued over endlessly by liturgical committees. They are by definition groans that words cannot express. But this does not let us off the hook – part of the struggle is to give voice to the voiceless.

When one member of the body, the community which is both church and Christ's own sacred body, cries in pain and despair against God this cannot be denied. 'There is no division in the body, but all its different parts have the same concern for one another. If one part of the body suffers, all the other parts suffer with it' (1 Corinthians 12.25–6). This is not sympathy but empathy, entering into the pain and suffering to share the burden. This is living in the community of God's Spirit. The anger and pain and despair are not to be denied but to be upheld as part of the experience of the holy people of God. The pain is inarticulate but this does not present a difficulty. The very cries of anger and pain and despair are presented to God by the Spirit's pleading. The cries and screams come out of relationship. The Spirit manifested in the community reflects pain as well as praise.

The body of Christ in history and locality includes the 'How long?' and the 'Why?' and the despair. These cries and groans are theology done on the right side of the brain, theology of stomach and emotion. Without them a community cannot have wholeness and holiness and haleness (health). The holistic community has a holistic theology. The healing community is where wounds are tended. Where God calls us to pray holistically, for health, for holiness, for wholeness, and calls us to release him from the 'surprise' of inaction. The Spirit pleads for us, allowing us to enter into negotiation and dialogue. At the prompt of God our prayer allows him to have his mind changed. 'Prayer is not to bring the petitioner's will into submission to the unchanging will of God, but prayer is to move God to do something he otherwise would not do.'[16] If we are not in a state of continual prayer, of relationship with God, how can we expect to change his mind?

But God too is under constraints. If this were not so, God would not only seem capricious and vindictive but would actually be evil. One of the constraints is the limit of our own free will as human beings, but this is not all. To ascribe God's weakness to our own power would be rank arrogance. Equally to ascribe it to our lack of faith or sinfulness would be conceit. There are obviously times when we look for the wrong answers to prayer (even as those of Jesus' day, including his cousin John, wrongly looked for the coming of a war-lord), but this too is not enough: 'there are situations where God's will seems so transparently evident that to assert that God says no is to portray God as a cosmic thug'.[17] As Walter Wink says, the death of approximately forty thousand children a day – over fourteen million a year – cannot be the will of God.

Paul writes in several places of the spiritual forces that, in the ancient world-view, controlled the world, the principalities and powers. He instructs us to put on the whole armour of God because 'we are not fighting against human beings but against the wicked spiritual forces in the heavenly world, the rulers, authorities, and cosmic powers of this dark age' (Ephesians 6.12). These are not ethereal creatures wafting about in the beyond, disembodied spirits or ghoulies and ghosties, but rather the faceless bureaucracies, the social systems and the 'thems' which seem to control our destinies. In the book of Daniel, the prophet prays but God takes twenty-one days to send him an answer, a vision of an angel. The angel explains that God has heard his cries from the very beginning but the answer has been delayed by a struggle between earthly powers in heaven. They are given the mythological form of angels but are really the powers of the nations which hold Israel in thrall – Persia and, once Persia is defeated, Greece.

This reflects the experience that we have when we pray. It feels as though God doesn't answer prayer or if he does he takes his time about it. Prayer feels like inaction when we look at the evil in the world. We have an overwhelming sense of our own helplessness and powerlessness under of the weight of so much evil. We are caught up in a struggle to engage with God but we are weighed down with the world that we live in. God engages in the struggle, reaching out to us, but he also becomes enmeshed in the web woven by the systems and structures that we face. 'In short, prayer involves not just God and people, but God and people and the Powers. What God is able to do in the world is hindered, to a considerable extent, by the rebelliousness, resistance and self-interest of the Powers exercising their freedom under God.'[18] God seems impotent. But we, Paul assures us, have complete victory through him who loved us!

> For I am certain that nothing can separate us from his love: neither death nor life, neither angels nor other heavenly rulers or powers, neither the present nor the future, neither the world above nor the world below – there is nothing in all creation that will ever be able to separate us from the love of God which is ours through Christ Jesus our Lord.
>
> (Romans 8.38)

In the present, however, God's struggle, which is our struggle, continues. The powers of this world seem ranged against us and threaten to overwhelm us – faceless bureaucracies, multi-national companies, governments, International Trade Organizations, Treaty Organizations, even the structures of the Church – those things that Walter Wink calls the Domination System. In our struggle to bring liberation to those imprisoned by illness we know that God hears our prayer, like Daniel's, on the very first day. However long it seems to take, however often we cry, 'O God, how long?' However distant and unhearing God seems, we continue to cry out, 'Rouse yourself, Lord.' And 'we cannot stop praying for what is right because our prayers are seemingly unanswered. We know that they are heard on the very first day that we pray. Yet we keep on praying, for even one more day is too long to wait for justice.'[19]

The Church is a community in which no instant healing and wholeness and holiness can be found. Physical healing is not even guaranteed, for Christianity is not 'a way of escape *from* suffering but a way of healing *through* suffering'.[20] But Jesus shows God's purpose in healing by including the outsider into the Kingdom. Sometimes he went to them, by invitation. Sometimes they came to him. Occasionally they were brought to him, perhaps by friends, like the man with paralysis or, perhaps, propelled by demons, like the man possessed by the mob. The person who is already within the body of Christ does not come to Jesus, they are already in Christ. The Christian healing ministry is only incidentally directed to the body of Christ; for the Christian the grace of God is sufficient. The ministry of healing is the same ministry as the ministry of proclaiming Good News. The ministry of healing is directed towards the 'nations'. It points outwards.

The healing ministry of Jesus proclaimed the Kingdom. Healing enlarged the boundaries to include the people who were sick. The boundaries of the healing community are flexible enough to include the person with mental illness, the person with physical illness, the person with moral illness, the person with social illness and the person with spiritual illness. Peter and John bring healing to the man at the Beautiful Gate, excluded from the Temple. By healing he becomes included. St Paul is included through the process of being both blinded and healed. Irenaeus wrote of the gifts of the Church exerted 'day by day for the benefit of the Gentiles'. But for Jesus and the early Christian communities there was a struggle to bring God's healing. It was not always instantaneous.

It is evening in the great city of Rome, the greatest city of the empire. In the gathered Christian community there are some people that we know. There is Phoebe, the president of the church at Cenchreae, a former slave. There are Priscilla and Aquila, wealthy multi-national merchants, who own this enormous house that we are in now! They are Pharisees like their friend Paul. Over in the corner sitting quietly is John Mark. He has two names like many of the Jewish Christians, a Jewish name and a Gentile name – a scribbler! Sitting next to him is Epaenetus, the first Asian person ever to become a Christian! The woman over there is Mary. See her and those other women over there? Deacons, they are. Mary and Tryphaena and Tryphosa and Persis. Appointed by the community for the community. There are Andronicus and Junia, they are both well known as apostles – yes, both of them. Yes, a woman who is an apostle! There is the Jewish Herodian, a client and freed slave of the Herods. There is the family of the Gentile, Narcissus. There are even the widow and the son of Simon of Cyrene – the one who carried Jesus' cross. There are lots of others, some of whose names we know and others, like Nereus' sister, whose name we do not.

What a mixed bunch! Jewish and Gentile, men, women, rich, poor, citizens, slaves, freeborn and freed. There are rich merchants and full-time church workers. There are dependent widows and independent women of influence. The church is divided along class lines. The church is divided along ethnic lines. The Jewish Christians returning from exile under Claudius found that the Gentiles had taken over. Like all expatriates they are in shock because of the changes. Like all expatriates they can't believe the state that things are in. Everything is changed utterly. And even though it is now several years since the return the division remains.

A freed slave has brought his mother to the meeting. She is a slave and she is blind. He has brought her for healing. Her master is thinking of getting rid of her. She is useless, he says, just sitting about, eating her head off and walking into the best pottery. The master has kept her on as her eyesight has faded. He has put up with her for the sake of the past, but he is not made of money, he cannot afford to keep such a useless slave. She can no longer wait at table or cook or even work in the fields. The other slaves mistreat her and think that nobody knows – it is bad for discipline! She is too much of a liability. Her son cannot afford to buy her medicines or pay for a doctor. Or buy her.

Whenever anyone walks past she flinches away as though stung. She cowers in the corner away from anyone in case of a passing kick or slap. Her son looks over at her and a frown creases his brow. He has brought her to the church for healing and freedom, like Jesus promises.

This is the signal for an argument to break out, any excuse really. Herodian starts laying down the law, as usual. 'Jesus didn't use any medicines, did he? He just touched people and wham! Bang! They were healed. It was instant and complete. If we have enough faith we can move mountains. There can be no argument about it. We just have to have enough faith and it will happen. Any of us can do it.'

Aquila the Pharisee tries to get his two penn'orth in but an excited Herodian shouts him down. 'Let not him who has faith touch medicines. The glory of the Lord Jesus is at stake here. If we allow the use of medicines we are only going to confuse people. We only need to lay hands on her and she will be healed. Jesus has promised and he will fulfil his promises.' He thumps his hand into his fist with an air of finality. 'So that's settled then.'

There is uproar. Aquila brusquely pushes his way forward. He shouts loudly for quiet and finally things settle down.

'What utter bilge,' he says. 'The Lord has clearly laid down a structure of authority for us. He authorized his disciples as representatives. And only they and their successors have his authority. The church must have order. Jesus said so to his brother James. James told Paul. And Paul told me.' At this there is a moment of silence followed by a general groan. Aquila is always name-dropping where Paul is concerned. And he thinks that Paul's name is a clincher.

'Oil and prayers and the elders laying on hands – that's the way to do it. As it's always been done. We send the elders round on our behalf. They lay on their hands, rub in oil, pray, forgive sins and that's what does the trick!' He rubs his scarred and calloused hands together. 'You've all heard James' circular!'

There is chaos. People are shouting across the floor. Those who favour ritual are shouting red-faced at those who favour a more charismatic approach. The more charismatically inclined are bawling back. Tempers are high. The woman huddles, cowered and forgotten in her blindness.

Junia steps into the centre of the room and stands silently. Her head is bowed and her eyes are closed. Then Phoebe steps across to join her. Mary stops arguing with Julia and Philologus, and the two women join the steadily growing group standing silently. Eventually, last of all, a shamefaced Priscilla, with an embarrassed look towards her spouse, joins the other women in prayer.

'Hear the word of the Lord Jesus, first-born child of the Most High, the Risen One,' says a surprised-looking elderly woman. She is the usually silent widow of Simon of Cyrene. 'Do my life and death and resurrection mean nothing to you? Is this what loving your neighbour means?' She sweeps majestically to face the men. She looks straight at Aquila.

'Be on your guard against the yeast of the Pharisees and' – she spins to face Herodian – 'the yeast of the Herods. Eat instead the Bread of Life. Eat together of my body broken for you.'

For a woman to speak out in the meeting is not itself shocking, though it is a tremendous surprise to the woman herself. But the women are standing together in a group. They are supporting each other and allowing the normally voiceless to be heard. Their solidarity gives them strength. By standing together the group allows the individual a voice and through them the voice of Jesus is heard in the community. The whole community turns together and shares the common meal of the faithful. They break bread together and share the broken body of the Christ.

After the meal Mark is invited to speak. He is their library of tales of the Lord's earthly life. 'Tell us', they say to him 'if Jesus said or did anything that might help us put into practice his will.'

'They came to Bethsaida,' remembered Mark. He thought back to what he had been told by Peter – the Peter who saw and heard all that Jesus did and said. 'Some people brought a blind man to Jesus and begged him to touch him. Jesus took the blind man by the hand and led him out of the village. After spitting on the man's eyes, Jesus placed his hands on him and asked him, "Can you see anything?"

'The man looked up and said, "Yes, I can see people, but they look like trees walking about."

'Jesus again placed his hands on the man's eyes. This time the man looked intently, his eyesight returned, and he saw everything clearly. Jesus then sent him home with the order, "Don't go back into the village."

Olympas, who often tried to mediate between feuding parties, spoke up. 'Even Jesus didn't always manage to heal on the first attempt, then.'

'Yes,' agreed Patrobus slowly. 'But it was a charismatic action, wasn't it? He didn't go through some ornate ritual, did he?'

'But he used medicine. His spittle,' said Tryphaena.

'What about what Ben Sirach says in Ecclesiasticus?' asked Aristarchus, an educated Jewish believer who was in prison with Paul. His wrinkled face creased up in concentration. He recited in something of a sing-song voice: 'Value the services of a doctor for he has his place assigned by the Lord. His skill comes from the Most High, and he is rewarded by kings. The doctor's knowledge gives him high standing and wins him the admiration of the great. The Lord has created remedies from the earth, and a sensible man will not disparage them. The Lord has created remedies from the earth and from them the pharmacist compounds his mixture.

'My son' – Aristarchus grins a little sheepishly at the women and shrugs his shoulders – 'in times of illness do not be remiss, but pray to the Lord and he will heal you.'

'That's all right for you,' offers Phlegon. 'You've got enough wealth to consult a doctor, but what about the rest of us?'

And so the debate continues. They started from the needs of the person who came to the church, identified those needs but lost sight of them in the ensuing argument. Like the disciples with the boy who had epilepsy, the Roman church was diverted from action by easier theological dispute. The partisan dispute stopped the woman's needs from being met. Then an individual beginning to pray stops the dispute and the community turn instead to prayer, to a common meal and finally to constructive dialogue. This may develop into a practice which meets people's needs.

While the details and individual motivations are imaginative, the broad brush-strokes fit the church in Rome in the middle of the first century. By thinking about our experience and looking at the way that two thousand years ago the church met its experience with stories about Jesus, we too can build a model for action.

> We read the New Testament for this purpose and this purpose only: [as] a resource for a community committed to the programme of Christ's kingdom, which faces problems and gets into trouble precisely because it is thus committed. [. . .] To treat it as merely an object of historical or literary study, or as a source of individual solace, is to misuse it.[21]

What does this story say about our theories and practices of health and healing? What does it say about how to bring the living Lord of the Church to the person who is sick? What does it say about the responsibility of the Church? Can we bring our imaginations to bear upon it and see a relevance for our own questions? Where do we go from here?

Healing is not necessarily instant. Jesus' repeated attempts to heal the man with blindness from Bethsaida show that this issue was important for the Marcan community. The very presence of this story in the Gospel seems to suggest that it was as much a question for the Marcan community as it is for us. Then and now, the issue of whether healing takes place instantly or whether healing takes place over a period of time is a question to be wrestled with.

Neither does spiritual healing take the place of medicine. Jesus ben Sirach, the author of Ecclesiasticus, writes that the doctor should be called when you are ill. Pray to God, yes, but also call the doctor and 'keep him by you, for you need him also. A time may come when your recovery is in his hands, then he too will pray to the Lord to grant success in relieving pain and finding a cure to save the patient's life' (Ecclesiasticus 38.12ff. REB) His example shows a multi-disciplinary approach: spiritual healing and medical healing are two sides of the same coin.

The woman came to the church to discover healing, she was not already a member of Christ. The man from Bethsaida who came to Jesus was not a disciple, he was brought to Jesus for healing. The healing ministry of the Christian community is primarily designed to bring people face to face with the living Christ. Healing has to do with entering into a relationship. Lifelong relationships are rarely instantaneous and neither is the journey to health. In the Gospels healing is through contact with the community centred on Christ, a community that is both Christ and the person marginalized by weakness. Faith is required, although not necessarily that of the person who is ill. The faith of the community is enough. However, physical healing is not guaranteed; nor is commitment to Christ demanded, but the prayer and dispute and arguing and struggling of the people of God to get God to act are. 'God will judge in favour of his own people who cry to him night and day for help.' Of the ten people that Jesus healed in Luke 17.11–19, only one returned to create relationship. The body of Christ in history and in the world is the community which reflects Christ, where Christ is discovered. It is a holistic community which addresses God from history and the world. The purpose of healing remains a sign of God's Kingdom coming/come. And as we pray daily

'Your kingdom come,' we join God in the struggle against the powers that restrain him and us. Health and healing anticipate the world to come. And until the kingdom comes in its entirety the person with a weakness remains the ikon of Christ for the community.

Leonardo Boff noted that it is not enough to know: new praxis must be implemented. The centrality in the community of the person who is weak or sick or who has an impairment and the missionary thrust of the healing ministry of the sick are both practical issues for the liberating gospel. And both need prayerful consideration and translation into action within the local church. All theology has at its human end the intention of making people free from oppression. In classical theology it is freedom from sin, interpreted in a highly individualistic way. This supported the political status quo. But if freedom from oppression is freedom from economic oppression it is about self-determination and release from poverty, about land reform and fair wages, about standing in solidarity against the oppression of the wealthy and powerful. Theology can also be done in the context of other forms of oppression: from the context of being black or being a woman, seeking release from captivity. But people who are oppressed by a society that marginalizes them because they are ill and people who are oppressed by society because they have impairments are not represented by liberation theology or black or feminist or womanist theology. Indeed, churches continue to promote their marginalization by their silence and inaction. Jesus saw his mission as being to those who were marginalized by poverty, by confinement, by impairment and by oppression. A theology reflecting the gospel needs to include the concerns of people with impairments and people who are oppressed and imprisoned by illness. To deliberately misquote and misapply James Cone, a theology for people who are ill or for people with an impairment is 'the theology of a community whose daily energies must be focused on physical survival in a hostile environment. [. . .] Therefore the central question for [people who are disabled or who are ill] is "How are we going to survive in a world which deems a humanity other than [the physically able] an illegitimate form of human existence?"'[22]

Healing is part of the everyday life of the local church. In the Gospels, people meet Jesus for a variety of reasons: idle curiosity;

driven by some inner compulsion such as demonic possession; out of despair; to be healed. Their motives are rarely simple or unselfish. They come because Jesus brings healing. Some stay and follow him. More go on their way. In the community centred upon Jesus, healing takes precedence over eating. The needs of the oppressed come first. The cries of the despairing and hurting and lost come before the body of Christ break bread together. The hungry need feeding before the merely peckish. Healing comes first because the person who is ill has a more urgent need. We extend the boundaries to include those who do not conform to our narrowly defined norms. The church is the body of the Christ who took the boundaries out to those on the edges.

Liberation theologies recognize that all human relationships are to some extent power relationships. And these relationships between people are often relationships that have an imbalance of power. Discrimination empowers some people while disempowering others. People who use wheelchairs can be easily disabled by simple things like the height of a light switch. Institutionalized racism is matched by institutionalized disabling.

> We should learn to resist the seductiveness of the helping role and acknowledge that the baggage that we carry can undermine the empowerment of people. The dynamics of power are multi-dimensional. [We] shape the daily experiences of many people [that we] serve and the quality of experiences and opportunities available to them. That is real power.[23]

This is not the pattern of the disabled, crucified Christ. He chose, even disabled by the cross, to empower the thief on the next cross. St Paul discovered that it was in weakness that he was empowered by God. A Christian people who are liberated are a people who live in the way of wholeness and haleness and holiness. This does not mean that they will never get a headache or flu. Wholeness and haleness and holiness are in engaging with God in the struggle.

The stories and sayings of Jesus and God's people are a map for our journey. We walk in the footprints left by those who have travelled the path before us. But the footprints have been obscured. While one person remains oppressed, the whole of the people of God are oppressed. We each participate in Christ and each sustains and supports the whole. If there are those that are prevented from full participation because the 'head says to the feet,

"I don't need you!"' then the whole body is diminished. We must acknowledge the valid experience of all people. The experience of the community is important. It is important because it gives the community identity and purpose. Every community has to write its own story of the living Jesus. Their account is the fifth Gospel. For this Gospel to give a valid account of the reality of the living Jesus it must reflect the experience of the whole. The real experience of real people in the real world needs to be expressed as part of the liturgy of liberation – a liturgy of personal testimony.

I once overheard a conversation between a gifted academic researcher and a woman with little formal education. While he had been debating over excessive alcohol in the student union, she had learned motherhood through practical experience. She felt disadvantaged by his intellectual argument and long words. She was trying to defend a cable television programme featuring gospel choirs and a show-biz style evangelist. The academic was highly critical of the programme and anyone who watched it. As I listened I began to realize that she watched it not for the ranting of the evangelist, not even for the exciting and compelling music, but for the testimonies. Experiences of ordinary people like her were being voiced. Ordinary people could walk with God and tell their own stories.

This liberation begins in the risen Christ met now and in the Gospels where suffering is real, where death is reality – but where love is possibility. And often our experience resonates with the experience of the people who first listened to the Gospel stories. We are all, in a sense, second-generation Christians. 'We are the early church for our time.'[24] Every generation is the early church for its time. We face new questions and situations. No other church community has ever faced precisely our dilemmas or problems or joys or successes. But the experiences of the first-ever second generation of Christian communities are recorded in the Gospels. They needed to meet their circumstances as much as we do our own. These communities were full of arguments and tensions. The people had tensions and disagreements. They too faced people who laid down the law or walked off in a huff, those that were disadvantaged and those not. They squabbled, forming parties and alliances against each other. They divided over church order and spiritual gifts. They argued over the question of political obedience and disobedience – how could one live in an unjust society? They divided over sickness and health and healing. The early church in the first century was full of the same people as the early church in the present. It was full of people who were ambitious or were quiet and unassuming. It was full of gossips and back-stabbers. It was full of the insightful, the holy, the prayerful and the joyful. It was the bride of Christ! It was the body of Christ! It was as bad and as good as it is today!

We must make a leap of the imagination to link our experience with theirs. We must ask, 'What is God saying to us about our church community? Is it a place of health and holiness and healing and wholeness? Is it enabling, for this locale, at this time? Is our community there "for the sake of the nations"? Does it "promote the welfare of others"? Is its stated and explicit reason for existing to serve the wider community?' Our primary resource is the gospel. But we come to the text of the Bible carrying a baggage of questions and preconceptions. The imaginative skill and the life experience of the whole people are required. The person who has spent her or his life in academic institutions has only one type of life experience. It is the arrogance of the academic theologian to make his or her viewpoint into the norm. Father Ed de la Torre said, 'You really need to hear the peasants and farmers telling in their own way the theological perceptions that they are coming to. I cannot go as deep or speak as clearly as they can. You see, I am an educated cripple – I had seminary training.'[25] The theologian will receive instruction when the people of the theological community get to work.

If we are to reinvent liturgy as the people's work then the story of ordinary people and their journey of faith must be given voice. Liturgy must reflect the needs and the aspirations and the experiences and the fears and hopes of the people and not just the academic liturgist. The liturgist has merely an advisory role in developing people's awareness of what 'might be built up, and what might be safely demolished'. New liturgies should '[l]isten to the needs of; and consult with, the whole body of worshippers, young and old, male and female, rich and poor, rural and urban, literate and non-literate: what do they want to express before God, and how?'[26] The sense of anger towards God, the sense of despair, the sense of anguish felt by many in the community, are not presently given voice. God cannot be approached by those who feel that he is guilty of neglect. The liturgy needs to include anger and joy. The liturgy needs to include the possibility of reaching out in response to God in forgiveness. As Brian Pattern wrote, our liturgy 'should be seen in the company of thieves and lovers rather than of journalists and publishers. On sighting mathematicians it should unhook the algebra from their minds and replace it with poetry; on sighting poets it should unhook the poetry from their minds and replace it with algebra; it should fall in love with children and woo them with fairytales.'[27] Our liturgy reflects our prayer, reflects our theology. We must be passionate, our prayer being the expression of our love for God and each other. We must go to war against the powers that restrain us and God with our prayer and our passion and our determination not to give up. Our prayer must not 'wimp out'! God calls us to pray unceasingly, unstintingly. We pray because even one more day is too long to wait for justice, for healing. The prayer of God's people fails because it is 'lukewarm, neither hot nor cold'. Our prayer must recapture the spontaneity, the vigour, the passion, the continuity of a first love.

In C. S. Lewis' Narnia stories, Aslan is 'not a tame lion'. His actions cannot be predicted with any certainty. He is rumour. 'They say Aslan is on the move – perhaps has already landed.' He is a wild and untameable creature. He refuses to be tamed. We continually try to domesticate God and prevent him from running wild and ruining our introverted club. Our buildings exclude the outsider – thick walls and strong doors designed as fortresses to protect those inside from bandits and marauders. Our hymn books and service books, full of stilted formal language, exclude those who are not church-speak literate. Our worship is full of tiny private symbols, arcane secrets known only to the initiates. Our response to God's call to struggle with him in the face of the unpredictability of life and death is to withdraw into our own world. Our fear is so overwhelming that we harden ourselves against being overwhelmed. The scale of the evil in the world is beyond our comprehension.

But our experience of God implicates God in the catastrophe that is our world. The Lion of the tribe of Judah, the great descendant of David, is the lamb who was slain. God is the lion who breaks the bones of the sick. He is the vengeful lion who attacks the proud and forgetful. God cannot be tamed, he is no domestic kitten.

The Church has treated God like a circus lion. The angels of the nations that oppressed Daniel's people and warred in heaven and so prevented God from even sending a messenger for twenty-one days find echoes in the New Testament. John's Revelation contains letters to the angels of the seven churches. The church structures too militate against God. The angel of Laodicea is himself 'lukewarm, neither hot nor cold'. The multi-national corporations, the international trade agreements, the governments and so on are not the only powers arraigned against God. The Church too confines the lion of Judah in a cage and forces him to do its embarrassing tricks. Bright lights and the harsh music disguise the filthy sawdust in the ring. The roaring lion which is God is forced to go through hoops held up by us, the lion-tamer. The Church, the same body of Christ that was once striped with the marks of the whip, now stands with the whip and turns it upon its Lord. The lion appears mangy and uncared-for. His teeth are pulled and his claws clipped. The glamorous garb of the lion-tamer is showing threadbare. The reality is that the lion-tamer is shabby and has lost the will to care.

The Church has become scared of what God might do; it has too many vested interests in the world to allow God to get free.

These four things – buildings, clergy, theological colleges and social responsibility – are all things we take for granted in the Church. We cannot conceive of the Church existing without them. If we did not have to raise money to build new buildings and to maintain old ones, if we did not have to train and maintain the clergy and undertake social service in our own country and elsewhere, what would members of the church do? What did the early church do when it did not have to trouble about these things? It converted the Roman Empire.[28]

While our energies are continually sapped by having to raise ever-increasing amounts to support old and crumbling buildings – we are not in the heritage business after all – and support a church bureaucracy as faceless as any at County Hall, we are diverted from our task of being the body of Christ, the healer and proclaimer of Good News.

The lion must be uncaged for his own sake and for the sake of the lion-tamer. The leash must be slipped. The wildness of God needs to be released from its restraints. That wildness needs to be acknowledged and sought and prayed into being. Freedom in

Christ is not a suburban garden. It is not tame freedom. It is wild, untamed and untameable, a wild ride.

> That ride was perhaps the most wonderful thing that happened to them in Narnia. Have you ever had a gallop on a horse? Think of that; and then take away the heavy noise of the hoofs and the jingle of the bits and imagine instead the almost noiseless padding of the great paws. Then imagine instead of the black or grey or chestnut back of the horse the soft roughness of golden fur, and the mane flying back in the wind. And then imagine you are going about twice as fast as the fastest racehorse. But this is a mount that doesn't need to be guided and never grows tired. He rushes on and on, never missing his footing, never hesitating, threading his way with perfect skill between tree trunks, jumping over bush and briar and the smaller streams, wading the larger, swimming the largest of all. And you are riding not on a road nor in a park nor even on the downs, but right across Narnia, in spring, down solemn avenues of beech and across sunny glades of oak, through wild orchards of snow-white cherry trees, past roaring waterfalls and mossy rocks and echoing caverns, up windy slopes alight with gorse bushes, and across the shoulders of heathery mountains and along giddy ridges and down, down, down again into wild valleys and out into acres of blue flowers.[29]

This is the wild ride of relationship – the heady first days of new love. It has passion. It has speed. It has strength. It is deliciously frightening. It is not safe. It is a wild relationship fraught with danger. It is a ride which has the racing headlong rush of Mark's narrative. It is a ride for the person who is pushed to the margins of life. The person who is sick and the person who is imprisoned and the person who is poor has no time for the lion in the cage. The lion for the marginalized is a wild lion, a liberated lion.

The liberation model of health and healing starts from a place of captivity. It begins from the person who has an impairment and the person whose health is instead unhealth. It starts from the woman with a dying baby. It begins the walk with the man whose legs are paralysed. It sounds in the ears of the girl who is deaf. It is seen through the eyes of the child who is blind. But it does not start from the dead baby or the paralysis or the deafness or the blindness. It starts from the viewpoint of a human being asking, 'How much longer will your anger last? Have pity, O Lord.' It is not about impairment or sickness but about being person. It grows out of the experience of suffering and pain and anger and isolation and disability. It takes seriously the stated aim of Jesus.

> The Spirit of the Lord is upon me,
> because he has chosen me to bring good news to the poor.
> He has sent me to proclaim liberty to the captives
> and recovery of sight to the blind;
> to set free the oppressed
> and announce that the time has come
> when the Lord will save his people.
>
> (Luke 4.18f.)

Taking as its starting point the needs of people and the stated aim of Jesus, the liberation model of health and healing is not careful of theological niceties. These are issues for the person who is safe. Theological niceties are for the insider. The liberation model is for the person who is outside as a consequence of sickness or impairment. The urgent task is to find healing.

The person who most clearly shows the model for praxis is the woman with fibroids. She has been marginalized for long enough. She takes matters into her own hands and without worrying about the niceties takes action. She risks rebuff from all the people that surround Jesus for she makes them share in her ritual uncleanness. She risks rebuff from Jesus for she makes him ritually unclean by her touch. Her need for healing is more important than the need of the crowd for ritual purity. Her need is greater than the mores of the community. Jesus' body is hijacked by her touch. She knows that even one more day is too long to wait for justice. Her struggle is with the powers that prevent her from reaching Jesus – with rituals, with people's dignity, with the disabling attitudes of those around her. And seizing the opportunity, she acts. Her determination is prayer in action. Prayer is not something we do – it is a response to what God is already doing in us and in the world. The community of faith which has Jesus in its midst, his resurrection body in history, the Church, must allow its agenda to be hijacked by the desperate needs of the outsider.

The boundaries of the community are elastic enough to include the person for whom society has no room. The liberation model recognizes the image of God in each individual and in recognizing this the community of faith becomes the servant. This means that the shape of the community is always changing and evolving. It is not a static community but a living and changing organism. The person does not need to change to be included, though meeting with the person of the living Christ brings change; it is the community that has to change to accommodate the individual. Even the person whose impairment is such that their common humanity is barely recognizable can become included in the community which takes the liberation model seriously. The recognition that they too are the ikon of Christ is a source of joy.

Jacob wrestling with a man at Peniel in Genesis 32.22–31 is symbolic of our action. He recognizes God in the face of the other; he struggles and doggedly holds on until he changes God's inaction into action – a blessing; he is changed into a new creation; and as someone with an impairment he is an ikon of God's liberation – the father of a nation and God's witness to them. This liberation model of health and healing recognizes all people for who they are as participants in a common humanity. The body of Christ, which is the community with Christ at its centre, recognizes the ikon of God in each person. Humanity is liberated by the recognition that this humanity is shared with the incarnate God. And God too is liberated by our sharing in that incarnation, in that struggle to defeat the powers that trap us. Our common humanity declares the living presence of the Lord and this means that the liberation model is about meeting that incarnate Lord. It is about mission. The risen Christ is met in the needs of others and in the community of faith.

Healing is found in the body of Christ. Holiness is found in the body of Christ. Wholeness is found in the body of Christ. They are all part of the *shalom*, the *sozo*. In the broken and limp body of the Christ the two worlds that are not two worlds meet and intermingle. Forgiveness crosses both ways across the Christ. In that broken body the 'now' is also the 'not yet'. And the 'not yet' is the 'now'. The prayer 'How long?' is heard on the very first day, while we continue to struggle with the powers of evil as the body of Christ in partnership with the Father. The body of Christ prays, at the prompting of God, that God's will be changed, that God will rouse himself and act. Prayer is no longer dismissed as being a 'time-wasting occupation'[30] suitable only for women. Prayer

214

becomes a focus of action not found only in silence and solitude. Prayer becomes a means of action found also in riot and crisis. Prayer is holding on and struggling and joining in the same conflict as the earthly Christ joined. An occupation for the whole body of Christ where nature and supernature become meaningless terms. Prayer is joined as God incarnate is impossibly and paradoxically dead on the cross. Praying in that horror is healing between humanity and God, and God and humanity, and humanity and humanity, and in oneself. In the cross the ghastly reality of human existence is taken into the Godhead.

This is not the sanitized crucifixion of art. This is the reality. The city dung heap. The broken body – not a glorious and heroic death but one that was so shameful that the early church did not portray it for centuries. The body is shattered and befouled and ugly. There is no modesty – his Jewishness and his manhood are simultaneously revealed. There are flies and stink. Over everything there hangs the heavy scent of dung and rotting food. It is this that is both the horror and the joy. For this death is ordinary. There are no heavenly choirs. No voice booms out from heaven. In this pain God forgives and is forgiven. And out of this comes healing.

Twisted, contorted face.
    Slack mouth, muscles a-twitch in spasm.
Broken, paralysed body.
    Loose-bowelled, blood-stained, bladder-empty wet.
Holiness is hung on these nails.

The Church is the body of Christ in the world. That body is broken on the cross. The blood and the urine and the faeces flow. In the body of Christ that is in the world, blood and urine and faeces cannot be avoided.

Twisted, contorted face.
    Slack mouth, muscles a-twitch in rictus-spasm.
Broken, paralysed body.
    Befouled, loose-bowelled, blood-stained, urine-wet.
Healing is hung on these nails.

The Church is the healing body of Christ for the community. We are a healing body which contains the broken as its centre. We bandage the bleeding. We sponge the urine and wipe the faeces for the beloved. We join in the struggle against the injustice of unhealth. In the body of Christ that is in the world blood and urine and faeces are to be the sign of God's presence.

Twisted, contorted face.
Slack mouthed, muscles all a-twitch in uncontrolled spasm.
Broken, paralysed body.
Stained with ordure, blood-spattered, wet with urine.
Here is hung wholeness.

## NOTES

1 Robinson, J. A. T., 'The Gospel and Health' (a sermon preached at the annual service of the Guild of Health in St Martin-in-the-Fields, London, 2 October 1958), in *On Being the Church in the World*. SCM, London, 1960, p. 123.
2 Robinson, *On Being the Church*, p. 123.
3 Dorothee Soelle commented that true theology begins in pain; see Soelle, D., *The Strength of the Weak*. Westminster Press, Philadelphia, 1984, p. 90.
4 'Simeon el Salo', *Penguin Dictionary of Saints*. Penguin, Harmondsworth, 1965.
5 Plank, K. A., *Paul and the Irony of Affliction*. Scholars Press, Atlanta, 1987, pp. 20f.
6 Robertson, A. and Plummer, A., *A Critical and Exegetical Commentary on the First Epistle of St Paul to the Corinthians*. T. & T. Clark, Edinburgh, 1978, p. 275.
7 See, for example, Orr, W. F. and Walther, J. A., *I Corinthians*. Doubleday, Garden City, NY, 1976, p. 286 for the association with genitalia.
8 See Irenaeus, *Adversus Haereses*, II. xxxii. 4.
9 Blue, L. with Magonet, J., *The Blue Guide to the Hereafter*. William Collins, Glasgow, 1988, p. 36.
10 Walsh, C. J., 'The History of the Rites', in Coyle, T., ed., *Christian Ministry to the Sick*. Geoffrey Chapman, London, 1986, p. 5.
11 *Tauchuma* fol. 15.3. See also Didache 8.3, 'Pray thus three times a day.'
12 Bradshaw, P., *Daily Prayer in the Early Church: a study of the origin and early development of the Divine Office*. Alcuin Club/SPCK, London, 1981, p. 135.
13 Barth, K., *Prayer*, cited in Wink, W., *Engaging the Powers*. Fortress Press, Philadelphia, 1992. p. 400n.
14 Weller, P. (ed), 'Pagans', *Religions in the UK: a multi-faith directory*. University of Derby/Interfaith Network for the United Kingdom, Derby, 1997, p. 674.

15 Wink, *Engaging the Powers*, p. 303.
16 Wink, *Engaging the Powers*, p. 302.
17 Wink, *Engaging the Powers*, p. 309.
18 Wink, W., *The Powers that Be: theology for a new millennium*. Doubleday, New York, 1998, p. 192.
19 Wink, *Engaging the Powers*, p. 313.
20 Frost, E., *Christian Healing: a consideration of the place of spirit healing in the Church today in the light of the doctrine and practice of the anti-Nicene Church*. Mowbray, London, 1949, p. 202.
21 Fraser, I. M., *Reinventing Theology as the People's Work*. Wild Goose, Glasgow, 1988, pp. 64f.
22 Cone, J., *A Black Theology of Liberation*. Maryknoll, Orbis, NY, 1990, p. 16.
23 Goldsmith, S., 'Gentle Teaching', in *Community Living*, 1991.
24 See Fraser, *Reinventing Theology*, pp. 63ff.
25 Fraser, *Reinventing Theology*, p. 28.
26 Gitari, D., ed., 'The Kanamai Statement', *Anglican Liturgical Inculturation in Africa, The Kanamai Statement with introduction, papers from Kanamai and a first response*. Alcuin/Grow, Bramcote, Nottingham, 1994, 1.1.i (a), p. 37.
27 Patten, B., 'A Prose Poem Towards a Definition of Itself', *Penguin Modern Poets 10: the Mersey Sound*. Penguin, Harmondsworth, 1974, p. 119.
28 Gibbs, M. and Morton, T. R., *God's Frozen People*. Fontana, London, 1964, p. 31.
29 Lewis, C. S., *The Lion, the Witch & the Wardrobe*. Penguin, Harmondsworth, 1959, p. 149f.
30 Sarah Coakley, 'Femininity and the Holy Spirit', in Furlong, M. (ed.), *Mirror to the Church: reflections on sexism*. SPCK, London, 1988.

217